The Woman's Guide to the
Catechism of the Catholic Church
∞

The Woman's Guide to the
Catechism of the Catholic Church

∞

SUSAN MUTO AND
ADRIAN VAN KAAM, C.S.SP.

CHARIS

SERVANT PUBLICATIONS
ANN ARBOR, MICHIGAN

Charis Books is an imprint of Servant Publications especially designed to serve Roman Catholics.

Imprimatur: Most Reverend Donald William Wuerl
                     Bishop of Pittsburgh
                     August 7, 1997
Nihil Obstat: Joseph J. Kleppner, S.T.L., Ph.D.
                     Censor Liborum

The Nihil Obstat and Imprimatur are declarations that this work is considered to be free from doctrinal or moral error. It is not implied that those who have granted the same agree with the contents, opinions, or statements expressed.

Published by Servant Publications
P.O. Box 8617
Ann Arbor, Michigan 48107

Cover design: Hile Illustration and Design, Ann Arbor, MI

97 98 99 00 10 9 8 7 6 5 4 3 2 1

Printed in the United States of America
ISBN 1-56955-004-2

LIBRARY OF CONGRESS CATALOGING-IN-PUBLICATION DATA

Muto, Susan Annette.
A woman's guide to the Catechism of the Catholic Church / Susan Muto and Adrian van Kaam.
    p.   cm.
Includes bibliographical references.
ISBN 1-56955-004-2 (alk. paper)
1. Catholic Church. Catechismus Ecclesiae Catholicae.   2. Catholic Church—Catechisms.
3. Catholic women—Religious life.   I. van Kaam, Adrian L., 1920-   . II. Title.
BX1959.5.M88   1997
238'.2—dc21   97-8595
                                                        CIP

This book is dedicated to
Our Lady of Epiphany

∞

Contents

∞

Preface

TEACHINGS OF GREAT DEPTH AND VALUE concerning women in the Church have permeated the consciousness of the modern world. The dignity of women, their tireless efforts as mothers and teachers, as women religious, as caregivers and friends, as advocates for justice, peace, and mercy, as creative innovators in family life, Church, and society, their work at home and in the marketplace, their dedication to the single life, marriage, and spiritual motherhood—all these accolades and accomplishments find a new voice in the *Catechism of the Catholic Church*.

Every woman who reads the *Catechism* with an eye toward becoming more fully a believing, celebrating, life-affirming, and praying person will relish its clear restatement of basic Church teaching and fresh presentation of important spiritual truth. Certainly catechists—of whom the majority are women—will feel the need not only to digest its contents but also to devise accurate and attractive ways to present them to the local church.

The teaching role of women in the Church, and their influence on the next generation, makes their appreciation for the universal *Catechism* an urgent necessity at this turn of the century. In undertaking this task, we bring together the gifts and experiences of a convinced Catholic laywoman and a dedicated priest, who believe that the *Catechism* must be viewed both as an instructional masterpiece and as an inspiration for spiritual deepening affecting our daily life of prayer and service.

Readers might wonder why a book clearly written for women has been coauthored by a man. For two reasons: first, we wanted to offer in this companion to the *Catechism* a living testimony to the importance of cooperation, collaboration, and collegiality in Church ministry today: male and female serving together as partners in the mystery of redemption. Secondly, we wanted to place our complementary fields of expertise (literature and formative spirituality, the human sciences, and formational theology) at the service of the universal Church.

In many years of writing and teaching together, the Holy Spirit made us sense the need for a healing, wholesome approach by contemporary authors to the growing resentments and misunderstandings between women and men. An approach of humble and respectful cooperation between male and female authors, committed to their calling, provides an enriching experience for them and their readers of either sex. Such an empathic collaboration serves to narrow, not widen, any currently experienced rift between women and men in the Church. It allows those who have strong intuitive abilities to complement those who tend to be more analytical. This is helpful and necessary when dealing with material as inspirational and profound as the *Catechism*.

In this spirit we patiently and prayerfully craft and recraft, draft and redraft together the content and style of each sentence and paragraph. In openness to each other's perspective, we try to create books that may prove to be helpful and enjoyable for all readers, even if a particular work like this one is intended primarily for women. The truth is, men will welcome it, too!

We think here of some of the writings of St. Teresa of Avila. She directed them to women religious, as in *The Way of Perfection,* but they clearly attracted the interest of male readers in her time and into the present age. It is not improbable that her collaboration with St. John of the Cross influenced in great measure the content and expression of her thoughts.

It is of paramount importance for men in the Church to become acquainted with a woman's lived experience of the *Catechism,* since women have such a key role to play in its teaching. Growth in sensitivity for her experiences of believing, celebrating, living, and praying the faith and its expression in her words will help to transcend a climate of conflict and competition that is a sore wound in the Body of Christ, his Church.

As contemporary spiritual writers we strive always in our many coauthored books for a blending in unity not only of feminine and masculine perspectives but also of our professional skill and knowledge. After so many years of dedicated service to the Church under the auspices of our cofounded Epiphany Association (1979 to date), after many opportunities worldwide to speak and teach and write together, it was a privilege to work on this book. We brought to it our combined perspectives in the literature of spirituality, in clinical psychology, in the theology of Christian personality formation—perspectives which after so many years of respectful collaboration have permeated one another. Being equally at home in the wisdom literature of spiritual formation and in the spiritually relevant facets of the human developmental sciences and disciplines in their feminine and masculine facets proved to be an invaluable aid to composition.

Last but not least, we came to appreciate anew the unbreakable bond between catechetical theology and the theology of formation. This same link undergirds the two previous books we wrote for Servant Publications: *Divine Guidance* (1994) with its emphasis on the Beatitudes and *The Commandments* (1996) with its reflective meditation on the Decalogue. Our experience of coauthoring these books gave us a wonderful start for this undertaking.

By focusing on the thematic, experiential, formative, and practical concerns of women, we have been able to reclaim in a fresh and provocative way the foundations of belief, celebration, pro-life proclamation, and deep contemplation that every Christian needs to know and act upon. In the process, we encourage women not only to read the *Catechism* for information but to meditate upon it for their personal and spiritual formation. We lift up for reflection and encouragement the oft-quoted words of women saints and martyrs. We see in every section the integrative, innovative presence of Mary, our model and mother, whom we fondly designate "Our Lady of Epiphany."

Throughout this presentation, we opted to attend in faith to the foundational teachings of the Church and not to use the *Catechism* as a forum for debate. Our purpose has been to dwell on its contents from a formative perspective with women in the forefront of our concerns. We chose to see each part of the *Catechism as* a reflection of the whole and to see women as the believing, celebrating, loving, and praying daughters of the Church they most fully are.

Themes guiding women through the *Catechism*, experiences of women evoked by the *Catechism*, invitations issued to women in the *Catechism*, and areas in need of women's gifts suggested by the *Catechism* were all taken into account. Thus, its four pillars—what we believe, how we celebrate, why we live moral and spiritual lives, and who we become when we pray from the heart—are treated in a comprehensive fashion so that by reading any one part of our book, a woman can be present, either implicitly or explicitly, to the whole. By virtue of this intertwining concentric approach, we strove to unlock the treasures of the *Catechism* for all readers, but especially for women whose love for the Church surpasses any lovers' quarrels they may have with her!

We trust that mothers and grandmothers, women religious, and lay catechists, spiritual guides and pastoral associates—indeed all women on parish teams and in positions of responsible leadership—take seriously their role as teachers of the faith and protectors of her story. May the *Catechism* be for them, as it has become for us, a powerful source of repletion and renewed hope for the future of

God's chosen people. Its pages reconfirm the freshness and boldness of Christ's message to the women of his time and to all the women he touches today in the Church universal.

We counsel readers to use this book as a *companion to* rather than as a *substitute for* the *Catechism.* Keep the *Catechism* by your side. Refer to it ideally before and after each of these chapters. Use it to help you respond to the questions for reflection and faith sharing we suggest. In this way you will receive benefits on the level of both mind and heart. You will perceive and feel a graceful rhythm growing between what you believe and how you live, what you think and how you pray. In brief, you will become at one and the same time an *informed* Catholic woman and a woman *formed* in Christ by virtue of her love and service.

It is our hope that this book will inspire its readers to listen anew to women's songs of faith, past and present, to the voices of known and unknown saints, who became spokespersons for a uniquely feminine way of discipleship modeled on the life of our beloved "Theotokos," the Mother of God, the bearer of Christ, the mediatrix who intercedes for us and the whole world. There is no room for discouragement in womanly hearts, for true femininity finds favor with God.

We want to acknowledge at the outset of this book our profound thanks to its initial readers and critics, to our Epiphany associates and women friends, to our colleagues in Pittsburgh and many other places. We acknowledge with gratitude the encouragement we received from the editorial staff at Servant Publications, especially from Bert Ghezzi and Heidi Hess, both of whom have encouraged this project from start to finish. Last, but certainly not least, we thank our administrative secretary, Mary Lou Perez, and her daughter, Sara, and our staff assistant, Vicki Bittner, for their immense help with the production of the interim and final drafts of this manuscript. We are grateful to God for the blessings we received while doing it from the other women in our courses and from our Epiphany volunteers and associates. Finally, none of this work could have been undertaken or accomplished without the guiding presence of Jesus and Mary. Their hearts are the most believing, celebrating, living, and praying guides one could ever hope to find. Fortunately, at exactly the right time, the Church has given us the new *Catechism* to enhance our search. For this gracious favor and for women of the Church everywhere we pray:

> Lovely Spirit,
> hear our plea
> in fidelity and gentle femininity
> to sink deeply
> with Jesus' humanity
> in the wellspring
> of divinity.
>
> Let us be cleansed,
> wholly drenched,
> by his divinized humanity
> miraculously quenching
> burning thirst,
> hearts about to burst
> with new hope and tender surrender.
>
> Fill our minds
> emptied of self-centeredness
> with the ointment
> of wondrous consent
> to the daily mystery

of what it means to be
a daughter of the Church.

Draw us with all the saints
in Jesus' warm embrace.
Turn each and every
womanly face
into a trace,
a shimmering refraction,
a quiet attraction,
a small epiphany
of the radiance
of the Trinity.

Temper our absorption
in too many daily tasks,
remove our masks
that we may taste and see
only your beauty
saturating memory, mind, and will,
until we grow still
while still moving
with motherly grace,
lacking any trace
of vehemence.

Behold the wellspring
from which increasingly,
prayer to your majesty
flows through time
into eternity.

Let divine oration sing
with daring melody
in spring or winter weather
of your fidelity
to women everywhere,
your upholding
of their dignity.

Let our prayer
orchestrate the care
women show
for all in need
for every limping life
longing to be freed from strife.

May women's voices
be like a soft refrain,
a chant of charity
heard with pristine clarity
under the canopy
of sun and stars.
Protect your suffering little ones
O Invisible One,
guiding all creation
to its mysterious destination.

ONE

Believing That a Loving God Loves Us

The dignity of every human being and the vocation corresponding to that dignity find their definitive measure in *union with God*. Mary, the woman of the Bible, is the most complete expression of this dignity and vocation. For no human being, male or female, created in the image and likeness of God, can *in any* way attain fulfillment apart from this image and likeness.

—Pope John Paul II
Mulieris Dignitatem, 5

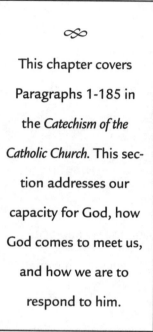

This chapter covers Paragraphs 1-185 in the *Catechism of the Catholic Church*. This section addresses our capacity for God, how God comes to meet us, and how we are to respond to him.

There are as many ways to read the *Catechism of the Catholic Church* as there are readers to study it, develop teaching tools from it, and adapt its contents to the needs of the local church. It is a storehouse of information, a treasure of formation. All four pillars of the *Catechism* stand on one strong foundation: that of love.

> *The whole concern of doctrine and its teaching must be directed to the love that never ends. Whether something is proposed for belief, for hope or for action, the love of our Lord must always be made accessible, so that anyone can see that all the works of perfect Christian virtue spring from love and have no other objective than to arrive at love [25].[1]*

Another feature of the *Catechism* is its rootedness in the writings of the saints and the spiritual masters. Many of them represent the undivided church the first Christians knew. We meet a panorama of women and men whose lives have been made holy by grace. They believed then, as we do now, that a loving God loves us.

Last but not least, from beginning to end, the *Catechism* compels us to see ourselves as a people bound together by sound doctrine, by the timeless splendor of a rich sacramental life, and above all by the transformation through grace offered to us in our Savior, Jesus Christ. Reading the *Catechism* offers women and men a marvelous opportunity for in-depth spiritual formation. A text of this magnitude draws its readers, under the guidance of the Holy Spirit, into a more intimate relationship with the Trinity. There are many times when one sentence, one paragraph, one section, read slowly and ruminated upon, can move us and change us.

The *Catechism* is a classic to be embraced, a treasure to be mined from beginning to end. Anyone who wants to be a true disciple of Jesus, a lover of the Church, a teacher of the faith will find in its pages ample wisdom for a lifetime. Were many voices to resound in one voice, women who hear anew might say:

We believe that we are called to intimate communion with the triune God. We believe in our adoptive participation in the life of the Trinity, in our sanctification through the redeeming love of Jesus Christ, and in the power of the Holy Spirit. When we say, "We believe," we experience a kind of homecoming to the heart of God's greatness and majesty. To be in communion with Father, Son, and Holy Spirit is to live in thanksgiving. It is to know the true dignity of all people in God. To believe means to trust God in every circumstance of our life—through all its peaks and valleys. It is to believe in God the Father Almighty, Creator of heaven and earth, and in Jesus Christ, his only begotten Son.

Called to Believe

The need for nearness to the mystery, implanted in us by God, is a distinctive mark of our humanness. At every time and in every place, God calls us to a relationship of love initiated not by us but by our Maker. As women of faith we readily accept that God wants us, scattered and shattered though we are by sin, to be in communion with the Trinity. We are heirs to the blessed life. As teachers of the faith, women believe that this Good News must be imprinted on our hearts, passed on to every generation, and imparted to all nations.

Formation in this sense cannot be separated from education. A well-formed faith is a solidly informed faith. Catechists who know the doctrine of the Church are happy to tell others why they believe in her teachings, celebrate the sacraments, experience the joys of Christian living, and become people of prayer.

In other words, information received from Holy Scripture, from the writings of the saints and spiritual masters, from the liturgy, and from the Magisterium of the Church has to become formation lived from the heart.

Thus the faith that forms us through and through first of all informs us. It reveals to us that Jesus is the Son of God, conceived by the power of the Holy Spirit and born of the Virgin Mary. Brought into the world through her womb, this child is God's gift to everyone who believes in his name. And his mother in her receptive and giving being remains the purest image of the Church. From the earliest era, our profession of faith has centered on the mystery of the Incarnation and on the women through whom it came to be.

Believing That We Are Called

Believing is not something we do; it is a response to something God has done for us. Faith is a gift to be received, a light that beckons, a call that demands a response. Three facets of faith formation help us to focus on the invitation and the challenge to believe: our capacity for God; God's revelation of a divine plan; and our response. Each facet can be considered separately, although any one is intrinsically connected to the other two.

Our Capacity for God

The desire for God is written on the human heart. Created *by* God, we are also created *for* God. No true happiness can be ours if the search for intimate communion ceases. Throughout history, human beings have been in quest of God. Their search changes them. At times it demands sacrifices; at other times it offers abundant rewards.

The longing for God does not go away, no matter how evil or indifferent the world may seem. It beckons women theologians intellectually. It moves women caregivers affectively. It challenges women mentors spiritually. No seeker ever understood the quest more clearly than a man whose conversion is attributed to the prayers of his mother, St. Monica. That is why St. Augustine's words echo the passion of every searching heart: "You are great, O Lord, and greatly to be praised: great is your power and your wisdom is without measure ... for you have made us for yourself, and our heart is restless until it rests in you"[2] [30].

One way in which Augustine came to know God was by observing the order and beauty of the world. He possessed an outlook of awe and wonder, which led him to rise above the many changing appearances of beauty, to the unchangeable Beautiful One who made them. Augustine did not try to prove the existence of God through endless and ultimately unsatisfying arguments. Rather, he observed the loveliness of creation and looked into his own heart.

As women, the way in which we come to know God is often through the lived experience of our openness to beauty combined with a sense of moral goodness, a longing for freedom from sin, and a deep desire for happiness. God implants in all people a "seed of eternity"[3] [33] that cannot be reduced to what is merely material. We refer to this as our innate openness to the "more than." This drive to "go beyond," this transcendence dynamic, comes from God and draws our soul to God. We are seekers because we know there is something—or, better still, Someone—to be sought.

As the Church teaches, "faith is not opposed to reason" [35]. However, mere analytical reasoning is not enough. It must be complemented by an intuitive comprehension. This truly womanly gift helps reason to come to full realization in faith. St. Augustine could never have believed had he not surrendered to God's revelation and sought eternal salvation.

God's Revelation of a Divine Plan

The divinely revealed and inspired information we find in the Bible is the best guide to God's plan of salvation. It is not so much that we go out to find God as it is that God comes to meet us. The Bible lays out the loving goodness of God's covenant in exquisite detail. From the beginning, God answered our most burning questions by giving us a new order of knowledge. The Bible is not a dry bundle of information sparking endless argumentation, but a disclosure of truth calling us first to adoration.

God did not reveal himself to us reluctantly or stingily, but generously, joyfully, and ecstatically, in the fullness of time. God orchestrated the incredible splendor of this plan out of pure goodness, handing over to the care of women and men alike lofty truths that would lead eventually to the Truth, to the Word made flesh through the power of the Holy Spirit and the cooperation of Mary.

In other words, God, like a good teacher, unfolded the divine plan step by step in a series of stages culminating in the Incarnation. God even deigned that we should become sharers in the divine nature. In the Book of Genesis, we catch hints of the intimacy between God and us that not even sin could destroy. The tender image of man and woman walking hand in hand with God in the Garden of Eden is imprinted on our minds.

Even when we disobeyed God and lost the right to friendship, God did not abandon us to the power of death. Time and again the covenant bond between us deepened, first with Noah, symbolizing God's tie with the nations; then with Abraham, our father in faith through whose descendants God would form a people, Israel. Later,

God gave the Commandments on Mount Sinai to Moses, their leader, implanting in their hearts the expectation of a new and lasting covenant. This was a hope so strong that it would be proclaimed by the prophets and heard by the poor, among whom the best listener would be a maiden named Mary. With her consent, Jesus, the Christ, the mediator and fullness of all revelation, would become incarnate.

How is divine revelation handed over to us? We have a road map, but how do we read it? The answer lies in Tradition, and women have been its carriers since the beginning of the Church. The passing on of the truth of the gospel from age to age happens in two ways: *orally*, by means of the word of God spoken and preached, and in *writings*, as in the texts of the Church's doctrine, her liturgy and prayers. The successors of the apostles, the Holy Father and our bishops, shepherd this sacred dimension of reality by virtue of their teaching authority. Through Sacred Scripture and Tradition, "the Church, in her doctrine, life, and worship perpetuates and transmits to every generation all that she herself is, all that she believes"[4] [78].

The two compasses of Scripture and Tradition flow from the same divine wellspring. Both move us toward the goal of union with God, and both need to be treated with reverence and devotion, not rigid critique or demeaning refusal.

Tradition, which comes to us from the apostles, has "to be distinguished from the various theological, disciplinary, liturgical, or devotional traditions, born in the local churches over time" [83]. Whereas the latter can be retained, modified, or even abandoned under the guidance of the Magisterium, the sacred deposit of the faith belongs to the whole Church.

In an era where people's opinions seem to carry more weight than the deposit of faith, the dogmas defined by the Church appeal to women of discernment. They want to advance on the road to transformation in Christ without getting lost in the tangled mazes of subjectivism, secular humanism, and moral relativism. The *depositum fidei*, the deposit of the faith contained in Sacred Scripture and Tradition, and the *sensus fidei*, the faithful's appreciation of and consent to this teaching authority, coalesce, resulting in right judgment and growth in the spiritual life.

Like Mary, women want to ponder these things in their hearts. As their knowledge of revealed truth deepens through thoughtful reading of the *Catechism*, they feel connected to the spiritual experiences of believers over the ages, who "contribute effectively to the salvation of souls"[5] [95].

For this to happen, the *Catechism* recommends that we pay attention to the content and unity of the Bible as a whole so as to grasp the unity of God's plan; that we read the Scriptures not alone but within the living tradition of the whole Church; and that we stay alert to the analogy of faith, that is, to "the coherence of the truths of faith among themselves and within the whole plan of Revelation" [114].

Two senses of Scripture—the literal and the spiritual—also enrich our reading. The literal meaning is conveyed precisely by the words of Scripture when we follow the rules of sound interpretation or exegesis. The spiritual sense of Scripture is revealed when we look beyond the events described on its pages to see the deeper, allegorical meanings contained just below the surface. For example, we can see the crossing of the Red Sea by the Israelites as a sign or type of Christ's rescuing us from inundation by sin and death.

The *Catechism* confirms that the Gospels "are the heart of all the Scriptures 'because they are our principal source for the life and teaching of the Incarnate Word, our Savior'"[6] [125]. Why we venerate them, why we give them our full attention, is articulated beautifully by St. Thérèse of Lisieux, a young woman wise beyond her years. She writes in her autobiography: "But above all it's the Gospels that occupy my mind when I'm at prayer; my poor soul has so many needs, and yet this is the one thing needful. I'm always finding fresh lights there, hidden and enthralling meanings"" [127].

Access to the Scriptures on the part of the faithful, especially in this Vatican II era, strengthens our belief, nourishes our hope, and deepens our love of spiritual life. Such reading, enjoyed by women and men in many faith sharing groups, is essential for ministry, preaching, catechetics, and all forms of Christian instruction.

Our Response

Because God created us as free persons, our response to divine revelation may be to resist the longing we feel or to refuse to let the truth touch us. Neither response makes us happy. An invitation from God calls for acceptance. It beckons women over a lifetime to keep closer company with our Beloved, who calls us to respond in faith. It requires something human pride is reluctant to give: the complete submission of our will and intellect to God. Nothing must be held back. Inspired by Our Lady, we strive to assent to God's invitation with our whole being—in a word, to be obedient. Only then can one say, "I believe."

Obedience, from the Latin *ob-audire*, means to hear or to listen to. It signifies by extension the submission of our willful tactics of control to God's plan. At times the way will be unclear, veiled by the mystery. We may feel torn between resistance and surrender, refusal and acceptance. We may not always be able to see very far ahead or know how long and arduous the journey will be. But it is always easier to travel if we have a companion like our Blessed Mother, whom the *Catechism* describes as the most perfect embodiment of the obedience of faith [148].

The deeper a woman's faith is, the less resistant she is to God's call. She runs toward God; she does not walk. God speaks and she responds—not by force but by freedom. She ceases trying to figure everything out and simply gives her heart to a Sacred Heart already in love with her. And if submission helps a woman to look anything like Mary, who would want to resist God's call?

Heeding the Call as a Mature Woman in Christ

What then are the characteristics of a mature faith? How do we recognize real belief when we see it? And how do we respond?

The *Catechism* tells us that faith with backbone, stature, and perseverance is a gift from God, "*a supernatural virtue infused by him*" [153]. Faith is a human act, a choice of what a woman will do with her freedom. She believes on the authority of God, but also in the fact that faith is not stagnant; it wants to understand more. At stake here is not "a blind impulse of the mind"[8] [156] but a sense of certitude, a spiritual experience stronger than the light of natural reason can give, that one is in the presence of truth. Of this certitude John Henry Cardinal Newman said, "Ten thousand difficulties do not make one doubt"[9] [157].

On this earth, to be sure, "we walk by faith, not by sight" (2 Cor 5:7). Though we see only dimly and in part, we believe. Faith lived in the darkness of not knowing, faith that is put to the test, matures and mellows.

Surrounded by the evil of the Holocaust, facing her own imminent death, Edith Stein, a Jewish convert to Catholicism and a Carmelite nun, became a modern witness to the faith, a woman who, in the night of not knowing, found the light she had been seeking. In a reflection on *The Mystery of Christmas*, she wrote these prophetic words:

> *"Thy will be done," in its full extent, must be the guideline for the Christian life. It must regulate the day from morning to evening, the course of the year and the entire life. Only then will it be the sole concern of the Christian. All other concerns the Lord*

takes over. This one alone, however, remains ours as long as we live.... And, sooner or later, we begin to realize this. In the childhood of the spiritual life, when we have just begun to allow ourselves to be directed by God, then we feel his guiding hand quite firmly and surely. But it doesn't always stay that way. Whoever belongs to Christ, must go the whole way with him. He/she must mature to adulthood: he/she must one day or other walk the way of the cross to Gethsemane and Golgotha.[10]

Faith's finest hour is lived at the foot of the cross. This powerful text from Hebrews 12:1-2 teaches us what Christian maturity really means:

Therefore, since we are surrounded by so great a cloud of witnesses, let us also lay aside every weight and sin which clings so closely, and let us run with perseverance the race that is set before us, looking to Jesus the pioneer and perfecter of our faith.

Just as the language of faith is the mother tongue of the Church, so the Church teaches the people of God how to best express that faith, how to hand it on and celebrate it in the community, how to live it out in prayer and action. Within the many languages, cultures, and nations that comprise the universal Church, there is but one faith confessed, received from the Lord, and transmitted by Baptism. Tongues may differ, but the content of our tradition is one and the same. No matter where we live, when we say, "We believe," it is as if we dwell in the same house or speak with one voice. As St. Irenaeus said long ago, the Church's message "is true and solid, in which one and the same way of salvation appears throughout the whole world"[11] [174].

Questions for Reflection
and Faith Sharing

1. "When I am completely united to you, there will be no more sorrow or trials; entirely full of you, my life will be complete" (St. Augustine[12] [45]. What do these words from the *Confessions of St. Augustine* mean to you in the context of this chapter?

2. How do you think God is asking you as a woman of this time to perpetuate and transmit "to every generation all that [the Church] herself is, all that she believes"[13] [98]?

3. "Your word is a lamp to my feet and a light to my path" (Ps 119:105). Why do you believe, in the light of the *Catechism*, that "The Church has always venerated the divine Scriptures as she venerated the Body of the Lord"[14] [141]?

4. "The Church is the mother of all believers" [181]. What does this sentence mean to you in the context of your present ministerial commitments?

Seeking Intimacy with the Trinity

As you beget children on earth, never forget that you are also begetting them for God. God wants their birth in the Holy Spirit. He wants them to be adopted children in the only begotten Son, who gives us "power to become children of God" (Jn 1:12). The work of salvation continues in the world and is carried out through the church. All this is the work of the Son of God, the divine bridegroom, who has given to us the kingdom of his Father and who reminds us, his disciples, that "the kingdom of God is in the midst of you" (Lk 17:21).

—Pope John Paul II
Letters to Families, 22

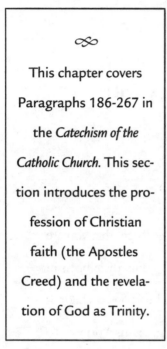

This chapter covers Paragraphs 186-267 in the *Catechism of the Catholic Church*. This section introduces the profession of Christian faith (the Apostles Creed) and the revelation of God as Trinity.

The Apostles' Creed is not only a splendid expression of the essential elements of our faith; it also is the basic point of reference for personality formation in Christ. "To say the Credo with faith is to enter into communion with God, Father, Son, and Holy Spirit, and also with the whole Church which transmits the faith to us and in whose midst we believe" [197]. In the words of St. Ambrose, "This Creed is the spiritual seal, our heart's meditation and an ever-present guardian; it is, unquestionably, the treasure of our soul"[1] [197]

How does this Revelation of God's creative fatherhood affect our spiritual formation? *Creation* is a key word in the *Catechism*. The first claim of the Creed is that God created the heavens and the earth, an act so full, fecund, and fertile that it is still unfolding in every nook and cranny of our planet. God did not contain his lofty greatness, but outpoured it in total and self-giving love. We cannot help but rejoice that "creation is the beginning and the foundation of all God's works" [198].

We Believe in One God

The first person of the Blessed Trinity is the beginning and end of all that is, the Creator of heaven and earth. Thus when we say "I believe" or "we believe" in God, it is the most fundamental affirmation of faith we can make. Whatever else we have to say about the final meaning of our lives and world, it begins and ends in God.

Every subsequent article of the Creed depends on this first statement of belief.

What we confess to first is God's oneness. We believe in a God who is "one in nature, substance, and essence"[2] [200]. Thus Israel, God's chosen, proclaimed with ringing sincerity, "Hear, O Israel: The LORD our God is one LORD; and you shall love the LORD your God with all your heart, and with all your soul, and with all your might" (Dt 6:4-5) [201]. Jesus proclaimed the same truth (Mk 12:29-30), but, as a distinctive mark of the Christian faith, he revealed that he himself is "the Lord" (Mk 12:35-37), and, consequently, that the Holy Spirit is the "Lord and giver of life" [202]. There is only unity, no division, in this one God in three persons whom we love and adore.

As women of faith, we know God not as an anonymous force but as a knowable, loveable Person. God did not reveal the mystery of his love all at once but progressively, through the Old, then the New Testament, and in a special way through a litany of saints into the present age. God would be to holy people a compassionate guide, a faithful spouse, a liberator wanting to free all who believed from slavery to sin.

"I AM WHO I AM" (Ex 3:13-15). These words spoken to Moses [205] were at once a stunning revelation and a preservation of the abyss of God's mystery. Our God is as near as this name, and yet more distant than the farthest star. Though ineffable, the Most High is closer to a woman's heart than she is to herself. Her past, present, and future are bound forever and for every day to God's creating, redeeming, and sanctifying love.

As women of faith we identify with the God of creation, who is also the God of ongoing divine formation. This means that God did not just set the world in motion and then leave it alone. Creation was only the start, only the foundation, of God's plan of salvation. From the first moment, God foresaw the grand design that would culminate in Christ Jesus, our Restorer and Redeemer. This economy of wisdom appeals to our womanly sense of how things should be: fruitful not wasteful, from start to finish.

The joy of creation, indeed the joy women of spirit feel as co-creators with God, is splendidly revealed both in the act of giving birth and in the continuation of the nurturing process. This suggests to us that it was not enough for God to draw the world and everything in it out of nothingness into existence, nor was it enough to fashion cosmic wonders and countless earthly creatures. God sought not only the splendor of creation but the pleasure of ongoing face-to-face conversation. Then, as Genesis relates, something wonderful happened. The Almighty created us, male and female, in his own image and likeness (Gn 1:26-27). God invited us to share in the act of creation, in the naming of what he had created. Though sin abounded more than obedience at the start, God never withdrew his favor.

A key to praying the Creed with conviction is to remember that "God is love," as John, the beloved apostle, teaches (1 Jn 4:8) [214]. God, like the good mother to whom he compares himself in Psalm 131, never stops loving us, however disobedient we may be. His love, unlike ours, is not fickle or arbitrary. It is everlasting, faithful, utterly unconditional, accepting us to such a degree that we become adoptive members of the Trinity. In response to such love a woman might say:

To know you is to love you,
    and to love you, my God, is to long to serve you.
To be your handmaiden means to accept the honor
    of being called and chosen by you.
This grace empowers me to revere the unity and dignity
    that is mine as a woman because of you.
You have entrusted to me the most marvelous epiphany

of your mystery: the creation of new life.
This trust inspires me to care for created things
    with the right balance of attachment and detachment.
In poverty of spirit I learn to trust in you
    at all times, in all places, and under every
    circumstance.
With your help I will make my goal the one St. Teresa of
    Avila prayed:

Let nothing trouble you
Let nothing frighten you
Everything passes
God never changes
Patience
Obtains all
Whoever has God
Wants for nothing
God alone is enough [3] *[227].*

We Believe in the Blessed Trinity

Our faith rests on the knowledge that God is one, and yet this one God is three divine Persons. The mystery of the Most Holy Trinity is "the source of all the other mysteries of faith, the light that enlightens them" [234]. Reason alone has no access to this mystery. Nor could we arrive at it merely by observing God's traces in creation or his revelation to Israel. Something more was needed—not human words but God's own Word in Christ Incarnate.

When we call God "Father" we acknowledge that God is the origin and transcendent source of everything. By this title we also profess, as Jesus taught us, that the Divine Forming Mystery we call "Abba, Father" cares for us intimately with all the tenderness of a loving parent.

The fatherhood of God is often linked with his supreme authority, the motherhood of God with his immanent intimacy. However, the *Catechism* asks us to keep in mind "that God transcends the human distinction between the sexes. He is neither man nor woman; he is God. He also transcends human fatherhood and motherhood, although he is their origin and standard:[4] no one is father as God is Father" [239].

In line with the apostolic tradition, the Council at Nicaea in 325 taught that the Son is "consubstantial" with the Father, or one in being with him. In line with this Council and that held at Constantinople in 381, we thus say in the Nicene Creed that Jesus is "the only-begotten Son of God, eternally begotten of the Father, light from light, true God from true God, begotten not made, consubstantial with the Father"[5] [242]. By virtue of his Incarnation, Jesus is truly and fully human, a man like all others, except for sin, and truly and fully divine, the Second Person of the Blessed Trinity.

The sending of the Holy Spirit, announced by Jesus before his Passover, "reveals in its fullness the mystery of the Holy Trinity" [244]. We believe in the Holy Spirit as the Lord and giver of life. He proceeds from the Father, and with the Father and the Son is worshipped and glorified. This affirmation of the *"filioque"*—that the Spirit "proceeds eternally from both [the Father and the Son] as from one principle and through one spiration"[6] [246]—no longer constitutes a point of disagreement with the Orthodox Churches. In the East and in the West, our faith is shaped by the doctrine of the Trinity. As the opening salutation of the Eucharistic liturgy reminds us: "The grace of the Lord Jesus Christ and the love of God and the fellowship of the Holy Spirit be with you all"[7] [249].

From the first century of Christianity to the present day, the Church has sought to clarify the Trinitarian nature of our faith and to defend it against errors while still declaring that this mystery is "infinitely beyond all that we can humanly understand"[8] [251].

"God is one but not solitary"[9] [254], for the divine unity is Triune. The persons of the Trinity, though distinct, coexist with one another. Because of their unity, "the Father is wholly in the Son and wholly in the Holy Spirit; the Son is wholly in the Father and wholly in the Holy Spirit; the Holy Spirit is wholly in the Father and wholly in the Son"[10] [255].

Creation, redemption, and sanctification are the outflow of God's wholly undivided goodness. God, who is eternal blessedness, wills to share this life of beatitude with all who believe. Women and men by virtue of their Baptism are conformed to the image of Christ. They are adopted daughters and sons of the Trinity (see Eph 1:4-5, 9; Rom 8:15, 29).

This plan of salvation was in the mind and heart of God before we came to be. It would be the mission of the Son to save us and the work of the Holy Spirit to sanctify us by conforming us to the image of the Son. Our creation by the Father would be continued and immensely elevated by means of our ongoing renewal in the Church, the body of Christ. Distinct as the "Trinitarian missions" are, "The whole divine economy is the common work of the three divine persons" [258], for the one nature unfolds in the same operation.

In the Incarnation of the Son, in the gifts of the Spirit, women see with eyes of grateful love all that our God has done for us, his family by adoption. Thus, as the *Catechism* states, "the whole Christian life is a communion with each of the divine persons, without in any way separating them" [259]. When we glorify the Father, it is through the Son in the Holy Spirit. When we follow Christ, it is because the Father draws us and the Spirit moves us. In this way, our lives are Trinitarian through and through, for "the ultimate end of the whole divine economy is the entry of God's creatures into the perfect unity of the Blessed Trinity"[11] [260]. No more beautiful tribute to this graced relationship could have been given than that by Elizabeth of the Trinity, whose prayer is a treasure all women share:

> *O my God, Trinity whom I adore, help me forget myself entirely so to establish myself in you, unmovable and peaceful as if my soul were already in eternity. May nothing be able to trouble my peace or make me leave you, O my unchanging God, but may each minute bring me more deeply into your mystery! Grant my soul peace. Make it your heaven, your beloved dwelling and the place of your rest. May I never abandon you there, but may I be there, whole and entire, completely vigilant in my faith, entirely adoring, and wholly given over to your creative action*[12] *[260].*

Questions for Reflection and Faith Sharing

1. As women of faith we are called to believe that God is "abounding in steadfast love and faithfulness" (Ex 34:6), even though "God remains a mystery beyond words" [230]. How have you experienced this sense of immanence and transcendence in your own walk with God?

2. If someone asked you to define the Trinity, how would you begin to explain this "central mystery of the Christian faith and of Christian life" [261]? If you are a mother or teacher, how would you explain it to a child? Someone of another faith?

3. The *Catechism* assures us that "we are called to share in the life of the Blessed Trinity, here on earth in the obscurity of faith, and after death in eternal light"[13] [265]. How do you experience the mystery of the Holy Trinity in your own personality?

4. The next time you make the sign of the Cross, in the name of the Father, and of the Son, and of the Holy Spirit, meditate on its meaning. What does this brief moment of blessing reveal to you about God's love?

THREE
∞

Belonging to the Trinitarian Family

Man—whether man or woman—*is the only being among the creatures* of the visible world *that God the Creator "has willed for its own sake";* that creature is thus a person. Being a person means striving towards self-realization (The Council text speaks of self-discovery), which can only be achieved "through a sincere gift of self." The model for this interpretation of the person is God himself as Trinity, as a communion of Persons. To say that man is created in the image and likeness of God means that man is called to exist "for" others, to become a gift.

—Pope John Paul II
Mulierus Dignitatem, 7

∞

This chapter covers Paragraphs 268-701 in the *Catechism of the Catholic Church*. This section continues to explore our profession of Christian faith (the Apostles' Creed), which reveals God as Creator of heaven and earth, his only begotten Son Jesus Christ, and the Holy Spirit, and how this faith comes to fruition in the life of the Virgin Mary.

God of mercy, God of love. Thank you for calling me, your beloved daughter, to intimacy with the Trinity. You ready me through grace to receive the gift of fidelity. I believe with all my feminine being, with every degree of receptivity in me, in God, the Father Almighty, in Jesus Christ, his only Son, in the Holy Spirit, Lord and Giver of life, in the Church, and in its doctrines and creeds. Bring me—as I read the Catechism—*to a loving knowledge of thee, O Trinity.*

I Believe in the Father

In this one article of the Creed, there are many meanings. The Father, our Creator, is omnipotence and majesty, absolute love, impenetrable mystery. The more we believe, the more we know. We experience with awe-filled faith that nothing is impossible with God and that nothing is possible without God. Our God is Lord of the universe and "master of history, governing hearts and events in keeping with his will" [269].

The fatherhood of God is about power, strength, and might, but it is also about compassion. God stoops to help us. The Almighty waits upon us in our need. God is infinite wisdom and forgiveness.

We can count as much upon the depths of divine mercy as upon the rightness of divine justice.

All these faces of God are turned toward us at various stages of our lives. They render our relationship with God challenging, appealing, dynamic. Especially when confronted by evil and suffering, or the sense of God's absence, we have the painful thought that perhaps we have been abandoned by God.

This crisis calls for faith at a new level of maturity. It is not easy to believe in the Almighty when we behold the suffering of the innocent. Yet Christ's victory over death, his breaking of its bonds on Easter morn, compels us to believe in the mystery best articulated by the apostle Paul, who understood that the foolishness of God is wiser than human wisdom, and that the weakness of God is stronger than human strength (1 Cor 1:25). Such paradoxes may give new meaning to the word "Father," which we pray in the first lines of the Apostles' Creed.

God the Almighty, the Maker of heaven and earth, comes to woman as Friend-to-friend. This paradox of distance and nearness is hard to grasp. St. Augustine best formulated it in his *Confessions* when he said, "[God is] higher than my highest and more inward than my innermost self"[1] [300].

A woman's intimate relationship with God is always unfolding. Her Maker did not set the world in motion and then leave it to the devices of men. God provided, despite the scandal of evil, for the glorious transformation and salvation of all who believe. The story began when God set the universe in motion, but its final outcome is still being told, for no sooner had sin entered the world than God set in motion a plan to defeat it.

Evil, whether physical, as in destructive forces unleashed by man's misuse of nature, or moral, as in disastrous decisions, is not and can never be God's doing. In fact, total goodness is so good that it can "bring a good from the consequences of an evil, even a moral evil, caused by [God's] creatures" [312]. Even out of the greatest evil ever perpetrated—when Love bled for us on the Cross—came the greatest good ever known—when Love rose from the dead and gave us new life. That is why with the apostle Paul women can say, "We know that in everything God works for good with those who love him" (Rom 8:28). St. Catherine of Siena confirms the same, saying, "God does nothing without our salvation in mind."

From our conception to our final Sabbath rest, our lives are guided by God. It is by divine ordinance, through the power of Jesus Christ, "who died and rose to vanquish evil" [324] that women of faith follow this divine itinerary, freed from anxiety, confident of forgiveness, and fully cooperative with grace.

The Value and Dignity of the Human Soul

Along with St. Catherine of Siena we ask:

> *What made you establish [us] in so great a dignity? Certainly the incalculable love by which you have looked on your creature in yourself! You are taken with love for her; for by love indeed you created her, by love you have given her a being capable of tasting your eternal Good*[2] *[356].*

Only in the light of love can we at one and the same time celebrate God's goodness and lament our sinfulness. Unworthy though we may be, we also know that we have been made in the image and likeness of God. Ours is a *human body* precisely because it is animated by a *spiritual soul*. As the classical Christian tradition puts it, *anima forma corporis* (the soul forms or besouls the body). It follows, therefore, that "the whole human person ... is intended to become, in the body of Christ, a temple of the Spirit"[3] [364].

Thus, from the first moment of our passage from essence to existence, from our being in God to our being in the world with and for God as other-centered lovers, we are responsible for our choices. The Church teaches that as regards equality and dignity there is no difference between us as human persons. Both women and men are of equal worth in the eyes of God. Both mirror uniquely God's wisdom and goodness, God's strength and tender-hearted love. Woman and man are meant by God not only for friendship with him but *for* one another. Equal though we are as persons, our gifts are unique. We need each other to be whole and complete. Hence in marriage a man and a woman form "one flesh" (Gn 2:24) and together they become "stewards of God" [373].

God created us good. He sought our friendship from the start, but betrayal stalked our hearts. Harmony was in our hands, yet disharmony prevailed. Radiance shone from human faces; then the light dimmed. Sin entered the world. Freedom loosened from obedience caused the fall from grace. We cannot grasp the dark reality of sin unless we comprehend at a deep and personal level the relationship God seeks to initiate and maintain with us. The problem is not God's rejection of us but our rejection of God. Love is a free choice, and God cannot make it for us. No one would deny that circumstances can and do contribute to our fallenness, but the fact remains that we must exercise our freedom in a way that draws us closer to God—or condemns us to a life of unhappiness.

Fortunately for us, the story of the Fall remains only half told unless it includes the rising of Jesus from the dead. However gross sin may be, it can never be greater than the grace of God. Whereas Satan's rejection of God was irrevocable and irredeemable, our fallen condition merits divine forgiveness if we are truly repentant. No wonder Satan would go to any length to destroy us. Jesus rightly calls him a "murderer from the beginning" (Jn 8:44), a liar intent on separating us from the love and mercy of God [394]. Thus women mystics like those cited in the *Catechism* accepted that their life on earth was to be one of continual vigilance. Teresa of Avila was not spared warfare with the Evil One. Holy women seldom are left in peace, but fortunately, demonic power, though formidable, is still finite. Though he is a pure spirit, Satan is still a creature, not a God. Despite the injury he causes to human and cosmic history, the victory over sin and death has been won by Jesus Christ [395].

Though original sin deprives us of our divine likeness, it does not corrupt us totally. Our natural powers are wounded. Ignorance of our true destiny in God blinds us to truth. We suffer. We die. We are inclined to sin. But God gives us a second chance. Just as all humans are implicated in Adam's sin, so are all dependent on Christ for salvation, for "as one man's trespass led to condemnation for all men, so one man's act of righteousness leads to acquittal and life for all men" (Rom 5:18) [402].

Baptism erases the stain of original sin. It offers us the fresh start we need to win the battle against Satan. No one should underestimate how hard this struggle will be. That alone is reason enough for spiritual formation to be ongoing.

We Believe in the Son

"We believe" that in the fullness of time God sent his only begotten Son to be our Savior. "We believe" that he "descended from heaven" (Jn 3:13; 6:33), that the "Word became flesh" (Jn 1:14), and that Christ is "the Son of the living God" (Mt 16:16). Thus, at the heart of catechesis, women meet Jesus Christ, for to catechize is to reveal in the Person of Jesus the fullness of God's grand design for our salvation [426]. What women teach is Christ. What women seek is to know Christ. What women suffer is to gain Christ.

"Jesus" means in Hebrew "God saves" [430]. This is the mission of Jesus. To invoke his name is to acknowledge that he is our

Redeemer. "Christ" in Hebrew means Messiah or the Anointed One [436]. In acknowledging Christ's divine Sonship, we accept our adoption as children of God and witness the power of his "glorified humanity" [445]. Never could we settle for mediocre spiritual lives when the Lord of life is at our side. He has sovereign "power over nature, illnesses, demons, death, and sin" [447]. To him we can say in a posture of perfect adoration, "My Lord and my God!" [448].

"We believe" that Jesus came among us to show us the depth and fullness of God's love. He became one of us to save us and to reconcile us with the Father. Of his healing mission St. Gregory of Nyssa said:

> *Sick, our nature demanded to be healed; fallen, to be raised up; dead, to rise again.... Closed in the darkness, it was necessary to bring us the light; captives, we awaited a Savior; prisoners, help; slaves, a liberator. Are these things minor or insignificant? Did they not move God to descend to human nature and visit it, since humanity was in so miserable and unhappy a state?* [457].

Unworthy though we may be, Jesus made us "sharers in his divinity." Belief in his incarnation, in the unity in Jesus of full humanity and full divinity, "is the distinctive sign of Christian faith" [463].

Who is this Jesus in whom women the world over place their belief, hope, and love? He was a man who loved his mother, cried with his friends, laughed at human foolishness. He was a devout Jew who fasted when appropriate but placed people's needs first, who knew when to speak and when to keep silent, when to pray and when to rest.

This man, crucified and crushed, this Christ, who is our God, is our friend, brother, teacher, and guide. He "expresses humanly the divine ways of the Trinity"[5] [470]. He did carpentry with Joseph and taught, already at the age of twelve, with the wisdom of a Rabbi. He used his mind, his will, his imagination, his reason. He obeyed his mother, Mary, and his foster father, Joseph. He loved his apostles and disciples warmly, wholeheartedly. The Jesus of history and the eternal Son are one and the same. As a rational being he increased in wisdom, as a physical being he grew in stature, and as a loyal, obedient son he found "favor with God and man" (Lk 2:52). His human knowledge, like his will and his body, "expressed the divine life of his person"[6] [473]. There was in Christ no opposition between his sonship with the Father and his being the son of Mary. His very presence lifted people toward the God they could not see, so much so that to see him was to see the Father.

When we contemplate so wondrous a Savior, we are drawn deeply into the mystery of pure, unselfish giving, symbolized for many by the Immaculate Heart of Mary. The Virgin Mary was pre-ordained to be the Mother of God by virtue of her own Immaculate Conception. Many women of faith and courage already in the Old Testament, women like Sarah, Ruth, and Esther, were marked by God for great missions, but Mary alone would be the one through whom "the new plan of salvation is established"[7] [489].

Redeemed from sin from the first moment of her conception, she is blessed among women: "… for Mary to be able to give the free assent of her faith to the announcement of her vocation, it was necessary that she be wholly borne by God's grace" [490]. More than any other created person, she is the great mediatrix between us and God. The spiritual life we seek gains depth and vigor when we bind our hearts to hers. Mary exemplifies the virtues that must become part of our Christian character—and none more so than obedience [494]. Mary reserved nothing of herself in the three words that will always be associated with her: "Let it be …" (Lk 1:28-38). Women pray for the courage to say these three words, too. They pray with gratitude in the name of the whole Church:

Thank you, dear Mother, for letting God manifest through your feminine being the gift of becoming the Mother of our Savior. Thank you for conceiving and bearing Jesus, and thus for inaugurating our new creation, our entrance into the family of the Trinity. Thank you for giving the undivided gift of yourself in surrender to God's will. As Virgin and Mother, you are the most perfect realization of what our life in the Church should be [see 502-507].

The Mystery of the Life of Christ

The *Catechism* stresses time and again that the mystery of Christ's life is at the center of the Creed. The *what* in which "we believe" is the Incarnation, conception, and birth of Jesus, true God and true man. It is the Paschal Mystery unfolding in his passion, crucifixion, death, burial, descent into hell, resurrection, and ascension. Though the Apostles' Creed does not focus explicitly on Jesus' hidden and public life, "we believe" that his whole life, from birth to death to risen glory, is a mystery so awesome words fail to express it. All of Jesus' life—his deeds, miracles, and words—reveal that "in him the whole fullness of deity dwells bodily"[8] [515]. His humanity is a sacrament, a sign, an instrument of his divinity and the salvation he brings. The core of the mystery in which we believe helps us to see that "what was visible in his earthly life leads to the invisible mystery of his divine sonship and redemptive mission" [515].

Is there a common thread that holds these mysteries of Jesus' life together? All that he is and does, his silence and his speaking, is a *revelation* of the Father [516]. His mission is consistently *redemptive* [517]. By his poverty we are enriched. By his submission he atones for our disobedience. In his healings he takes on our infirmities. Most important for our formation is the fact that Christ's life is a mystery of *recapitulation*. This means, in the words of St. Irenaeus, that:

> *When Christ became incarnate and was made man, he recapitulated in himself the long history of mankind and procured for us a short cut to salvation, so that what we had lost in Adam, that is, being in the image and likeness of God, we might recover in Christ Jesus.*[9] *For this reason, Christ experienced all the stages of life, thereby giving communion with God to all*[10] ... *[518]*.

Every woman's life can be a revelation of the Father's love, an epiphanic manifestation of the redemptive riches of Jesus' self-gift to her, a recapitulation of his oneness with God. Jesus is the most perfect model of pure love. That is why the "imitation of Christ" becomes not a duty but a delight. It is he who draws us to pray with passion and to serve with compassion. It is his poverty that calls us "to accept freely the privation and persecutions that may come our way"[11] [520]. Christ calls us to do all that we can to realize our original vocation to obedience. If we live in him, he will live in us, for we are members of his Body.

No woman can absorb in one lifetime the depth and range of the mysteries of Jesus' infancy and hidden life she strives to emulate. What she can do is to prepare herself at all times for the coming of Jesus into her life. She can awaken in a heart already bound to Christ in covenant love the expectation of his coming [522].

At present, the Church lives in the time of the Spirit. She struggles to find peace amidst distress and trial, for the Evil One will not spare her. That is why as women of faith we must watch and wait, be vigilant to the signs of the times, and stay on guard. Believers and unbelievers will be witnesses to Christ's second coming, but, for as much time as God allows, "the Church must pass through a final trial that will shake the faith of many believers"[12] [675].

What we await is the true historic victory of God and the Church over evil. This moment of triumph "will cause [the] Bride to come down from heaven"[13] [677]. After "the final cosmic upheaval of this passing world"[14] [677] will come the Last Judgment, when the heart's secrets will be brought to light and the living and the dead will be saved or justly condemned. Whether people have accepted or refused grace will be revealed, for they will have already judged themselves, according to their works.

"Let us live on earth from now on," one might hear women of faith say, *"as if we were already in eternity. Let us accept—never reject—the Spirit of love. Let us share with our neighbors, and never fail to ask for the grace we need to win the war between good and evil in our own hearts and in the world."*

We Believe in the Holy Spirit

St. Paul tells us, "No one can say 'Jesus is Lord' except by the Holy Spirit" (1 Cor 12:3). In the Letter to the Galatians (4:6), he reminds us, "God has sent the Spirit of his Son into our hearts, crying, 'Abba! Father!'" In these startling teachings, Paul tells of a knowledge that is not of our own making. It comes through faith, as God's gift to us. The giver of this gift is the Holy Spirit.

As believers, our deepest desire is to be in touch with Christ. Yet we know from revelation that this communion with him is only possible if we have the faith to move mountains. The Holy Spirit initiates this meeting between Jesus and us. The Spirit enkindles our faith and keeps its flame burning brightly. By virtue of our Baptism, the Holy Spirit in and through the Church communicates to us a new life that has its origin in the Father and its full blossoming in the Son.

The Spirit speaks to women through Christ and the Church. There is about the Spirit a kind of "divine self-effacement" [687]. The Spirit works in the background, as it were, to unveil Christ to his daughters. The vehicles of this unveiling are the inspired Scriptures; the Tradition of the Church; her liturgy and sacraments; her prayers, charisms, and ministries; her apostolic and missionary life; her lifting up as exemplary the witness of the saints [688].

The mission of the Spirit and the Son are beheld by women as one. In the words of St. Gregory of Nyssa, there is "no distance between the Son and the Spirit"[15] [690]. Therefore, we honor the Third Person of the Trinity with the names, titles, and symbols so dear to the Church, saying:

> *You are cleansing water, purifying us of sin. You are the breath of life. You come to us as a refreshing wind. You stand beside us, O Holy Companion on our journey in faith, as a Comforter and Advocate. With Jesus you are the Spirit of truth who leads us to truth. We adore you, living water, welling up from the wellspring of Christ crucified. You give him to us as the source and promise of eternal life. You anoint our head with oil in deep confirmation. Fire, cloud, and light are you, transforming energy, theophany, transcending glory. You place the life of Jesus as a seal on our heart through the holy sacraments of the Church. You are the hand that holds us, the finger that guides us, the dove that hovers over us [690-701].*

The Holy Spirit, who rules, sanctifies, and animates creation, is a special companion on our spiritual journey. It is he who protects and guides our whole formation story, who draws our Christian character and personality back to the glory of God, who restores our divine likeness in the light of the image and form of God in which we were made.

The anchor of our faith is thus the mystery of the Most Holy Trinity. We are empowered by the Father, our Creator, to initiate within ourselves and in our relationships whatever it takes to advance in spiritual maturity. The Eternal Son enables us to reform, because of his redeeming love, the vices that invade our personal and social characters. He graces us beyond all deserving with the power to deepen and expand the good character virtues we already enjoy. The Holy Spirit inspires us to open our hearts, characters, and personalities increasingly to the transforming fullness of Christ himself, to such a degree that we, too, become other Christs *(alter Christus)*.

Thus the whole mystery of belonging to the family of the Trinity moves the heart from intimacy to community. Together the Father, the Son, and the Holy Spirit are one burning, purifying kiln of divine love in which a woman's Christian heart, her matching character and personality, are constantly being formed, reformed, and transformed, drawn from glory to glory, until with all the saints she beholds in beatific splendor the vision of her Beloved.

Questions for Reflection and Faith Sharing

1. How do you see God's "plan of his loving goodness" [315] unfolding in your life here and now as a woman of the Church? Do you trust in "the providence of [your] heavenly Father" (see Matthew 6:24-34)? Are you aware of any life experiences that make it difficult for you to trust?

2. According to the *Catechism*, the "partnership of man and woman (see Genesis 1:27) constitutes the first form of communion between persons"[16] [383]. How do you live out this partnership, this friendship, as a married or a single woman?

3. All of us have struggles with particular sins—some are hidden, some more obvious. Are you able to give testimony to the victory Christ has won over sin in your own life? [420] Why is there "no other name under heaven … by which we must be saved" (Acts 4:12) [452]?

4. Mary, the woman God chose "to be the mother of his Son" [508], is our mother, too. What aspects of her life and faith are most meaningful to you? Her motherhood? Her obedience? Her long-suffering?

FOUR

Enjoying Oneness with a Faith Community

Christ has entered this history and remains in it as the Bridegroom who "has given himself." "To give" means "to become sincere gift" in the most complete and radical way: "Greater love has no man than this" (Jn 15:13). According to this conception, all human beings—both women and men—are called through the Church, to be the "Bride" of Christ, the Redeemer of the world. In this way "being the bride," and thus the "feminine" element, becomes a symbol of all that is "human," according to the words of Paul: "There is neither male nor female; for you are all one in Christ Jesus" (Gal 3:28).

—Pope John Paul II
Mulieris Dignitatem, 25

> ∞
>
> This chapter covers Paragraphs 702-870 in the *Catechism of the Catholic Church*. This section continues to explore our profession of Christian faith (the Apostles Creed), with special emphasis on the Holy Spirit and on how the Church grows under obedience to the Spirit s guidance.

The feast of Pentecost, the birthday of the Church, marks the turning point from fear to faith Christ had predicted. Belief did not belong behind closed doors. The Holy Spirit, with tongues of fire, set aflame the apostles' capacity to proclaim God's word from that hour until the "last days" [732]. Because we live in the era of the Church, we dare to proclaim with the Byzantine liturgy: "We have seen the true Light, we have received the heavenly Spirit, we have found the true faith: we adore the indivisible Trinity, who has saved us"[1] [732]. Women who enjoy to the full their oneness with this community of faith pray from the heart:

Holy Spirit, Spirit of Fire and Light, thank you for pouring into our hearts the love of God as your first gift to us. Dead and wounded though we were by sin, you oversaw the course of our redemption. You left your signature, the gift of charity, in our hearts. We embrace this love as the way to intimacy with Christ—an intimacy only possible because of the power to love we received from you. Thank you for the fruits you allowed to blossom in our life: "love, joy, peace, patience, kindness, goodness, faithfulness, gentleness, self-control" (Gal 5:22-23). You planted these seeds of Christian character in us, and you help them to grow. Let us always listen to you, and be restored to holiness by you. Teach us, as adopted daughters of God, as children of light, what it means to be given a share in eternal glory [736].

We can best participate in the mission of the Holy Spirit by participating in the mission of the Church, for the Church is the very sign and sacrament of the life of the Trinity. Its mission is to make the Trinity known to all members of the *ecclesia* and to initiate them into the family of God. As St. Cyril of Alexandria says, "... the one and undivided Spirit of God, who dwells in all, leads all into spiritual unity"[2] [738].

Christ, as the head of the Body, pours out the Spirit among the members of the believing community, especially through the sacraments. The Church thus attributes to the Holy Spirit the sanctification of the assembly. As members of the Mystical Body of Christ, we believe the holy Catholic Church is the place "where the Spirit flourishes"[3] [749]. The Church is not confined to a building because she is first and foremost a community of believers committed to Christ. She "draws her life from the word and the Body of Christ and so herself becomes Christ's Body" [752]. She is "the spotless spouse of the spotless lamb,"[4] uniting the many to the one Christ, who nourishes them with the bread of life [757].

The Church has taken shape like an intricate tapestry, woven by the Spirit from age to age during various phases of its growth in history—not haphazardly, but in accordance with the Father's plan. In its unity and diversity, the Church represents the "family of God" [759]. As the *Catechism* reminds us, "The world was created for the sake of the Church"[5] [760], that we might witness God's saving plan and enjoy communion with each Person of the Trinity.

As women of faith, we can celebrate the New Covenant instituted by Christ [762] in worship and in the world of everyday life. Our liberation in him is an accomplished fact. Our beloved Lord broke through all boundaries. By an act of total self-gift, he gave birth to the Church in the deepest sense. Both her origin and growth "are symbolized by the blood and water which flowed from the open side of the crucified Jesus"[6] [766]. An apt analogy extends our understanding of her destiny: "As Eve was formed from the sleeping Adam's side, so the Church was born from the pierced heart of Christ hanging dead on the cross"[7] [766], a heart willingly wounded for our sins.

By revealing God's purpose and plan, the Church helps every seeker to find the way to holiness. She is a sign and an instrument of communion with God. It is her desire "that the whole human race may become one People of God, form one Body of Christ, and be built up into one temple of the Holy Spirit"[8] [776]. Women resonate with the vision that we are "a chosen race, a royal priesthood, a holy nation" (1 Pt 2:9). We share with all the faithful in the priesthood of Christ, a priesthood characterized not by power but by poverty. To share in Christ's priesthood is to share in his cross and to serve others with love. In the words of St. Leo the Great: "… apart from the particular service of [the ministerial priesthood], all spiritual and rational Christians are recognized as members of this royal race and sharers in Christ's priestly office."[9] The saint goes on to say: "What, indeed, is as royal for a soul as to govern the body in obedience to God? And what is as priestly as to dedicate a pure conscience to the Lord and to offer the spotless offerings of devotion on the altar of the heart?"[10] [786].

The *Catechism* likens intimate communion with Jesus at the level of the heart to the bond of intimacy between Christ and the Church [789]. To be united with him as members of the one Body is to feel, amidst the diversity of many formation traditions, the unity of belonging to the same faith tradition. Through Baptism, through belief in the Lord's death and resurrection, God's people stand always on the threshold of transformation. We can trust Christ's word that the unity of his Mystical Body will triumph over all divisions, "For as many of you as were baptized into Christ have put on Christ. There is neither Jew nor Greek, there is neither slave nor free, there is neither male nor female; for you are all one in Christ Jesus" (Gal 3:27-28).

As the Head of his Body, the Church, Christ calls women and men over a lifetime to become other Christs. Every day of our lives we must strive to grow in resemblance to the One under whose sovereign rule we live. No closure to the quest for union is possible "until Christ be formed" in us (Gal 4:19). We are to be imitators of his way in this world. Membership in the Church assures our growth in the life of the Spirit, for the faith community to which we belong is one with Christ now and for all ages to come. "Head and members form ... one and the same mystical person"[11] [795], as St. Thomas Aquinas said. When, at another time in history, St. Joan of Arc stood before her judges she said with equal vigor, "About Jesus Christ and the Church, I simply know they're just one thing, and we shouldn't complicate the matter"[12] [795].

The love relationship between Christ and the Church is tenderly captured in the imagery of the marriage union: Christ is the Bridegroom of the Church. So great is his love that he will do all he can to sanctify her, binding himself to her in an everlasting covenant, caring for her as for his own body (see Eph 5:29). That is why the Church is "the temple of the living God" (2 Cor 6:16). As St. Irenaeus puts it: "For where the Church is, there also is God's Spirit; where God's Spirit is, there is the Church and every grace"[13] [797]. As coworkers with Christ in the mystery of redemption, women and men undertake a variety of tasks and offices to renew and build up the Body of Christ. The Church has the authority to test these "spirits" so as to assure that they serve the common good and contribute to the holiness of all believers.

The Church Under the Guidance of the Spirit

In the Creed we confess that the Church of Christ is *one, holy, Catholic,* and *apostolic.* These four characteristics are inseparably intertwined since "unity is of the essence of the Church" [813].

The Church is one. It might seem bold to make this claim when we witness internal divisions in the Church as we know it today, for example, the conservative-liberal polarity, the controversy surrounding certain teachings like the laws governing the beginning and end of life, and even the conflicts one sees on the parish level. What we witness daily is the human face of the Church; what the *Catechism* draws us to consider are the Church's foundational faith traditions and her unity in faith. This unity weaves its way through a variety of formation traditions like a binding thread in an intricate tapestry. Polish Catholics and East African Catholics, to cite but one example, may express their beliefs in different kinds of customs, but they are one in the faith. While it is always possible that a formation tradition may not be in time with the foundations of our Catholic faith traditions—a fact that could lead to war between ethnic and religious factions as we see in places like the former Yugoslavia, Northern Ireland, and Rwanda—the oneness of the faith remains the same from age to age. In short, the Church is home to many people who give form to their faith in terms of their own cultures and customs, but she is ultimately one in Christ Jesus.

St. Clement of Alexandria calls the mystery of the unity of the Church "astonishing" [813]:

> *There is one Father of the universe, one Logos of the universe, and also one Holy Spirit, everywhere one and the same; there is also one virgin become mother, and I should like to call her "Church."*[14]

Rifts, dissensions, ruptures, heresies, apostasies—all such wounds afflict this unity, but none can ever undo it. Remarks the early Church Father Origen [817]:

Where there are sins, there are also divisions, schisms, heresies, and disputes. Where there is virtue, however, there also are harmony and unity, from which arise the one heart and one soul of all believers.[15]

The Church is holy. We dare to make this claim because he who is holy [823] sanctifies her and draws her by grace to the fullness of holiness. Despite human imperfection the children of God share the same foundational call: to be saints. Teresa of Avila taught that the soul of holiness, the first fruit of contemplation, is charity. It was her vision of sanctity that drew Thérèse of Lisieux to this unforgettable meditation on her vocation:

If the Church was a body composed of different members, it couldn't lack the noblest of all; *it must have a Heart, and a Heart BURNING WITH LOVE.* And I realized that *this love alone* was the true motive force which enabled the other members of the Church to act; if it ceased to function, the Apostles would forget to preach the gospel, the Martyrs would refuse to shed their blood. LOVE, IN FACT, IS THE VOCATION WHICH INCLUDES ALL OTHERS; IT'S A UNIVERSE OF ITS OWN, COMPRISING ALL TIME AND SPACE— IT'S ETERNAL![16] [826]

As a way of keeping in the foreground of our faith journey the universal call to holiness, the Church recognizes in women like Teresa of Avila and Thérèse of Lisieux the practice of heroic virtue. Saints are models and intercessors [828] whose presence has at all times in the Church's history spurred the people of God on to sanctity, as has the all-holy presence of the Mother of God whose praises are sung by her daughters and sons.

The Church is catholic. The *catholicity* of the Church refers not only to her universality but also to the fact that there subsists in her the fullness of Christ's body, and that from Christ comes "the fullness of the means of salvation"[17] [830]. It is the Church's mission to bring this Good News to the whole human race, which exists under the one God and Lord of all. Each local church in each diocese is like a microcosm of the macrocosm of the universal Church, for "it is in these and formed out of them that the one and unique Catholic Church exists"[18] [833].

Communion with the Church in Rome is the basis of the universality of the Roman Catholic Church. Pope Paul VI offers a fuller explanation of what "Catholic" means when he says that in the mind of the Lord, "the Church is universal by vocation and mission, but when she puts down her roots in a variety of cultural, social, and human terrains, she takes on different external expressions and appearances in each part of the world"[19] [835]. In other words, though we share the same Roman Catholic faith tradition, we have to respect the many formation traditions that express its underlying universality. Disciplines, rituals, and heritages, proper to the local churches, are "unified in a common effort [to show] all the more resplendently the catholicity of the undivided Church"[20] [835].

The Church is apostolic. The apostolic mission of the Church is to evangelize all nations [848]. In some way every Christian falls under what the *Catechism* calls "the missionary mandate" [849], which sparks in women and men alike the motivation to bring to fulfillment "God's universal plan of salvation" [851]. This dynamic commitment to "make disciples of all nations, baptizing them in the name of the Father and of the Son and of the Holy Spirit" (Mt

28:19) requires patience and *"respectful dialogue* with those who do not yet accept the Gospel"[21] [856]. Evangelization is not a plan to push people to believe by means of clever proselytizing but a presentation, in convincing and uplifting ways, of the truth and goodness of God.

The deposit of faith, traceable to an unbroken line of leadership beginning with Peter, continues to be handed on under the guidance and inspiration of the Holy Spirit. Jesus instructed the apostles that their ministry would be a continuation of his mission. That is why he said to the twelve, "He who receives you receives me" (Mt 10:40). Just as Jesus received everything from the Father, so his followers receive everything from him. They are ministers, servants, and "ambassadors for Christ" (2 Cor 5:20).

Within this one, holy, catholic, and apostolic Church, we pray:

Lord, let us live up to the divine mission you have entrusted to us. Whatever our ministerial role in the Church may be, help us to hand on the true teachings of your Church and never to deviate from them. Give us a spirit of humble obedience that we may respect the successors of your apostles and remain open to all they have to teach us.

Questions for Reflection and Faith Sharing

1. "The Holy Spirit ... builds, animates, and sanctifies the Church" [747]. What womanly gifts of yours enable you to cooperate with the Spirit in this threefold mission?

2. Scripture tells us that "all members [of the Body of Christ, the Church] are linked to one another, especially to those who are suffering, to the poor and persecuted" [806]. In what way do you feel part of this mystery, and how are you called to serve?

3. Of whom do you think when you read in the *Catechism* that "[the Church's] holiness shines in the saints," and when you recall that "in Mary she is already all-holy" [867]?

4. In what way have you experienced the "missionary mandate" of the Church? What are the defining qualities of *"respectful dialogue* with those who do not yet accept the Gospel"²² [856]?

FIVE

∞

Forming Our Lives in Christian Fidelity

The eyes of faith behold a wonderful scene: that of a countless number of lay people, both women and men, busy at work in their daily life and activity, oftentimes far from view and quite unacclaimed by the world, unknown to the world's great personages but nonetheless looked upon in love by the Father, untiring laborers who work in the Lord's vineyard. Confident and steadfast through the power of God's grace, these are the humble yet great builders of the Kingdom of God in history.

—Pope John Paul II
Christifideles Laici, 17

This chapter covers Paragraphs 871-1065 in the *Catechism of the Catholic Church.* This is the concluding section of our profession of Christian faith in the Apostles Creed. It summarizes Church teaching on the consecrated life, the communion of saints, the forgiveness of sins, the resurrection of the body, and life everlasting.

Women—the baptized of the Lord, his priestly, prophetic, and royal daughters—are called to permeate "social, political, and economic realities with the demands of Christian doctrine and life" [899]. Of this noble calling Pope Pius XII said:

Lay believers are in the front line of Church life; for them the Church is the animating principle of human society. Therefore, they in particular ought to have an ever-clearer consciousness not only of belonging to the Church, but of being the Church, that is to say, the community of the faithful on earth under the leadership of the Pope, the common Head, and of the bishops in communion with him. They are the Church [899].[1]

A woman's life in the Church in these post-Vatican II times can be rich, inviting, rewarding, and challenging. Alone and together with others, she can use her gifts to ensure that the work of the Church is carried out in a way that both builds unity and nurtures spiritual well-being within the body of Christ.

"You 'are a chosen race, a royal priesthood, a holy nation, a people of his own.'" The words of the apostle Peter echo through the centuries of Church history (1 Pt 2:9, NAB). As children of

God, we also have a role to fulfill as prophet, priest, and king—an office uniquely our own, which is not only accepted but encouraged by the Church.

"To fulfill your priestly office," the teaching Church seems to say in the *Catechism, "be dedicated to Christ. Allow yourself to be purified and anointed by the Holy Spirit, not only at Baptism and Confirmation but all the days of your life. Rich are the fruits of the Spirit if you live them to the full: work and prayer, friendship and family, relaxation and production—all done out of love and service to God. Bear the hardships of life patiently, as sacrifices acceptable to the Father. Celebrate the Eucharist as often as you can. Reveal Christ's presence everywhere by your holy actions. Consecrate the world to God. Ask him to transform it into his holy house. Be holy yourself and witness to this way with your children. If you are married, lead a conjugal life in the spirit as God decrees. If you are unmarried, lead a faithful single life. See to the Christian education of the children entrusted to your care. Accept the call to lay ministry if God gives it to you and prepare yourself for it by ongoing education and spiritual formation [901-903].*

"To participate in Christ's prophetic office, follow the Catechism and maintain your sense of the faith, even in the face of opposition. Remember the words of St. Thomas Aquinas: 'To teach in order to lead others to faith is the task of every preacher and of each believer"[2] [904]. Proclaim the Word of God by teaching and by the testimony of your life. Prepare yourself for the task of evangelization by proper study. Occasions for announcing Christ to believers and unbelievers alike are already works of grace. Be ready to receive them. Collaborate in catechetical formation and seek the training you need to do so. Teach the sacred sciences in accordance with your educational background. Be

faithful to the Church, especially if you use the media. Express your opinion respectfully for the upbuilding of the Church. Always consider the common good and the dignity of persons [904-907].

"To participate in Christ's kingly office, be obedient to his teachings. This is the first rule you must follow. Freedom can only flower in the garden of responsibility. Pray that you can overcome sin in yourself. Then unite with other laity to remedy conditions in unjust institutions, to 'impregnate culture and human works with a moral value'[3] *[909]. Serve the ecclesial community in accordance with the graces and charisms the Lord has bestowed on you. Strive to unite your work to the teachings of the Church, but be willing to make hard choices when necessary. Remember that 'in every temporal affair [you] are to be guided by a Christian conscience, since no human activity, even of the temporal order, can be withdrawn from God's dominion'*[4] *[912]. Be a living instrument of the mission of the Church in the world, a channel of divine transformation."*

Women in Consecrated Life

Everyone is called to the perfection of charity, but only to some is it given to practice this call in chastity and celibacy, in poverty and obedience, for the sake of the kingdom. "It is the *profession* of these counsels, within a permanent state of life recognized by the Church, that characterizes the life consecrated to God"[5] [915]. Women renewing their profession might thus be inspired to pray:

Lord, make my consecration to you more intimate and recollected, ready for action rooted in contemplation. Don't let me lose the initial fervor of my dedication. Sustain my commitment with special graces so I can continue to give my all in service of your kingdom. Let my life

"signify and proclaim in the Church the glory of the world to come"[6]
[916]. Help me to be an epiphany of the sacred wherever you place me.

"From the God-given seed of the counsels a wonderful and wide-spreading tree has grown up in the field of the Lord, branching out into various forms of the religious life lived in solitude or in community"[7] [917]. One branch is the eremitic life, characterized by silence, solitude, assiduous prayer, and penance [920]. Though hidden from the eyes of the world, hermits preach silently the Word of the Lord. Though in the desert, they are "in the thick of spiritual battle" [921], assuring that the victory will be his.

The same tree branches out into the lives of Christian virgins. These women are solemnly consecrated by sacred vows to Christ. Vowed virgins, be they lay women living alone or nuns living in a community, "are betrothed mystically to Christ, the Son of God, and are dedicated to the service of the Church"[8] [923]. Religious life for those so consecrated is canonically recognized by the Church and "is distinguished from other forms of consecrated life by its liturgical character, public profession of the evangelical counsels, fraternal life led in common, and witness given to the union of Christ with the Church"[9] [925]. This life is a call, a gift received from the Lord, and a form of commitment to the Church that signifies "the very charity of God in the language of our time" [926].

Complementing their service to the Church are other branches of the same tree: secular institutes made up of Christian faithful living in the world, committed to evangelization and the evangelical counsels [928-929]; and societies of apostolic life whose members, without religious vows, pursue the particular apostolic purpose of their society as sisters who in their own way embrace the counsels and strive for the perfection of charity. All women who live the consecrated life might thus pray:

Lord, give us the grace to surrender more fully to you in all that we are and do. Let our lives be mirrors and manifestations of Trinitarian love. Help us to live to the full the threefold path of obedience, poverty, and chastity. Use us, in fidelity to our call, to serve the Church in the desert and the city, near at home and far away. Let our self-emptying be so filled with the spirit of the counsels and the Beatitudes that in us others see Christ. In public and in private let your Son be the origin and "rising sun" of our existence. Let what we do here and now give witness to the "new and eternal life which we have acquired through the redemptive work of Christ." Let our short sojourn on earth be but a prelude to "our future resurrection and the glory of the heavenly kingdom"[10] [933].

Believing in the Communion of Saints

Looked at from the perspective of the Church as a whole, women see a special communion between heaven and earth: between those still being formed as pilgrims on earth; those who have died and are being purified or reformed in purgatory; and those who are transformed in ultimate glory, enjoying the everlasting state of deification. Wayfarers are we in communion with those who sleep in Christ. That is why in our faith tradition we believe so firmly in the intercession of the saints. It was Thérèse of Lisieux who said to her sisters in her final conversations, "I want to spend my heaven in doing good on earth"[11] [956].

We remain in communion with the saints when we cherish their memory, practice devotions associated with their gifts, and call upon them to intercede before the Father on our behalf. By the same token, we remain united to those who have died before us when we treasure their memory, pray for their release from purgatory, and ask them to pray for us who are still on the way. Communion with the dying often prompts women who are caregivers to beseech God to have mercy on those entrusted to their care and to give them the grace of a peaceful death.

Living in fidelity to the Lord changes the way we look at life. We must often step back and take a careful look at our past and present, as well as our hope in the life to come. As members of the one family of God, we all share in the one life call: to seek holiness by living in love and serving our Lord [959].

As we stay in close communion with Mary, who is "the mother of the members of Christ"[12] [963] whose "role in the Church is inseparable from her union with Christ and flows directly from it" [964], we will become more and more fully formed in the faith. With this in mind, with confidence we can pray:

Mary, my Mother, from the time of the Annunciation to your glorious Assumption, you were united with the source of life itself. Through your unfailing intercession, deliver my soul from the jaws of death. Teach me the way of "complete adherence to the Father's will" [967]. Let me be sensitive to my role in his redemptive work and to stay faithful, as you did, to every prompting of the Holy Spirit. Let your courageous consent to the order of grace in your life encourage me to cooperate with the Spirit's leading. Quell all resistance so that I, too, may mediate the work of our Redeemer on earth. Mother of God, blessed by all generations, protect me, your faithful daughter, in all my dangers and needs. In contemplating you, let me envision already what the Church is "in her mystery on her own 'pilgrimage of faith,' and what she will be in the homeland at the end of her journey" [972].

Believing in the Forgiveness of Sins

Through Baptism we are purified from the stain of original sin, and in the case of adult Baptism, of any offenses against God committed prior to this grace-filled release from bondage. What Baptism does not remove is the weakness of our human nature. Cleansing does not preserve us from combat. Until the end of our life it will be necessary to battle the inclinations in us to live in sin and ignorance. Though our sins are forgivable and forgiven in the Sacrament of Penance, we cannot grow slack. Though reborn, we must continually reform.

The best sign of ongoing conversion of heart is continual repentance. This core disposition of the heart makes us more open to receive the "ministry of reconciliation" [981]. In grateful repentance a woman loosened by grace from sin's imprisoning power might pray:

> Lord, I believe there is no offense so great that you cannot forgive it through your ministers, the priests of your Church. Burdened by sin as I may be, you give me the confidence that conversion is possible, the hope that forgiveness is forthcoming, the trust that you will not scorn or reject my repentant heart. The gates of your forgiveness are open wide. Incomparably great is your gift of mercy and compassion. Of it St. Augustine wrote: "Were there no forgiveness of sins in the Church, there would be no hope of life to come or eternal liberation." Let us, let every woman alive, "thank God who has given his Church such a gift"[13] [983].

Believing in the Resurrection of the Body

This act of faith, this belief in the resurrection of the dead because Jesus did what he said, marks the culminating point of Christianity. The risen Lord is with us now as the Christ-form of our soul. The entire cosmos is transfigured by his presence. He is the Lord of the living and of the dead.

What we believe on the basis of divine revelation is not only that our "immortal soul will live on after death, but that even our 'mortal body' will come to life again"[14] [990]. Women believe, despite every temptation to doubt, that the covenant of love binding them heart and soul to God does not end when they die physically, for God "is not God of the dead, but of the living" (Mk 12:27). This emphasis on life, now and forever more, prompts the life-givers women are to pray:

> *O my Jesus, remove from us all fear of death. Make our faith as strong as the tombstone you pushed away on the third day. Show us that with you we shall enjoy life eternal. Even now bring what is dead in us to life through your sustaining grace. Many are the holy ones who have encountered you in risen glory. Let their testimony keep alive our hope of resurrection. It is a struggle to believe that this body of ours, too, will rise, that what is mortal will become immortal, yet your word gives us all the hope we need to seek heaven [997].*

This meditation reminds us that all will rise—those who have done good and those who have done evil. This bodily resurrection will happen because Christ, who rose with his own body, "'will change our lowly body to be like his glorious body,' into a 'spiritual body'"[15] [999]. The "how" exceeds anything one can understand or imagine. Only faith can leap across this ultimate abyss of transformation. For now believers must continue to partake of the Eucharist as a sign of their hope in the resurrection and their willingness to await the last day [1000]. For now, while we live on earth, we must conduct ourselves as is fitting of people who participate in Christ's own life, death, and resurrection. We must remain hidden with Christ, as

Christ is hidden in God (see Col 3:3), anticipating already here and now an eternity of intimacy with the Trinity in the life to come.

What, then, can be said of death if our faith places so much emphasis on life? There is nothing unnatural about bodily death. It is inevitable. By accident, or simply due to the aging process, death puts an end to life as we know it. However old we become, "we have only a limited time in which to bring our lives to fulfillment" [1007].

To see death as a consequence of sin is also to understand that it is contrary to God's plans [1008]. Herein resides our hope. For death, our "last enemy," has been conquered and transformed by Christ. As a human being, he faced death in an agonizing way. He did not fight its natural course. He accepted his dying in total and free consent to the will of the Father. Just as our disobedience brought on the curse of bodily death, so Christ's obedience transformed this curse into a blessing [1009]. As the apostle Paul said, "For to me to live is Christ, and to die is gain" (Phil 1:21). Physical death completes our dying in Christ and reveals its deepest meaning.

Death invites the people of God to a new stage of transforming union. It is not an end but a beginning, not a departure but a homecoming, not a descent into darkness but a being drawn into pure light [1010]. St. Teresa of Avila said with the simplicity of a child, "I want to see God and, in order to see him, I must die"[16] [1011], words later echoed by St. Thérèse of Lisieux when she said, "I am not dying; I am entering life"[17] [1011].

At the appointed time death marks the end of our pilgrimage on earth; there is no turning back from this normal course of things, no reincarnation. All we can do is die a little daily, detaching ourselves from all that is less than God so that we will be ready to meet the "more than" that God has in store for us at the hour of our death. It is proper to pray for a happy parting that does not come upon us unexpectedly, but when we are prepared. Ask Mary, your Mother, to intercede for you. Entrust yourself to St. Joseph, patron of a happy death [1014]. Try to do all you can to be free from sin by living in hope and repentance. Be ready to go to God when your time comes. Remember what Thomas à Kempis wrote in *The Imitation of Christ*, "If you aren't fit to face death today, it's very unlikely you will be tomorrow"[18] [1014].

Believing in Life Everlasting

What happens after death? Life everlasting begins, we believe, with a particular personal judgment for each one of us. The time is over when we were open to "either accepting or rejecting the divine grace manifested in Christ"[19] [1021]. Immediately after we die, each of us will be rewarded in accordance with our works, our faith, and our love. This "eternal retribution" [1022] in our immortal soul determines whether we shall enter into the blessedness of heaven—either through the purification of purgatory or immediately—or into everlasting damnation. This is the moment, in the evening of our life, when, as St. John of the Cross said, "... we shall be judged on our love"[20] [1022].

To live in God's grace is in principle to be in heaven already. And to die in God's grace is to go to heaven. All our life we must strive for heaven. It is the goal for which we pray in the Apostles' Creed. There we shall see God as he is, face-to-face (1 Jn 3:2; 1 Cor 13:12; Rv 22:4). For this privilege women inspired by the great cloud of witnesses to the faith may pray:

Lord, bless our life with you here and now. Let it be a foreshadowing of the eternal bliss that shall be ours one day. Thank you, Beloved, for opening heaven to us, for inviting us to enjoy in full the fruits of your redemption. To believe in you, to remain faithful to you, is the royal road to everlasting glory. O blessed mystery beyond all understanding! O place of beauty beyond description. More delightful than a wedding feast. More intoxicating than the finest wine. Such is our Father's house, this paradise beyond compare, for "no eye has seen, nor ear heard, nor the heart of man conceived, what God has prepared for those who love him" (1 Cor 2:9). Transcendent as the mystery of your Trinity is, you open it to our contemplation in the "beatific vision" [1028]. In heaven our joy will be to continue to fulfill your will for this world and to intercede, as your blessed ones have always done, for all the creatures in it.

What if we are not yet ready for the beatific vision? God, so to speak, gives us a second chance to be transformed. What if we have died in his grace and friendship but are still "imperfectly purified" [1030]? We are assured of eternal salvation, but not until we have undergone the purification we still need "to achieve the holiness necessary to enter the joy of heaven" [1030].

In our tradition we name this place of final purification of the elect *purgatory* [1031]. We image it, as did St. Catherine of Genoa, as a purifying fire. We, the living, pray, therefore, for the dead, asking God to deliver them from their suffering as we hope one day our fellow Christians will pray for us.

The saving union with God we hope to enjoy forever in heaven depends on our freely choosing to know, love, and serve God on this earth. Grave sin of any sort is the opposite of the obedience God asks and deserves. How can a woman be pleasing to God if she deliberately sins against her best self or her neighbors? She has probably already made a hell of her life if she dies in mortal sin without repenting and accepting the gift of divine mercy, even in her final hour.

Sin of this grave a nature means "remaining separated from him for ever by our own free choice" [1033]. Hell is "this state of definitive self-exclusion from communion with God and the blessed" [1033]. No wonder we think of it as a place of "unquenchable fire" where people who refuse the gift of faith, whose hearts are hardened against conversion, are lost in soul and body [1034]. No words could be more devastating than these: "Depart from me, you cursed, into the eternal fire!" (Mt 25:41); no words more consoling than those we pray with the whole Church: "Grant us your peace in this life, / save us from final damnation, / and count us among those you have chosen"²¹ [1037]. Then Christ will come in his glory accompanied by angelic hosts to gather all the nations and to separate sinners destined for eternal punishment from the righteous who will enter eternal life [1038].

In the presence of Christ the truth of each person's relationship with God will be laid bare (see Jn 12:49). On that Judgment Day not only will our final end be set; Jesus will also "pronounce the final word on all history" [1040]. At last we shall know the ultimate meaning of "the whole work of creation and of the entire economy of salvation" [1040]. What was hidden of God's wondrous ways with us will be revealed. Then we will see "that God's justice triumphs over all the injustices committed by his creatures and that God's love is stronger than death"²² [1040]. Women uplifted by this vision will not fail to pray:

Lord Jesus, in the light of our belief in the Last Judgment, let us live every day as the day of salvation. Inspire in us the transforming virtue of holy fear. Give us the courage to commit ourselves to the justice, peace, and mercy that ought to characterize your reign on earth. Let our lives give witness to the blessed hope of your return. Place on our tongues this heaven-sent prayer, "Come, Lord Jesus."

These prayers signify that women who form their lives as Christ's faithful truly believe in and hope for the coming of a new heaven and a new earth, a "mysterious renewal, which will transform humanity and the world" [1043]. Then God's plan to bring under a single head "all things in [Christ], things in heaven and things on earth" (Eph 1:10) will be realized. Envision the heavenly Jerusalem. See it as a place of epiphanic splendor where God dwells with you, where you will once again walk together hand in hand with your Beloved. Let God "wipe away every tear from [your] eyes, and death shall be no more, neither shall there be mourning nor crying nor pain any more, for the former things have passed away" (Rv 21:4).

While we do not know the day or the hour of this consummation—"nor the way in which the universe will be transformed"[23] [1048]—we do know that "the form of this world, distorted by sin, is passing away, and ... that God is preparing a new dwelling and a new earth in which righteousness dwells, in which happiness will fill and surpass all the desires of peace arising in the hearts of men"[24] [1048].

Thus far we have made a journey together on the inroads of our faith and formation tradition. Like the disciples accompanying Jesus on the walk to Emmaus (Lk 24:13-35), we have recalled the deepest truths of the revelation, beginning with how much we are loved by God. As beneficiaries of his saving plan for our lives in Christ Jesus, we are invited with all our womanly gifts to pursue intimacy with the Trinity. God wants women to play a major role in building the community of faith. History attests to this intention. Now we see with enlightened eyes the fruits of that fidelity in everything from the forgiveness of sins to the enjoyment of life everlasting.

Only when we as faithful women meditate on each and every mystery of the Creed can we say our final "Amen," a word that expresses both God's faithfulness to us and our trust in God [1062].

The greatest "Amen" is the one we say to Jesus. In this one word we confirm the first two words of the Creed, "I believe." From this point on, we live to the full the faith we accepted at Baptism, the faith we have pledged to profess to our dying breath.

Questions for Reflection and Faith Sharing

1. At a time in history when faith and fervor are on the wane, how can you as a lay woman fulfill the call to make your "apostolate, through the vigor of [your] Christian spirit, a leaven in the world"[25] [940]?

2. Are you ready not only to hear the call to holiness and commit yourself to its fulfillment but to consecrate yourself as a lay person or as a woman religious "more intimately to God's service and to the good of the whole Church" [945]?

3. Why do you believe in, and what is your experience of, the truth that the saints, living among us and mercifully in heaven, are "always [attentive] to our prayers"[26] [962] and that Mary, our Mother and the Mother of the Church, "continues in heaven to exercise her maternal role on behalf of the members of Christ"[27] [975]?

4. Do you think about your death amidst the daily demands of life in the conviction that Christ shall come to judge the living and the dead [1051]? Can you envision that day when God will be "all in all" (1 Cor 15:28, NAB)? Are you trying daily "to achieve the holiness necessary to enter the joy of God" [1054]?

SIX

Celebrating the Liturgy

In the more specific area of evangelization and catechesis the particular work that women have in the transmission of the faith, not only in the family but also in the various educational environments, is to be more strongly fostered. In broader terms, this should be applied in all that regards embracing the Word of God, its understanding and its communication, as well as its study, research and theological teaching.

—Pope John Paul II
Christifideles Laici, 51

∞

This chapter covers Paragraphs 1066-1209 in the *Catechism of the Catholic Church* on The Sacramental Economy. It concerns many aspects of worship, including its Trinitarian source, the Paschal Mystery in the Church s sacraments, and how we celebrate the Church s liturgy.

Liturgy is a dynamic realty; it is a celebration of our presence to God, of our communion with Christ, of our participation in a mystery of faith, hope, and love so profound words fail to describe it. Liturgically speaking, the Holy Spirit enables women to share in Christ's ministry in a threefold way: in his priesthood by worship, in his prophetic mission by proclamation, and in his kingly compassion by charity [1070]. Liturgy is thus a source of Christian life formation in Church and society.

The heart of worship, proclamation, and compassion is prayer, "Christ's own prayer addressed to the Father in the Holy Spirit" [1073]. Power flows from his prayer, for the liturgy is "the privileged place for catechizing the People of God." In the words of Pope John Paul II: "Catechesis is intrinsically linked with the whole of liturgical and sacramental activity, for it is in the sacraments, especially in the Eucharist, that Christ Jesus works in fullness for the transformation of [all]"[1] [1074].

Trinitarian Transformation through the Liturgy

In a tradition common to the churches of the East and the West, the action of Christ through the sacraments is referred to as "the sacramental economy" [1076]. It accounts for the communication or "dispensation" of the fruits and graces Christ wants to give us as a sign of his love. In its economy and dispensation, in every facet of its unfolding, the liturgy is the work of the Trinity. The source of all blessing, as Jesus acknowledges, is the Father whom we adore and thank, worship and praise. We stand in awe because of what our God has done for us. In the liturgy these divine blessings, formed and informed by the Trinitarian shape of our faith, are fully revealed and communicated.

Christ's holiness, in which we share, is that which we offer in love to the Father. The sacraments are perceptible signs, words, and actions, accessible to us—signs that make present the grace they signify. That Christ has conquered death is happening here and now. That he is risen is the cause of our joy. That he will come again is a truth that fills the universe. Since the Resurrection unbinds Christ from the confinements of space and time as we know them, he is present always and everywhere. The liturgy, understood as one great act of love, thus gathers all that is dead in us and brings it to life.

In every sacrament of the Church, Christ acts to put to death sin and to raise women and men to new life in him. He is really present in the bread and wine consecrated by the Eucharist [1088]. This miracle of grace can only occur because he is risen. The Lord can fill all things with his epiphanic light, his saving love, his glorified life. In tender compassion for our suffering, he sent us the Holy Spirit. He inaugurated the apostolic succession. Though he vanished from our sight, he placed before us as a visible sign of his presence his shepherds, the apostles, his vicar the Pope, the bishops and the priests, who serve God's people. We the faithful meet the risen Lord when we gather together in his name. We receive his Body and Blood in Holy Communion. That is why the liturgy is not something the Church does, like a social gathering or a memorial service; it is a celebration of Christ with us and among us.

We are participants in the heavenly liturgy, for God is perfectly glorified by Christ acting in us [1090]. Our teacher in faith and the artisan of "God's masterpieces" (the sacraments) is the Holy Spirit [1091]. It is in and through the power of the Spirit that women yield their whole life, their thinking, willing, and remembering self to Christ. This yielding prepares women of spirit at every moment to encounter Christ and to make his mystery present to people here and now. The Spirit guides our reading of the Old Testament, our praying of the Psalms, our recalling the saving events in the Hebrew Scriptures and the New Testament that constitute the economy of salvation [1093]. The Spirit awakens our sometimes sleepy faith, converts our resistant hearts, and readies our stubborn wills for adherence to the divine will [1098].

The Spirit is "the Church's living memory"[2] [1099], helping us to recollect "God's saving interventions in history" [1103] and sending us forth to live and tell the Good News.

At the heart of the liturgy is the *Epiclesis* or "invocation upon" [1105]. It is the special prayer of the priest in which he begs the Father to send the Holy Spirit upon the offerings of bread and wine so that they may become the Body and Blood of Christ [1106]. This perfect offering to the Father cannot possibly occur unless the Holy Spirit comes upon these gifts and transforms them.

In every liturgical action women are brought into communion with Christ through the power of the Spirit. An intimate coopera-tion between the heart of a woman and the Head who is Christ is accomplished in the liturgy. From her communion with the Trinity flows her communion with other believers. If she is truly *there* when the liturgy is being celebrated, she can never be the same again. Her love of God grows by leaps and bounds; she notices a real change or transformation in her relations with others; and she recommits her-self to make Christ's saving work present in the Church "through the witness and service of charity" [1109].

What the Seven Sacraments Have in Common:

A Woman s Rumination

Lord, it is you who institute these seven ways to salvation: Baptism, Confirmation, Eucharist, Penance, Anointing of the Sick, Holy Orders, and Matrimony. By your words and actions, hidden and seen, you announced and prepared the way for what the Church would accomplish. Through your ministers, all your mysteries are dispensed. Your sacraments are like rays of love and mercy flowing forth from your mystical Body. The actions of your Spirit are at work in the Church through the sacraments. They are the master-works of the new and everlasting covenant [1114-1116].

1. Church. Lord, your Church recognizes what a treasure of grace is hers. She is to be the faithful steward of your mysteries. They are to be dispensed by her and they are also "for her." It is her respon-sibility to bring all in the Church into communion with you. Through the ministerial priesthood, and the apostolic succession in which it is rooted, your baptismal priesthood is to be served. Ordained ministers receive the call, O Jesus, to act in your name and in your person. When we, your people, are baptized and con-firmed, just as when your priests are ordained, we receive not only special graces but also a sacramental character or seal. These indel-ible marks make us sharers, O Lord, in your priestly, prophetic, and kingly life. They configure us to you and to your Church. You place in us a positive disposition for grace. You promise us that we shall be divinely protected. You call us to worship and ready us to serve your Church in ways that are unique and complementary [1117-1121].

2. Faith. Lord, you formed us into one body by virtue of your liv-ing word. You empowered us to evangelize the nations by giving us the gift of faith. You originated these seven sacraments to nourish, strengthen, and express our belief, our hope, our love. That is why they are called "sacraments of faith." Give us the courage we need in today's world to confess our faith with the fervor of the apostles. Let the law of prayer be the law of faith so that as we believe so we pray. Watch over your ministers so that they never modify or manipulate arbitrarily or at will any sacramental rite of your Church. Let obedience be our guide. Let respect for the mystery of the liturgy be our light [1122-1126].

3. Salvation. Lord, gratitude swells our hearts when we remember that your sacraments confer on us the grace they signify. How efficacious are your works, O Lord, because you are at work in them! The Father hears your prayers for us in our celebrations. As fire transforms into itself everything it touches, so your Holy Spirit transforms into divine life whatever is subjected to this light. Thus our Church affirms that the sacraments act "by the very fact of the action's being performed." No wonder the efficacy of these divine works is not dependent on the righteousness (though we hope it is there) of the celebrant or the recipient. You and your Spirit act independently of our personal holiness—though the goods coming forth from the sacraments depend on the dispositions we bring to these sacred rites. Let us be good bearers of their blessed fruits. For the sacraments are not rites added on to our formation, reformation, and transformation. They are necessary for our salvation. Heal us with the healing grace proper to each sacrament. Help us to conform our lives to Christ's in the spirit of adopted daughters and sons. Unite us, dear Father, in living union with Jesus [1127-1129].

4. Eternal Life. This, Lord, is our common sacramental destiny. We celebrate your mystery until you come, until you become "everything to everyone." Hear our groaning as we pray: Come, Lord Jesus! Remind us that what we partake of now shall only be brought to fulfillment in heaven. Yet insofar as we worthily receive your sacraments, we are guaranteed a share in everlasting life. Now we await with blessed hope the appearance of your glory (see Ti 2:13); then we shall see with the eyes of the blessed its shining epiphany for all eternity [1130].

Celebrating the Church s Liturgy

Who? How? When? Where? These questions point to the unity found in every liturgical celebration, however diverse its expression may be.

Who Celebrates?

Every time we celebrate the mystery of salvation in the sacraments, we—the Body of Christ—join in a heavenly chorus honoring God most high in the liturgy of eternity. Our roles are different, but we celebrate as one body this "sacrament of unity" [1140]. We, the baptized, are regenerated and anointed by the power of the Holy Spirit. We share the same spiritual household as the common priesthood of the assembly, though we do not all have the same function.

Christ, our High Priest, calls men consecrated to the priesthood by the reception of the Sacrament of Holy Orders, to act in his person for the service of all. Our tradition is unbroken on this point, for the ordained minister, the priest, "is, as it were, an 'icon' of Christ" [1142]. Since it is in the Eucharist that Christ's presence is made most visible, "it is in his presiding at the Eucharist that the bishop's ministry is most evident, as well as, in communion with him, the ministry of priests and deacons" [1142].

Assisting in this work of celebration are all the members of the common priesthood. Some are assigned to particular ministries; others to meet a variety of pastoral needs (servers, readers, commentators, choir members, teachers), but all act in the "unity of the

Spirit" [1144] to honor Christ, to witness to his living tradition, and to obey the Church by carrying out his or her part according to the established rites and norms of the liturgy.

How Do We Celebrate?

Think of the liturgy as a beautiful tapestry "woven from signs and symbols" [1145], stretching from the dawn of salvation history to the present day. The formative power of these signs stems from their four foundations. The first is our human world. The liturgy appeals to our bodily senses—to seeing, hearing, touching, tasting, and smelling—even as the rites, symbols, and ceremonies lift our spirits. Words, gestures, and actions bind us in worship to God and in social presence to one another. In the matter of creation we behold the mystery of our Creator. "Light and darkness, wind and fire, water and earth, the tree and its fruit speak of God and symbolize both his greatness and his nearness" [1147]. Rituals like the washing of hands or the breaking of bread point beyond themselves to our desire to give honor to God and to express our thanks for his saving grace. The signs of celebration help to imprint on our hearts the truth of our "new creation in Jesus Christ" [1149].

The second set of liturgical signs reconfirms the covenant. God gave the Chosen People certain symbols to mark this bond and to commemorate the wonder of the divine initiative on our behalf. Signs of the Old Covenant like circumcision are seen by the Church as prefigurations of "the sacraments of the New Covenant" [1150].

Comprising the third set of liturgical signs are those offered by Christ to reveal divine mysteries unknown before his revelation. For us Christ himself "is the meaning of all these signs" [1151].

Since Pentecost the fourth group of signs are sacramental because it is the Holy Spirit who "carries on the work of sanctification" [1152]. The liturgy is by definition transcendent. Every aspect of it is more than sensory or cosmic or social. We worship on earth in the light of the glory of heaven. Thus women might pray before, during, and after the liturgy:

> *Father, Son, and Holy Spirit, we thank you for welcoming us into this holy circle of celebration where we meet you more intimately in the words we speak and the actions we perform: serving at the altar, reading your life-giving Word, distributing Holy Communion, serving in decision-making positions. Let our actions reveal the source of our faith, the reason for our hope, the sign of our love. Let us be present to the wonders unfolding before us: processions, candle lightings, proclamations, sermons, meditations, music—all means of professing our faith, increasing our understanding, and fulfilling our longing for you [1153-1155].*

Among the many ways in which women and men give honor to God, music has a privileged place, for "the musical tradition of the universal Church is a treasure of inestimable value, greater even than that of any other art"[3] [1156]. Who of us could forget the famous words (Eph 5:19), echoed by St. Augustine, that one "who sings prays twice"[4] [1156]. The saint also said in his *Confessions:*

> How I wept, deeply moved by your hymns, songs, and the voices that echoed through your Church! What emotion I experienced in them! Those sounds flowed into my ears, distilling the truth in my heart. A feeling of devotion surged within me, and tears streamed down my face—tears that did me good[5] [1157].

Here Augustine confirms not only the formative but also the transformative power of prayer and solemn participation in sacred celebrations. For they stir transcendent desires; they express our love for God in echoes of celestial harmony.

Music and good singing inspired by Holy Scripture can be

instruments of conversion as Augustine testifies. So, too, can holy images. Liturgical icons represent Jesus Christ in such a way that images and words illumine each other, confirming that "the incarnation of the Word of God was real and not imaginary"[6] [1160]. Images of the Blessed Mother and the saints, of angels and the whole "cloud of witnesses" (Heb 12:1) are also important to us. We feel ourselves to be part of a dynamic, ever unfolding tradition of faith and sacrifice. We hope what we experience will do for us what it did for St. John Damascene, who said, "The beauty of images moves me to contemplation, as a meadow delights the eyes and subtly infuses the soul with the glory of God"[7] [1162].

When Do We Celebrate?
The answer is daily, weekly, seasonally, and on solemn feasts. In fact, over the course of the year, there unfolds before us "the whole mystery of Christ"[8] [1163]. These riches are not merely past events; they are made present to us age upon age, opening us to the Divine and making it possible for us to avail ourselves of God's saving grace. We fix these feast days to commemorate the actions of our Savior, to thank him for thinking so much of us, to make sure every generation remembers what God has done for us, and above all, to teach us to conform our conduct to Christ's.

All of this happens, to emphasize a word precious to the Church, "Today!" [1165]. This is the "today" of the living God. We are called to enter into intimacy with Jesus now, at this "hour." The "now" reaches across the ages and undergirds our entire history. Special to us is the celebration of the Lord's Day on Sunday with the Lord's Supper at its center, "for there the whole community of the faithful encounters the risen Lord who invites them to his banquet"[9] [1166]. Here and now, in this present hour, women, conscious of the guiding light of Christ, pray:

Lord, may we celebrate your day as a "day that knows no

evening"[10] *[1166]. When we gather to listen to your word, to take part in your Holy Eucharist, let us be mindful of what it is that we do, of how this day brings us closer to you. Let the great Sabbath rest be for us a "little resurrection," a quiet oasis in the busy stream of daily life, that restores our vision of what will be. Let this day be our renewal, as we move from darkness to light, glimpsing the gates of paradise and going through them free of fear [1167].*

Such are the dispositions that can carry our lives in Christ through the liturgical year, from the dawning of Easter morn through the cycle of feasts (Annunciation, Christmas, Epiphany) that surround the mystery of the Incarnation. The liturgy transfigures our entire year, just as the brilliant light of the Resurrection "permeates with its powerful energy our old time, until all is subjected to [Jesus, the Lord]" [1169].

Women give a special place of honor to Mary, their Mother, for she is inseparably "linked with the saving work of her Son"[11] [1172]. With the whole Church, we set aside days of the year to honor martyrs and saints in the hope that we, too, might emulate all who have suffered and been glorified with Christ [1173].

Yet another formative purpose is served by the Liturgy of the Hours or the "divine office." In it the mystery of transforming love permeates each hour of the day, transfiguring time and helping those who pray the office to praise God without ceasing. All who recite its psalms and prayers come away with a deeper understanding of the Paschal Mystery, of the liturgy, and of the Bible, "especially of the Psalms"[12] [1176]. Such praying on a regular basis, in a meditative fashion, is an exercise in *lectio divina*. It helps us to enter more fully into the "meaning of the mystery being celebrated" [1177]. Devotions, adoration, worship of the Blessed Sacrament become for us "an extension of the Eucharistic celebration" [1178].

Where Do We Celebrate the Liturgy?

Certainly our celebrations are not bound exclusively to one place, since the whole earth is holy. We who assemble to worship God are the "living stones," gathered to be "built into a spiritual house" (1 Pt 2:4-5). For, as Paul writes in his Epistle to the Corinthians, "we are the temple of the living God" (2 Cor 6:16). When churches are built, they are not just buildings or worship sites but dwellings of the Divine, where praying people meet their God and seek deeper union with Christ and one another.

Thus the Church is a "house of prayer." It is a holy place where the community celebrates the liturgy and reserves the Eucharist for constant adoration and consolation [1181]. Every part of the church speaks to us of God: the *altar* is the Lord's cross; the *tabernacle* is the place of Christ's presence; the *sacred chrism* signifies the seal of the Holy Spirit; the bishop's *chair* expresses his office of presiding over the assembly; the *lectern* reminds us of the dignity of the Word of God. Each sacrament has its own place of celebration as well, for special parts of the Church invite, as the case may be, remembrance, repentance, recollection, and prayer [1182-1185].

Unity in Diversity

While the mystery we celebrate in the liturgy is one, the forms by which we do so are diverse [1200]. No one expression can ever exhaust a mystery as profound as Christ's Passion, Death, and Resurrection. Each liturgical tradition in its singularity still represents a remarkable unity and complementarity. All threads of this rich tapestry interweave in fidelity "to the common mission of the whole Church"[13] [1201]. So rich is the "deposit of faith" (2 Tm 1:14, NAB) that no one tradition can capture it.

Parts of the liturgy are immutable; others can be changed by the power invested in the Church, but on one point there is full agreement: In the words of Pope John Paul II, "... diversity must not damage unity. It must express only fidelity to the common faith, to the sacramental signs that the Church has received from Christ, and to hierarchical communion"[14] [1206].

Questions for Reflection and Faith Sharing

1. When you celebrate the liturgy, when you receive the sacraments, are you aware of encountering Christ, of making his saving work present and active, of allowing it to bear fruit through your womanly presence in the Church [1112]? Do you see in yourself an "increase in charity" [1134]?

2. How have you come to understand your own "baptismal priesthood" [1188] as a woman in this post-Vatican II era?

3. Do you celebrate the "Lord's Day" in your household as "the day of the Christian family, and the day of joy and rest from work" [1193]? Can you think of ways your family might embrace "Sabbath rest" more fully?

4. Have you ever celebrated the liturgy in a country other than your own? What was your experience of the way in which "the diverse liturgical traditions ... manifest the catholicity of the Church, because they signify and communicate the same mystery of Christ" [1208]?

SEVEN

Revisiting the Sacraments of Initiation

As the Redeemer of the world, Christ is the Bridegroom of the Church. The Eucharist is the Sacrament of our Redemption. It is the Sacrament of the Bridegroom and of the Bride. The Eucharist makes present and realizes anew in a sacramental manner the redemptive act of Christ, who "creates" the Church, his body. Christ is united with this "body" as the bridegroom with the bride. All this is contained in the Letter to the Ephesians. The perennial "unity of the two" that exists between man and woman from the very "beginning" is introduced into this "great mystery" of Christ and of the Church.

—Pope John Paul II
Mulieris Dignitatem, 26

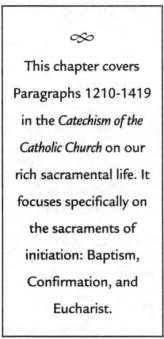

This chapter covers Paragraphs 1210-1419 in the *Catechism of the Catholic Church* on our rich sacramental life. It focuses specifically on the sacraments of initiation: Baptism, Confirmation, and Eucharist.

As the word "initiation" implies, these three sacraments represent the beginning stages of our path to maturity in Christ. They "lay the *foundations* of every Christian life" [1212]. That is why we use the expression "born anew" for Baptism. We speak of Confirmation as strengthening our faith through the power of the Holy Spirit. Partaking of the Eucharist nourishes us spiritually and also readies us for eternal life. All three sacraments find fulfillment in "the perfection of charity." They form the cornerstone of our faith and formation tradition.

The Gift of Baptism

The first of these "masterpieces," Baptism, has been called by St. Gregory of Nazianzus "God's most beautiful and magnificent gift" because

> it is conferred on those who bring nothing of their own; *grace* since it is given even to the guilty; *Baptism* because sin is buried in the water; *anointing* for it is priestly and royal as are those who are anointed; *enlightenment* because it radiates light; *clothing* since it veils our shame; *bath* because it washes; and *seal* as it is our guard and the sign of God's Lordship[1] [1216].

Many events in salvation history can be seen as prefigurations of this first gift: the Genesis account of the Spirit breathing on the waters; the parting of the waters so the Israelites could cross the Red Sea and escape the bondage of Egypt; the crossing of the Jordan River into the Promised Land. Yet no event of rebirth could have been more epiphanic than Jesus' own baptism by John. By this solemn gesture Jesus forecast the depth of his self-emptying love. He, the "beloved Son" (Mt 3:16-17), would one day submit to death on a cross to atone for our sins. By his Passover he would open for us the purifying fountain of Baptism, enabling us to pass over from death to new life.

From the birthday of the Church on Pentecost to the present day, the imperative of St. Peter has been fulfilled: "Repent, and be baptized every one of you in the name of Jesus Christ for the forgiveness of your sins; and you shall receive the gift of the Holy Spirit" (Acts 2:38). In the early Church, all who believed could be baptized, provided they met the requirement of faith: "Believe in the Lord Jesus, and you will be saved." So said the apostle Paul to his jailer in Philippi (see Acts 16:31-33). To be baptized meant then, as it does now, to "put on Christ" (Gal 3:27). In the water of Baptism, through the power of the Holy Spirit, we are changed irrevocably. We are purified, justified, and sanctified [1227].

Whether a person is baptized as an infant or initiated into the faith as an adult, certain essential elements by sponsorship or mature consent have to be in place. The Church identifies these as: "proclamation of the Word, acceptance of the Gospel entailing conversion, profession of faith, Baptism itself, the outpouring of the Holy Spirit, and admission to Eucharistic communion" [1229].

Infant Baptism abridges the process of preparation, but it presupposes and requires, as the *Catechism* states, "a *post-baptismal catechumenate*" [1231], for such instruction is necessary if the grace of Baptism is to flower and bear fruit in one's ongoing spiritual formation.

Carrying this formation forward initially, like a slow starting symphony that builds to a resounding crescendo, are the rich symbolic rites that transform the unbaptized into the baptized. The "mystagogy of the celebration" [1234] begins, of course, with the *sign of the cross*; it puts on the person who will soon be baptized the "imprint of Christ" [1235]. All the other rituals follow from this one, including the proclamation of the Word; one or more *exorcisms*, signifying the renunciation of Satan and one's readiness to *confess the faith of the Church* [1237]; the consecration of the *baptismal water*; the administering of the *essential rite* of Baptism by immersion or pouring water on the head of the candidate, baptizing her or him in the name of the Father, and of the Son, and of the Holy Spirit.

At this beautiful moment we enter into the central mystery of our faith and formation tradition: the life of the Trinity. Intimacy by adoption, a life-transforming relationship with the Triune God, can now be enjoyed by the newly baptized. At Baptism they receive a first *anointing with sacred chrism* (the second will come at the time of Confirmation) [1241-1242]. The white garment worn for this occasion signifies identification with the risen Lord. The *candle* is a reminder that we are to be "the light of the world" (Mt 5:14). The newly baptized are now eligible to receive their Confirmation and first Holy Communion, depending on the practices customary in the Latin or in the Eastern Churches. Regardless of ritual differences on this point, the result is the same: the baptized are solemnly blessed, drawn into the community of faith, and set on the path to graced transformation in Christ.

That is why the Church insists in the case of adult Baptism that the initiates receive adequate preparation and formation to bring "their conversion and faith to maturity." [1248]. To receive the three sacraments of initiation those in the catechumenate must first receive "a formation in the whole Christian life"[2] [1248], a life described in all its salvific, evangelical, liturgical, and charitable splendor in the *Catechism* itself.

Faith cannot grow in a vacuum; it requires the presence of a believing, hoping, loving community. Faith cannot merely be taught; it has to be caught. Renewing our baptismal promises as we do each Easter vigil night is our way of pledging to keep faith alive in family life. Its ideal unfolding can only happen if Christian parents accept their role to nurture and form in the faith the children God entrusts to their care [1250-1252].

An excellent way for parents of a newborn to prepare themselves for this rite would be to review in detail this section of the *Catechism*, especially if one of the parents is not a practicing Catholic. Many pastoral situations present themselves at this time. Grandparents whose children have left the Church may grieve when they refuse to have their own child baptized (or to wait until their child is old enough to decide for him or herself). Consultation with a priest can diffuse some of their anxiety and encourage them by prayer and example to try to win their children's hearts once again to Christ.

If all is well and the child is ready to be baptized, the parents ought to take time to ponder who will be the most suitable godparents. Are the people ready to assume responsibility in some way for the child's faith formation?

Though bishops, priests, and deacons are the ordinary ministers of Baptism, so necessary is this sacrament for salvation that anyone—even one who is not baptized—can still baptize if one has the right intention and uses, as the Church does, the "Trinitarian baptismal formula" [1256]. The necessity of our being "reborn of water and the Spirit" [1257] explains why the Church holds to the efficacy of the *"Baptism of blood"* for those who die for their faith without having been baptized previously [1258]. The "Baptism of desire" applies to souls who, though ignorant of the gospel of

Christ and of his Body, the Church, seek the truth and do the will of God in accordance with their understanding of it. They, too, can be saved on the premise that "such persons would have *desired Baptism explicitly* if they had known its necessity" [1260].

What about the fate of children who die without being baptized? What then? The answer given by the Church is simple and direct: entrust these little ones to the mercy of God whose desire is that all children be saved, especially the innocent who, through no fault of their own, come into the world under less than propitious circumstances. Jesus' own tenderness toward children (see Mk 10:14) gives the faith community reason to hope for their salvation, even if they die without being baptized.

Gratitude for the grace of Baptism wells up when a woman looks to God and asks in words all of us understand:

Lord, of what worth would life be without this gift of divine forgiveness? You offered it to us not because of any merit of ours but solely out of your gratuitous love. It was you, Almighty Father, who took the initiative in your Son, Jesus Christ, and through the power of your Holy Spirit, to break down the walls of sin separating us from you.

Father, you did not remove the consequences of sin. We still suffer sickness in body and soul. The battle harms us and cannot be won without the help of Jesus [1264]. Yet, for all of this struggle and its unfortunate consequences in our life and world, you still work miracles in Baptism. Not only are we purified from all our sins; we also become new creatures, sons and daughters adopted by you, partakers in your own divine nature (2 Cor 5:17), members of the Mystical Body of Christ (1 Cor 6:15; Eph 4:25) coheirs with you, and temples of the Holy Spirit.

O Most Holy Trinity, you give us as the greatest of all these gifts that of "sanctifying grace, the grace of justification"

[1266]. Thus we are able to believe in you, to hope in you, and to love you. From this point forward, we remain open to the theological virtues. We can live and act according to the promptings, the stirrings, the inspirations, the gifts of the Holy Spirit. Since by our fruits others will know us, we are also granted by this saving grace the chance "to grow in goodness through the moral virtues" [1266]. And as if membership in the Body of Christ were not gift enough, you made us as well members of your Church, people of the covenant, who, by virtue of the bond of Baptism, "[transcend] all the natural or human limits of nations, cultures, races, and sexes: 'For by one Spirit we were all baptized into one body'" (1 Cor 12:13) [1267].

Now we share in the priesthood of your Son and in the common priesthood of all who believe. Christ's prophetic and royal mission also extends to us, his baptized disciples. Give us the courage to die and rise with you, Lord Jesus. Show us that we are called uniquely and communally to serve others, to submit to the leaders of our Church, and to be sustained in all of our endeavors by your holy word and by all the sacraments of salvation [1268-1270].

Once we are baptized a change happens to us we cannot undo: We are sealed with the indelible spiritual mark (or *character*) of our belonging to Christ. As the *Catechism* teaches, not even sin can erase this mark. Sin may prevent the grace of Baptism from bearing fruit, but it cannot change our initial configuration to Christ. Therefore, reception of this sacrament cannot be repeated. Once incorporated into the Church, women and men must choose to live and act as committed Christians, consecrated to their divine Master, giving witness to this relation by the holiness of their lives and the practice of charity [1273].

These fruits of Christian formation produce a bountiful harvest throughout a woman's life. We must maintain fidelity to this seal to the end, for we have been "marked with the sign of faith"[3] [1274]. On that day we will behold the vision of God, and rise to a new dawn in the glory of the resurrection.

The Gift of Confirmation

To complete the grace of Baptism, Christians need to receive the sacrament of Confirmation, for through it the Holy Spirit strengthens our faith, deepens our love and our loyalty to the Church, and helps us to be witnesses to Christ's way in the world [1285].

The very name "Christian" means "anointed" [1289]. Thus the Eastern Churches still call this sacrament *Chrismation,* whereas in the West *Confirmation* suggests also the ratification and strengthening of baptismal grace and the outpouring of the fruits of the Holy Spirit [1289-1292].

Various symbols and rites surround this precious sacrament, but none more important than "the sign of *anointing* and what it signifies and imprints: a spiritual *seal*" [1293]. The apostle Paul explains: "It is God who establishes us with you in Christ and has commissioned us; he has put his seal on us and given us his Spirit in our hearts as a guarantee" (2 Cor 1:21-22). Now we belong wholly to Christ. Now we are worthy to be in his service for the rest of our lives. Now we can expect divine protection even as we await the trials of life and the rewards of eternity [1294-1296].

In the ceremony itself, the actual words by which the bishop invokes the outpouring of the Holy Spirit are these:

All-powerful God, Father of our Lord Jesus Christ,
by water and the Holy Spirit
you freed your sons and daughters from sin
and gave them new life.

Send your Holy Spirit upon them
to be their helper and guide.
Give them the spirit of wisdom and understanding,
the spirit of right judgment and courage,
the spirit of knowledge and reverence.
Fill them with the spirit of wonder and awe in your presence.
We ask this through Christ our Lord[4] [1299].

These words precede the essential rite, which in the Roman
Catholic tradition consists of the anointing with chrism on one's
forehead; this is done by the laying on of hands and through the
words the bishop speaks: "Be sealed with the Gift of the Holy
Spirit"[5] [1300]. The sign of peace shared at the conclusion of the
sacrament signifies that between the bishop and all the faithful there
is a bond of unity, an "ecclesial communion" [1301], whose wondrous effects we ought to feel over a lifetime. For this grace women
of spirit pray:

Spirit of the living God,
let your Spirit rest upon us
as on that first Pentecost day.
Increase our baptismal grace
until its waters fill the reservoir
of our soul. Root us so deeply
in the spirit of our adoption that with Jesus,
we, too, can cry out, "Abba! Father" (Rom 8:15).

Spirit of patience and perseverance,
unite us to Christ gently and firmly.
Let the gifts and fruits of your Spirit
yield in us a rich harvest of good deeds.
Bind our hearts to the Church victorious

so that from our mouths may come words
that both evangelize and defend the faith.
Let us witness to the risen Lord
and confess his name as Redeemer and Savior,
even when this means, as it always will,
that we must carry the cross of suffering.
Let us think often of the indelible seal
Confirmation imprints on our womanly or manly character,
since it marks us once and for all
as disciples of Christ, as his friends
and coworkers on the road to salvation.
May this special sign, seal, and character
perfect our common priesthood and give us
the power from on high
to understand and teach
your precious Word in the privacy
of our homes as well as in the public
sphere [1302-1305].

The parish, like the family, is responsible for preparing young people and adults for Confirmation. Some serious questions and concerns can arise at this time, and catechists have to be prepared for them. What if a child says that he or she does not want to receive this sacrament? Should a parent force the child to go through with it anyway? Coercion is hardly the best step toward Confirmation. With time and the kind of instruction that is not only informative but also formative, parents and children may come to a better understanding of this sacrament and be open to receive its myriad blessings. What matters is not so much perfect understanding of every mystery surrounding the sacraments (this is the work of a life-time) but a spirit of docility—a conviction on the part of the priests, parents, and sponsors that the children and adults concerned are willing to be taught, that they truly believe in God, that they want to receive through this and the other sacraments the help they need. Thus family members ought to be offered many occasions for ongoing education and spiritual formation, marked especially by more intense prayer. Young and old need to develop a willingness and a readiness to stand up for their faith as disciples of Jesus Christ.

To receive this holy sacrament, one has to be in a state of grace. One ought, therefore, to receive the Sacrament of Penance prior to its bestowal [1309-1310]. For Confirmation one has also to seek the spiritual support of a *sponsor.* He or she in the ideal case should also be one's baptismal godparent [1311]. Growing up under the influence of such a faithful witness is good for the child. In this way he or she continues to catch in action the faith being received in instruction.

It is the bishop who ministers this sacrament ordinarily in the Latin rite. By conferring Confirmation himself, the bishop "demonstrates clearly that its effect is to unite those who receive it more closely to the Church, to her apostolic origins, and to her mission of bearing witness to Christ" [1313]. For grave reasons, the bishop can concede to priests the faculty of administering confirmation but it is "appropriate from the very meaning of the sacrament" that the bishop confer it himself [1313]. If a Christian is in danger of death, a priest can be the minister of Confirmation, the reason being that "the Church desires that none of her children, even the youngest, should depart this world without having been perfected by the Holy Spirit with the gift of Christ's fullness" [1314].

The Gift of the Eucharist

This holy sacrament not only completes our Christian initiation; it also draws all who receive it into the Lord's own sacrifice both personally and communally. Christ himself instituted this living offering. He gave up for our sake the bread of his Body and the wine of his Blood. He wants to unite us to his cross in full thanksgiving for the redemption. Each time we go to the altar, he reminds us of his Death and Resurrection with all the graces and glory they grant [1322-1323]. The presence of Christ in the Eucharist by the power of the word and the Holy Spirit lays before us a veritable banquet of graces.

The Eucharist is the fountainhead of all the other sacraments, of our ecclesiastical ministries and apostolic works. Containing as it does Christ himself, the Eucharist brings all who believe into communion with the divine life of the Trinity, the Church on earth, and the heavenly liturgy [1325]. Celebrated in time, this sacrament always points to eternity. Faith, hope, and love find their "all in all" in the Eucharist [1326].

This holy sacrifice is an act of benediction and praise, prompting women to pray: "*We bless you, Father, for your great work of creation. We thank you, Jesus, for the miracle of our redemption. We praise you, Holy Spirit, for the grace of our sanctification.*"

The Eucharist is the Lord's Supper: "*We remember, Beloved, how you broke the bread of salvation with your disciples on the eve of your Passion—a night of suffering that gave way on Easter to the Lamb's wedding feast.*"

Holy Communion is a feast of thanksgiving. "*We thank you, Lord, for blessing the bread and giving it to your friends. They saw then that you are the Christ, the Son of the living God. It was bread broken that helped them to know you after the Resurrection. Let us see each time we participate in this celebration what it is that we do, for to receive your precious Body and Blood is to enter into communion with you"* [1328-1329].

It is in *the eucharistic assembly* that we celebrate this sacrament together, as a faith community, for all to behold. The Eucharist is the *memorial* of Christ's Passion and Resurrection and the *holy sacrifice of the Mass* because at its center is Christ's sacrifice surpassing all the sacrifices of the Old Covenant. These are *sacred mysteries*, for words fail to express the wonder of this sacrament, its commingling of humanity and divinity [1330].

Because the Eucharist is the sum of all the sacraments, we say that we worship Christ's presence in the *Most Blessed Sacrament;* that we come to receive *Holy Communion* in union with Christ and in communion with the saints. Indeed this is *"the bread of angels, bread from heaven, medicine of immortality,⁶ viaticum"* [1331]. Our Mass (*Missa*) is thus called "holy," for at its center the mystery of our salvation is accomplished; we are then sent forth (*missio*) to fulfill God's will in fidelity to the life form (our call) and the life style (our situation) to which God has beckoned us from the beginning.

What makes the Eucharist so central a sacrament is its institution by Christ himself when he knew that the hour to leave us had come [1337]. It was Christ who said to those at table, "This is my body which is given for you. Do this in remembrance of me.... This cup which is poured out for you is the New Covenant in my blood" (Lk 22:19-20).

As Jesus passes over to the Father by his Death and Resurrection, he leaves us with the extraordinary gift of the new Passover, celebrated in the Eucharist [1338-1340]. He asks us to do what we do in memory of him until he comes again in glory [1341]. So essential is this celebration that we could not live as Christians without it— not only on Sunday but daily, at least in intention. As the Eucharist is "the center of the Church's life," so must it be the center of our spiritual lives [1343].

The essential structure of the Eucharist unites all the faithful throughout the world. When we gather for the *liturgy of the Word*, the readings, homily, and general intercessions, when we proceed to celebrate the *liturgy of the Eucharist*, we experience "one single act of worship"[7] [1346]. All parts of our celebration form one gracious and graced movement.

We gather together in the presence of the bishop or priest who acts *in the person of Christ the Head*, to preside over the assembly. Everyone, from the people in the pew to the eucharistic ministers, has an important role to play [1348], culminating in the offerings of bread and wine that will become at the moment of consecration Christ's Body and Blood. This sacrifice brings to perfection any and all human sacrifices we may ever make [1350].

The Eucharistic Prayer (the *anaphora*) is the prayer of thanksgiving and consecration [1351-1352]. It consists of the *preface*, where we join in unending praise to the Father, Son, and Holy Spirit; the *epiclesis*, where the Church asks the Father to send his Holy Spirit to bless the bread and wine; the *institution narrative*, where Christ's Body and Blood become present under the species of bread and wine; the *anamnesis*, where the Church calls to mind Christ's Passion and Resurrection and his glorious return; the *intercessions* celebrating the communion of the Church with the living and the dead; and the Lord's Prayer, which precedes the reception of Holy Communion [1353-1355].

Priests and people together offer thanksgiving and praise to the *Father* as they share in the sacrificial memorial of *Jesus Christ* and as they dwell reverently in the presence of the Most Holy Trinity by the power of his *Spirit* [1358]. Thus women of spirit may sense welling up within them this litany of grateful love:

We thank you, Lord, for having accomplished by your holy cross the salvation of the world. At every Eucharist we offer our thanks and praise to the Father for the work of creation. Everything in it—all the bounty of human hands—is presented to the Father in the name of Jesus, our sacrificial Lamb.

We remember on this occasion Christ's Passover—not only as a recollection of past events but as a proclamation of the astounding works wrought by you for us and with us. We remember that these events are not to be relegated to the distant past but must become present and real to us here and now. Help us to treasure their memory so that we may conform our lives to them, remembering that because of what we do our redemption is at hand.

Every time we remember, we recall the sacrificial character of the Eucharist, for "what we receive" is Christ's own Body and Blood "poured out for many for the forgiveness of sins" (Mt 26:28). Our memorial ceremony makes present the sacrifice of the cross and applies its fruit in the form of a living memory perpetuated until the end of the world [1362-1366].

We remember, too, Beloved, that your sacrifice on the cross is one and the same with the sacrifice of the Eucharist. There is no difference in their efficacy, only in their manner of offering. Remind us when our mind wanders that the Eucharist is not only your sacrifice but that of the Church, who offers herself whole and entire with you for the sake of the salvation of all people everywhere.

Body and Blood, soul and divinity, you, O Christ, are contained in this sacrament, truly, really, and substantially. We believe in the truth of your presence in the Eucharist, of your real abiding with us, of your substantial presence every time bread and wine are changed into your Body and Blood. This is the faith of the Church to which we adhere, the faith upheld by all who believe in the efficacy of your Word and the action of the Holy

Spirit to bring about this "change of the whole substance of the bread into the substance of the body of Christ our Lord and of the whole substance of the wine into the substance of his blood"⁸ [1376].

O holy presence of Christ in the Eucharist, we kneel before you in pure adoration at the moment of the consecration, knowing that as long as the eucharistic species subsists, so your presence there endures whole and entire in each part in such a way that the breaking of the bread does not divide the Christ we receive. How can mind and heart contain so wondrous a mystery as this! Though the priest, in the role of Christ, pronounces the words, "This is my body," says St. John Chrysostom. "This word transforms the things offered."⁹ [1375].

We pray these truths, as we do so many in the *Catechism*, because for us the liturgy is not a routine occurrence but a transformative event calling for profound worship. It calls for the solemn veneration of Christ in our midst, of Christ whole and entire in the tabernacle, in hosts reserved for our edification and for distribution to the sick. The tabernacle reminds us whenever we see the flame burning before it of the real presence of Christ. In the words of Pope John Paul II:

Jesus awaits us in this sacrament of love. Let us not refuse the time to go to meet him in adoration, in contemplation full of faith, and open to making amends for the serious offenses and crimes of the world. Let our adoration never cease¹⁰ [1380].

Adoration is the only right response to this mystery of love. For this reason, the altar around which we gather to celebrate Holy Mass represents two aspects of the same mystery. It is, as the *Catechism* explains, "the altar of the sacrifice and the table of the

Lord" [1383]. The altar symbolizes Christ himself, present in our midst when we assemble to worship; the table signifies the food from heaven we receive in Holy Communion. Are we worthy to "eat the flesh of the Son of man and drink his blood" (Jn 6:53)? This invitation to transformation merits that we examine our conscience. Are we ready to receive so great a sacrament as this? Are we conscious of grave sin? If so we must receive the Sacrament of Reconciliation before we approach the communion table. Then we may be able to pray as women of faith do:

Lord, let every Communion augment our oneness with you. Let us come in this way to know you more intimately, for "What material food produces in our bodily life, Holy Communion wonderfully achieves in our spiritual life" [1392]. This life-giving interformation with you preserves, increases, and renews the grace we received at Baptism. How grateful we are for the nourishment we receive now and at the hour of our death. Your body "given up for us," your blood "shed for the many for the forgiveness of sins" [1393], both cleanses us of past iniquities and preserves us from future sins. How healing a remedy this is for the likes of us! May your Eucharist not only remove our resistance to sin. May it strengthen our capacity to love, break our disordered attachments to creatures, and give us the grace we need to die to sin and live for you.

We thank you, Lord Jesus, for the fruits of the Eucharist we feel growing in us day by day. It commits us to the poor, for in it we recognize the poverty and humility of Jesus, who emptied himself for our sake. It helps us likewise to give ourselves up for the sake of our brothers and sisters in need. And it is this sacrament above all which signifies and carries to heaven's door our plea for Christian unity [1397-1398].

In the divine plan for our redemption, the Eucharist affects our remembrance of the past (the whole economy of salvation), calls us to cherish the present (the practice of charity), and invites us to anticipate the future (the pledge of glory to come). The world as we know it will pass away, but not the words of our Savior. Every time we celebrate the Eucharist, we await his coming in glory. We believe in that time beyond time "when every tear will be wiped away. On that day we shall see you, our God, as you are. We shall become like you and praise you for ever through Christ our Lord"[11] [1404].

The Eucharist is a sure pledge, a clear sign, that the prayers of women are not in vain, that their hopes shall be fulfilled. Every time we celebrate this mystery, the work of our redemption is carried on. We break "the one bread that provides the medicine of immortality, the antidote for death, and the food that makes us live for ever in Jesus Christ."[12] [1405].

Questions for Reflection and Faith Sharing

1. How are the fruits of your Baptism bringing you even now to new life in Christ, incorporating you into the Church, the Body of Christ, and making you a "sharer" in his priesthood [1279]?

2. How are the graces perfected in you at the time of your Confirmation bearing fruit as you strive to carry on the mission of the Church in the modern world? How is this anointing helping you to bear witness to the Christian faith in words accompanied by deeds [1316]?

3. How would you explain to someone who asks you why the Eucharist is "the heart and the summit of the Church's life" [1407]?

4. Do you visit the Blessed Sacrament? What brings you before the tabernacle? Is your experience, as Pope Paul VI said, "... a proof of gratitude, an expression of love, and a duty of adoration toward Christ our Lord"[13] [1418]? What else do you feel when you sit, stand, or kneel in the presence of the living God?

EIGHT

∞

Seeking Sacramental Healing

If anyone has this task of advancing the dignity of women in the Church and society, it is women themselves, who must recognize their responsibility as leading characters. There is still much effort to be done, in many parts of the world and in various surroundings, to destroy that unjust and deleterious mentality which considers the human being as a thing, as an object to buy and sell, as an instrument for selfish interests or for pleasure only. Women themselves, for the most part, are the prime victims of such a mentality. Only through openly acknowledging the personal dignity of women is the first step taken to promote the full participation of women in Church life as well as in social and public life.

—Pope John Paul II
Christifideles Laici, 49

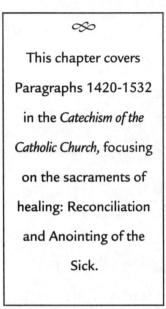

This chapter covers

Paragraphs 1420-1532

in the *Catechism of the*

Catholic Church, focusing

on the sacraments of

healing: Reconciliation

and Anointing of the

Sick.

New life in Christ comes to us through the sacraments of initiation, but, alas, we carry this treasure "in earthen vessels" (2 Cor 4:7). We drink the draught of likeness to the Divine from cups that are chipped by every imaginable sin. We fracture our relationship with God and others into fragments too numerous to count. This side of heaven women and men are "subject to suffering, illness, and death"[1] [1420]. Children of God though we are, we walk on legs weakened by sin. Gluttony and lust, avarice and envy, vanity and sloth are but a few of the stumbling blocks on our path to holiness. We are like lost children wandering in unmarked woods. Foolishly we flaunt the Ten Commandments. We forget the Beatitudes and the evangelical counsels. We argue endlessly about the teachings of Christ and resist letting their truth and beauty touch and transform our hearts. We need desperately to be healed—and we have a divine Physician in Jesus Christ. He is the healer of the soul and the body of those who seek his help. Remember the paralytic (Mk 2:1-12). Jesus forgave his sins and restored his ability to walk. And this power to save and heal continues today in his Body, the Church, through the power of the Holy Spirit. Two sacraments have healing as their purpose. One is Reconciliation (or Penance), the other, Anointing of the Sick.

The Gift of Reconciliation

The more our sins wound Christ's Body, the more the Church labors to forgive the offenses we have committed against him.

Tirelessly, by charity, by example, by prayer, she labors for our conversion [1422]. Women of faith voice for all of us our grateful, repentant response to the Sacrament of Reconciliation:

> *Spirit of transforming love, help us to avail ourselves sacramentally of Jesus' call to conversion. Let this turning around of our lives, this metanoia, be the first step we take on the journey home to our Father's house. Sin caused us to stray. Now we long for God's embrace.*
>
> *Spirit of repentance and contrition, help us to receive worthily the Sacrament of Reconciliation. Let it be for us the definitive destination of the steps your grace has already enabled us to take toward conversion.*
>
> *Spirit of integrity and humility, be with us when we go to confession. Let this sharing of our deepest self with our confessor be at once an act of acknowledgment ("Yes, Lord, this is what I have done... This is what I have failed to do...") and an act of praise for your mercy. May your loving forgiveness flow in an unending stream toward our sinful condition.*
>
> *Spirit of forgiveness, through the grace of sacramental absolution we are granted the privilege of "pardon and peace"[2] [1424], lifting from our repentant hearts the burden of sin and enabling us to start anew.*
>
> *Thank you, Lord of life, for bringing us to these healing moments that correct our course before it is too late. Change us. Redirect us. Impart to us sinners the unmerited grace of transformation. Let our reconciliation be twofold: to you and to our neighbor. As the apostle Paul tells us, "Be reconciled to God" (2 Cor 5:20). Only to the degree that we live in the light of your merciful love can we be reconciled to our sisters and brothers (Mt 5:24). Help us to show all in need the boundless love you've shown to us. For only insofar as we forgive others can we receive the forgiveness of sins God wants to grant us.*

Let us meditate for a moment on the enormity of what God has done for us. Through the regeneration of Baptism, the celebration of the Eucharist, the Confirmation of the Holy Spirit, we underwent a profound *conversion*. In God's eyes we were "holy and without blemish" (Eph 1:4; 5:27). Yet for all the new life we received, thanks to Christian initiation, we were not freed from "the frailty and weakness of human nature, nor the inclination to sin that tradition calls *concupiscence*" [1426]. This inclination clings to us like barnacles on a ship, but it cannot sink our vessel; on one condition, that we avail ourselves continually of the grace of God. Our efforts to be faithful never go unnoticed by the Trinity. Our struggle to reform meets with the warm glow of forgiveness. Our *conversion*, therefore, has to be ongoing. What is at stake, as women of prayer know, is no less than life eternal.

Lord Jesus, you have called us to conversion. You have proclaimed in the Scriptures that your kingdom is at hand; you have told us to repent and believe in the Good News (Mk 1:15). You address your call first of all to those who do not yet know you and your gospel. For those of us so blessed, whom you have given ears to hear, "Baptism is the principal place for the first and fundamental conversion" [1427]. Here our faith and formation journey begins, for it is only by faith that we have the courage to renounce evil and seek salvation. Through the power of your Spirit and the ongoing transformation in Christ it enables, you forgive us our sins. You offer us the gift of a life made new in you.

Lord Jesus, let your call to conversion resound in every corridor of our Christian life. Let this "second conversion [be] an uninterrupted task for the whole Church..." [1428]. We are at once a holy people and a people in need of continual purification. We have no choice, if we would be saved, but to follow the path of penance. Reformation, renewal, and reconciliation are essential.

You teach us through the Church that "This endeavor of conversion is not just a human work. It is the movement of a 'contrite heart,' drawn and moved by grace to respond to the merciful love of God who loved us first"³ [1428].

There is something else women seeking reconciliation need to proclaim about Jesus' teaching on repentance: True repentance is evidenced not by our exterior actions (walking around in sackcloth and ashes, aiming at heroic feats of fasting and mortification), but within our hearts as we seek conversion [1430]. If this inner turning to God does not occur, all our outer works risk remaining false and sterile. Provided we feel genuinely contrite, really sorry for our sins and pained at heart because we have offended God, then we may move toward expressing this inner conversion in visible signs, in sacramental confession, in appropriate gestures, in works of penance.

What does interior repentance look like? The *Catechism* graphically portrays it as "a radical reorientation of our whole life, a return, a conversion to God with all our heart, an end to sin, a turning away from evil, with repugnance toward the evil actions we have committed" [1431].

Accompanying this feeling of heartfelt remorse are two affective movements: One is an "affliction of spirit" called *animi cruciatus;* the other is "repentance of heart" called *compunctio cordis* [1431]. As women of the Church, we empathize with both responses:

Lord of life and breath, I can no longer bear the weight of this heart of mine, so heavy and hardened by sin. Please give me a new heart, a heart not of stone but of flesh (Ez 36:26-27). I rely wholly on your grace to start this work of conversion in me. Make my heart return to you. Give me the strength to begin anew. When I behold the greatness of your love, its boundless reaches, I feel the horror of sin, its sheer weight pressing me down. Fear of offending you by sin, fear of being separated from you forever, is a profound deterrent to evil doing. Rightly I should fear your wrath, but now I ask you to replace this fear by love. Let me look upon you, who died on the cross for my sake. Let me repent a thousand times over for the sins I have committed, sins that pierced your heart.

Spirit of my Lord, release the world also from its unbelief. Let all behold you, the Crucified, whom the Father has sent into this world to redeem us from our sins. Give us now and forever the grace of repentance, leading us to true conversion [1432-1433].

In our Christian life, interior penance can take many forms. It can be expressed in many ways. Three of these forms, oft reiterated as efficacious in Holy Scripture and in the writings of the spiritual masters, are fasting, prayer, and almsgiving. They point to conversion in relation to oneself, to God, and to others [1434]. Other means of penance might be to make peace (to seek reconciliation) with our neighbor and to shed tears of repentance, tears that connote at the same time sorrow for sin and joy in redemption. We can show concern for the salvation of others and intercede for them before God. And of course, we can practice charity, for, as St. Peter says, it "covers a multitude of sins" (1 Pt 4:8).

The *Catechism* identifies other ways to express conversion of heart. These may include showing concern for the poor; exercising and defending what is just and right; admitting our faults to another person; offering admonition or fraternal correction; correcting the wrong turn one's life has taken; examining one's conscience; seeking spiritual direction; accepting suffering as a formation opportunity; enduring persecution for the sake of righteousness. As a short summary of all these ways, the *Catechism* reminds us that "Taking up one's cross each day and following Jesus is the surest way of penance"⁴ [1435].

Common ways of returning to the Lord are offered to us daily when we celebrate the Eucharist, understood as "a remedy to free us from our daily faults and to preserve us from mortal sins"⁵ [1436]. Of great help, too, are the formative reading of Holy Scripture and the praying of the Liturgy of the Hours along with the prayer that Jesus taught us. In the Our Father we ask God to forgive us as we have forgiven others. It is consoling to remember that "every sincere act of worship or devotion revives the spirit of conversion and repentance within us and contributes to the forgiveness of our sins" [1437]. The Church helps us in this regard by setting aside in the course of the liturgical year seasons and days of penance, for example, Ash Wednesday and Good Friday in Lent. Penitential services, even pilgrimages and voluntary acts of self-denial like fasting and almsgiving, renew the call to live in repentance and ask for God's mercy.

Thus our conversion has to repair a double breach: with God through his forgiveness and with the Church through reconciliation. Both "healings" are "expressed and accomplished liturgically by the sacrament of Penance and Reconciliation"⁶ [1440].

As God hears the cry of the poor, so God attends to the prayers of women for the release all seek from the imprisoning power of sin:

God, it is you and you only who end our bondage through your Son, Jesus Christ, to whom you gave "authority on earth to forgive sins" and to say, "Your sins are forgiven" (Mk 2:5,10). By the same divine authority, you gave this power to our priests to exercise in your name (Jn 20:21-23). You paid the price of our forgiveness with your blood, and you want the whole Church, by her life of prayer and action, to witness to the grace of reconciliation. Thank you for entrusting to your apostolic ministry the power of absolution in which penitents can truly "be reconciled to God" (2 Cor 5:20).

When you forgave people's sins, my Lord, you did something else: you made forgiveness effective by reintegrating forgiven sinners into the community from which sin had exiled them. You received repentant sinners at your table and addressed the lost as your own daughters and sons. We thank you with all our heart for imparting to your apostles the power to forgive sins and to reconcile sinners with the Church, for to Simon Peter it was said: "I will give you the keys of the kingdom of heaven, and whatever you bind on earth shall be bound in heaven, and whatever you loose on earth shall be loosed in heaven" (Mt 16:19). For this reason we believe that "Reconciliation with the Church is inseparable from reconciliation with God" [1445].

Our merciful God awaits us in the Sacrament of Reconciliation. Why wait any longer? Our Beloved calls. Let us respond by showing *contrition*. When we admit to sinning, when we face up to our guilt and take responsibility for our actions, we are on the way to reopening our relationship with God and restoring our communion with the Church. Disclosure of sins to a priest can be a wonderfully freeing experience, bringing us to inner peace and initiating our reconciliation with others.

Diligently and sincerely examine your conscience. Recount grave sins in confession. Receive the grace of divine mercy and pardon. Knowingly withhold nothing, "for if the sick person is too ashamed to show his wound to the doctor, the medicine cannot heal what it does not know"[7] [1456]. Remember that confession is meant to be not a duty but a joy. Reception of our heavenly Father's mercy spurs us on to be more merciful.

Sin never involves us alone; its tentacles spread to others. We gossip about a neighbor; we scandalize the community; our lies infect a family circle; we take what belongs to another person. The list is almost inexhaustible. That is why our tradition speaks not only of contrition and confession but also of reparation or satisfaction. It may feel like the hardest thing we have to do, but we must try to repair the harm we have done. Simple justice demands, for example, that a repentant thief return the stolen goods; that a reputation cruelly and jealously slandered be restored; that the injured party receive compensation. Tragically, the person most harmed by sin is the sinner herself. Spoiled until sacramental renewal occurs is our relationship with God and with our neighbor.

Sin is a one-way ticket to isolation. What removes us from its lonely prison walls is confession, followed by absolution, but the consequences linger. Not even the grace of forgiveness can remedy "all the disorders sin has caused"[8] [1459]. We have a long way to go before we can recover full spiritual health. God asks something more of us: a firm purpose of amendment.

The penance imposed by our confessor respects our personal situation, aids our spiritual growth, and takes into account the gravity and nature of our sins. A priest may ask us to say prayers for penance or to perform spiritual or corporal works of mercy, thus serving the needs of our neighbor. We may be asked to choose for penance some practice of self-denial, to bear patiently with a difficult situation, or to meet with fidelity the challenges God sends. Penance always serves to "configure us to Christ, who alone expiated our sins once for all" [1460]. Only through Jesus can we bring forth the lasting fruits of a repentant heart: obedience, poverty of spirit, chaste love, justice, peace, and mercy. The effects of making a good confession draw women of faith to thanksgiving as well as contrition:

Thank you, Lord, for restoring us to your grace, for sealing once more our bond of friendship. You have reconciled us to yourself, thanks in great measure to the contrition you aroused in our heart. What peace we feel! What serenity of conscience! What strong consolations! It is as if we are undergoing a true "spiritual resurrection." Dignity you restore. Blessings you bestow. Does your love know no bounds, ever gracious Lord?

One can almost hear the angels singing for joy! For we have placed ourselves before the merciful judgment seat of God; we have been courageous and trusting enough in his mercy to antici-pate our eternal judgment day. We have chosen not death but life, as God asked us to—and all this is the work of grace. God paves the road to conversion; we walk on it. God opens the door of the kingdom; we close it by sin. Now it is opened again, thanks be to God!

The Gift of the Anointing of the Sick

Respect for life and the body, for its incarnated sacredness, is what makes the Sacrament of Anointing so special. The Church cares for the sick, prays for the dying, helps women and men in their most vulnerable state to identify with the risen Christ. This holy anointing reminds its recipients that in and with Christ they will come to life again, that through him they shall be ultimately healed and saved.

One tragic consequence of our fallen human condition is illness and suffering. No one escapes this reality. All of us have to face it either personally or with the people we love. The blessing in this is that there is no pain, no crisis moment, that does not have its coun-terpart in some form of meditation. We ask, "What does this mean?" We pray for answers when there is no logic to explain why we feel so powerless, so limited, so fragile and finite. Being sick is a sobering reality calling for faith because "Every illness can make us glimpse death" [1500].

How we respond to illness can be either character deflating or character building. We can abandon ourselves to God—or to anguish and self-absorption. We can surrender to the mystery or live in sullen revolt and despair. How we handle life's limits can lead to more maturity if these experiences enable us to discern what is and is not essential to a wholesome existence. What really matters? What is lasting? What is only passing?

Many spiritual writers, among them Catherine of Siena, Teresa of Avila, and Thérèse of Lisieux, blessed the times they were ill because their illness created the climate of detachment that led in turn to a deeper search for God and a wholehearted adherence to the divine will. Many figures in the Old Testament, such as Job, endured sickness and suffering in the sight of God. The Most High was for them the Master of life and the Master of death. Hence, it was to God that they could address their pleas for healing. In many texts of Scripture we find the same formative pattern: "Illness becomes a way to conversion; God's forgiveness initiates the healing"[9] [1502].

Both illness of body (due to physical debilitation) and illness of soul (due to sin) can serve to remind us that ours is a faithful God, who seeks to restore life and well-being to his people. In Exodus 15:26, God calls himself "the Lord, your healer." Suffering, we learn from a prophet like Isaiah, can have a redemptive value for expiating the sins of others (see Isaiah 53:11). Great is our fault and guilt, but greater still is God's healing power.

In the New Testament Christ's compassion for sick people, his healing of every manner of infirmity, is a sure sign that "God has visited his people" (Lk 7:16). The power to heal physically belongs to Jesus as much as does the power to free the heart spiritually by forgiving our sins. A woman of faith receiving this sacrament might thus be inclined to pray:

Lord, you heal the whole of us, body and soul. You do not stand aloof from our condition. You identify with it in all things but sin. In your presence, no matter how intense our pain, we feel comforted. In our fragility you lead us to new levels of faith, if we are open to your touch. In this holy sacrament you heal us again.

We feel your nearness, for you have made our misery the magnet that draws down your mercy. The healings you enable for some are meant by you to point to "a more radical healing: the victory over sin and death through [your] Passover" [1505]. When on the cross you took away the "sin of the world" (Jn 1:29)—of which illness is a consequence—you gave to suffering a new meaning. Now we ask you: let our suffering, in whatever form it comes, configure us to you. Let it unite us with your redemptive Passion.

After your death, and especially when you had shown your apostles your risen glory, you gave them a share in your ministry of compassion and healing. As a result of their faith in you, "they cast out many demons, and anointed with oil many that were sick and healed them" (Mk 6:13).

Every time hands are laid on the sick, it is in the hope that they will recover, at least in spirit if not in body, for a cure is not always meant for them in God's holy providence. You are there in that sick room when we invoke your name. You are rightly called by your faithful the God who saves (Mt 1:21; Acts 4:12).

To some the Holy Spirit gives the special charism of healing (1 Cor 12:9), but always and only to make manifest not their own power but the power of the risen Lord, who gives this grace or withholds it for reasons best known to him. Of this we can be sure, even if a cure is not effected, no matter how hard we pray for healing, God's power will be "made perfect in weakness" (2 Cor 12:9).

In our encounters with others, compassion must prevail. We need to take seriously Christ's imperative to "heal the sick!" (Mt 10:8). We do so by caring for them until they are well; by being with them when all medical help has been tried and failed; by praying and interceding for them as we trust they will do for us [1509]:

Jesus, we believe in your life-giving presence. We submit our whole being to you, Divine Physician of body and soul. We need to be fed by the bread of the Eucharist. The hope it gives us of eternal life helps in the healing process. We believe, even in our infirmity, that more than death awaits us. Thank you for giving us a rite and a sacrament for the sick, performed compassionately in the company of loving others as our priest prays over the sick person and anoints her in the name of the Lord. We wait quietly, in all our vulnerability, as he brings us the bread of life, the sacrament of our salvation [1510]. Partaking of your food, we know that you are with us there. We are not alone anymore.

At the point of death, the efficacy of this sacrament, alluded to by the evangelist Mark and promulgated by the apostle James (Mk 6:13; Jas 5:14-15), leads Catholics to call it "Extreme Unction." The minister continues to ask that the dying person recover, if that is God's will, but he also understands how necessary a sacrament this is to women and men facing imminent death. Who of us would not want to hear the following words at this time? "Through this holy anointing may the Lord in his love and mercy help you with the grace of the Holy Spirit. May the Lord who frees you from sin save you and raise you up"[10] [1513].

Happily for us, this sacrament is not reserved only for people at the point of death. One can receive it when one is seriously ill and still has time to prepare for her passing, should that be God's will, or to thank God for her recovery, if that should occur. One is eligible, if grave illness once more overtakes her, to receive the sacrament again [1515]. Opportune times would be prior to a serious operation or when she becomes increasingly frail and aged. Caregivers ought to encourage people, especially if they tend to be stubborn or superstitious, to call a priest when grave illness strikes. Many miss the chance for anointing because they live in denial or put off seeing a priest until it is too late.

Word and sacrament, silence, laying hands on the sick person, praying over her, anointing her with oil—all these liturgical actions "form an indivisible whole" [1518], whose effects sustain one whatever one's state of health. Four such effects are noted by the *Catechism*: *a particular gift of the Holy Spirit [1520]; union with the passion of Christ [1521]; an ecclesial grace [1522];* and *a preparation for the final journey [1523].* In their light, women pray:

> *Spirit of the living God, we thank you for granting us what we most need: strength, peace, and courage to meet the challenge and condition of serious illness, of inevitable frailty, of our final hour. Renew in us, O Spirit, our trust and faith in God. Let these virtues grow stronger now when we are most in need of resisting the tempter, the demon of doubt, despondency, and discouragement. Assist us, O Lord, by the power of your Spirit in the most important process: the healing of our soul. Heal our body, if you will, but more than this, forgive us our sins.*
>
> *Christ crucified, as we lie on our bed of weakness and pain, grant us the grace to identify at the deepest level with your Passion, Death, and Resurrection. Consecrate us to bear fruit even now by configuring us to your redemptive mission, O Savior. Let our suffering become for us a participation in your own saving work.*
>
> *Father of our Lord Jesus Christ, help us to see how we are contributing to the good of all people. Help us to feel in communion with the saints, known and unknown, who now intercede for us. Let our life, or what is left of it, be raised up to you as a worthy offering to contribute to the sanctification of the Church and the good of all.*

Holy Trinity, one God, be with us when it is time for us to depart from this life. Let this blessed sacrament then complete our conformity to Christ's Paschal Mystery, to his dying and rising. Baptism began our anointing; now Extreme Unction or "sacramentum exeuntium" (the sacrament of those departing) completes it [1523]. Let this last anointing fortify "the end of our earthly life like a solid rampart for the final struggles before entering the Father's house"[11] [1523]. Let the Eucharist we receive be the clearest sign of our "passing over from death to life, from this world to the Father"[12] [1524].

Questions for Reflection and Faith Sharing

1. When you receive the Sacrament of Reconciliation, of what feelings and experiences are you most aware: conversion of heart, return to communion with God; abhorrence of sins; hope in God's mercy [1486, 1489, 1490]? Can you describe a time when you were especially moved by God's free gift of forgiveness in the Sacrament of Reconciliation?

2. Our motives and emotions are often conflicted, even when we come to the Lord for forgiveness. Are there times when your repentance arises from "love of charity for God" and times when it is "founded on other motives" [1492]?

3. Have you personally or has anyone close to you received the Sacrament of the Anointing of the Sick? What was your and their experience? How would you describe in your own words "the special grace of this sacrament" [1531]?

4. The *Catechism* reminds us that suffering unites "the sick person to the passion of Christ," and that good can come from it. Have you seen in your own life, or in the lives of others, this miracle of God wresting peace from pain, gain from loss [1532]?

NINE
∞

Celebrating the Sacraments in Service of Communion and Community

When we say that the woman is the one who receives love in order to love in return, this refers not only or above all to the specific spousal relationship of marriage. It means something more universal, based on the very fact of her being a woman within all the interpersonal relationships which, in the most varied ways, shape society and structure the interaction between all persons—men and women. In this broad and diversified context, *a woman represents a particular value by the fact that she is a human person,* and, at the same time, this particular person, among others, *by the fact of her femininity.* This concerns each and every woman, independently of the cultural context in which she lives, and independently of her other spiritual, psychological, and vital characteristics, as, for example, age, education, health, work, and whether she is married or single.

—Pope John Paul II
Mulieris Dignitatem, 29

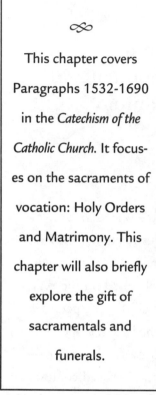

This chapter covers Paragraphs 1532-1690 in the *Catechism of the Catholic Church*. It focuses on the sacraments of vocation: Holy Orders and Matrimony. This chapter will also briefly explore the gift of sacramentals and funerals.

As women of faith we share a common vocation to be disciples of Christ, to witness to his way in this world, to strive for holiness. As recipients of the sacraments of initiation, we are full-fledged members of the faith community, who accept the need for continual healing in spirit and body, for reconciliation and anointing.

Two other sacraments serve the earthly goal of universal discipleship and the eternal goal of salvation. These are Holy Orders and Matrimony. Both sacraments touch upon sensitive, often misunderstood, truths and traditions that may seem countercultural to many today. Common to both sacraments, more profound than any controversy surrounding them, is the sense of the mystery of one's unique, communal life call and its embodiment in a vocation. The call to priesthood, the call to marriage, the call to celibacy in the world or in a religious congregation comes from God.

Regardless of gender, human beings are equally called to love God and neighbor. Neither celibacy nor marriage can be lived in fidelity unless one adheres to the fullness of the Church's teaching under the guidance of the Holy Spirit. Celibate or married, one is called, gifted, and sent by Christ to live in a way that does not endanger the salvation of one's own soul or the souls of others. In the matter of vocation, it is God who chooses, God who initiates. Though ministerial roles may differ, the call to serve in love stays the same.

The challenge facing women is to remain faithful to their call in Christ within the limits and possibilities allowed and blessed by the Church. As mothers and catechists, women exert a major influence on their children's choice of vocation.

Since these two sacraments pertain to lifelong decisions and commitments, since they deal with issues that are particularly sensitive for some women (roles in the Church, birth control, repentance from abortion), we must respond with empathy to the questions people have. If you also have a teaching role to play, please do what you can to prevent this rich teaching about ordained ministry, vowed religious life, and marriage or single life in the world from falling on deaf ears. The *Catechism* will greatly aid you as you help others as well as yourself to live your call in Christ to the full. Try always to remember that, different as these sacraments are, they both confer "a particular mission in the Church and serve to build up the People of God" [1534].

All of us are holy people. We have been consecrated to the Sacred by virtue of our reception of the Sacraments of Baptism, Confirmation, and Eucharist. God may further call men to the priesthood to stand in the person of Christ—not to judge or condemn but to serve the faithful in ministerial priesthood in imitation of his goodness and love. Their ministry confers on them the Sacrament of Holy Orders.

The Gift of Ordained Ministry

When Christ's ministry on earth began, he entrusted to the twelve apostles a mission that would be exercised until the end of time. It has three degrees: the order of bishops, of presbyters, and of deacons. The rite of ordination is the sacramental act that integrates a man into one of these three orders, conferring on him a gift of the Holy Spirit, a "sacred power" that is more than a simple election or delegation. This special call comes from Christ himself through the Church. It sets a man apart for service, consecrating him in Christ's name "to feed the Church by the word and grace of God"[1] [1535], while encouraging the collaboration of lay women and men as their call and giftedness allow. In keeping with an unbroken tradition in the Churches of the East and the West, ordination to the priesthood makes a man thus called and chosen a visible sign of Christ. It is only the laying on of hands by the bishop that "constitutes the visible sign of this ordination" [1538].

The ministerial priesthood is the means Christ uses to build up and lead his Church. In the ordained minister, "it is Christ himself who is present to his Church as Head of his Body, Shepherd of his flock, high priest of the redemptive sacrifice, Teacher of Truth" [1548]. This is what the Church means when it says of its priests that they act *"in persona Christi Capitis"*[2] [1548]. In other words, they act in the person of Christ himself, making him present to the community of believers. Ordination does not mean that a bishop or priest is freed from the cross of human weakness. Life shows, however, that the grace of God is greater than any one person's faults and failings. To be sure, sin cannot impede the fruit of God's love, but it can cause scandal. That is why a priest who lives in fidelity to his call, to the gospel, and to the Church is a treasure. He is a "model of Christ, who by love made himself the least and the servant of all"[3] [1551]. He deserves the heartfelt prayers of every person in ministry. Thus we pray:

Lord, may our pastors and priests have the courage to be shining mirrors of your sacred humanity, your priestly divinity. May their holy and wholesome lives draw us into deeper communion with your Church. The "sacred power" [1551] invested in them by you has nothing to do with "power trips" as the world knows them. Rather a priest's power resides in service modeled after the life and example of the Suffering Servant who was the least of all (Mk 10:43-45).

Lord, give your priests the grace to heal, teach, guide, and preach as your representatives on earth. Let them act in your name so as to raise our faith to new heights of divine desire, culminating in their offering of the Eucharist and our reception of this heavenly food. Let us join with our priests in offering ourselves through, with, and in Christ, in the unity of the Holy Spirit, to God, our Father. Give our priests the grace they need to represent your divine Son and in so doing to lift us to new levels of intimacy with him, for all of us together form his Body, the Church [1552-1553].

Every ordination is a celebration, not only because a bishop, priest, or deacon embarks on a lifelong journey of service to the Church, but also because we, the faithful, reap the benefits of his ministry of love and service. As a liturgical event that returns us to the time of Christ, ordination assures the continuity of the Eucharist for all our tomorrows.

The rites and symbols surrounding the solemn act of ordination may differ liturgically [1574], but the anointing thereby accomplished is consistent with Christ's own institution of the Eucharist. In the light of this miracle of God's manifest love, women may be drawn to pray in support of Christ's teaching:

Lord, you know how great our need is for living witnesses to your presence, and so you do not leave us alone and forsaken. You protect us as a shepherd watches over his flock. You see to it that we have in our midst pastors and guides. By their ordination they assure the continuity of the mission of mercy and redemption you made possible for a people lost in the misery of sin. In our bishops, priests, and deacons, we behold with eyes of faith "Emmanuel,"

God-with-us. The sacrament conferred on your servants forms one unbroken "apostolic line" [1576], succession by succession. You choose these servants to act in your stead and to work with the laity, to bring to fruition your holy mission. Help those who receive this call to accept in humility the Church's teaching. Raise up for ordination in our Roman Catholic tradition celibate men, truly called by you and committed to this state of life "for the sake of the kingdom of heaven" (Mt 19:12). Let their hearts belong to their Lord in undivided love. Let their love in turn be magnanimous, inclusive, and generous enough to embrace all people in need of the new life you give. Let your priests be other Christs, willing to work hand in hand with the laity to spread your word, to teach and evangelize, to address social needs with justice and mercy, with charity and self-initiative. May all their own and our efforts be strengthened by the worthy consecration and reception of the Eucharist for which we praise and thank you daily [1575-1580].

When a future deacon, priest, or bishop is ordained, he is configured to Christ not only by "a special grace of the Holy Spirit" [1581] but by "an *indelible spiritual character*" [1582]. This mark, as in the case of the Sacraments of Baptism and Confirmation, is bestowed once and for all; it cannot be given, so to speak, on a temporary basis nor can it be repeated. Even someone validly ordained, who for justifiable reasons leaves the priesthood or—in the case of scandal—is forbidden to exercise his functions, retains the mark of ordination. For this reason, much vocational discernment and many years of study and preparation precede a man's ordination, though nothing but this person's own heart can guarantee fidelity.

Even if an ordained minister is living in sin, since it is ultimately Christ "who acts and effects salvation" [1584] through him, the sacraments he dispenses are still valid. As St. Augustine explains, just because a minister is proud, "Christ's gift is not thereby profaned: what flows through him keeps its purity.... Those to be enlightened receive [the spiritual power of the sacrament] in its purity, and if it should pass through defiled beings, it is not itself defiled"[5] [1584]. Prompted by Christ-centered love for the Church and only too aware of the problems she faces with vocations, women pray:

Holy Spirit, Spirit of fire and light, let the grace of this sacrament configure him who receives it to you in every facet of his priestly life. Rush to the aid of your ministers when they are most in need of your presence. Hear the prayers of your faithful for their well-being said at every Mass. Give each of our bishops the grace to guide and defend the Church, to be prudent and yet lavish in their love for all, especially the poor, both those in need of material sustenance and spiritual direction. Enlighten them in mind and heart so that their proclaiming of the gospel paves the way for our sanctification. Let there be the closest identity possible between the priest and you, the Lamb of God, in the Eucharist so that he, too, is willing to lay down his life for his friends.

Lord, instill in your people renewed respect for the Sacrament of Holy Orders and the servants on whom it is conferred. Let us see you in their faces. Let each of them feel the urge to daily conversion and constant prayer. May the Holy Spirit be with them until that day when their entire life becomes one song of conformation to Christ.

Inspired by the words of St. Gregory of Nazianzus: let your priests purify themselves before purifying others; let them be instructed so as to instruct others; become light so as to illuminate; draw close to God to bring God close to others; be sanctified so as to sanctify; be led by you so as to lead; and take counsel themselves so as to counsel others [1589].

Lord, listen to our needs. Send us, especially in this time of transition in the Church, priests who are defenders of truth and sharers in the priesthood of Christ, men completely committed to their vocation, working in creative collaboration with us whom you also call, gift, and send. Help us to see in them the radiance of your epiphanic light. Remind us that he who is divinized by the Sacrament of Holy Orders is but an instrument used by you to divinize your people. As the Curé of Ars, St. John Vianney, reminds us, "The priest continues the work of redemption on earth.... If we really understood the priest on earth, we would die not of fright but of love.... The Priesthood is the love of the heart of Jesus"[6] [1589].

The Gift of Matrimony

God's love for us is seen most visibly in the covenant of love that binds a man and a woman in Holy Matrimony. Their lifelong partnership is an exercise in self-giving in which the good of the other overrides all self-centered concerns. With the miracle of procreation, if God so allows, husband and wife experience a special fulfillment. Their love comes to fruition when they become life-givers. What follows must be a firm commitment to educate and form their children in the love of the Lord. They should teach them how to use their gifts for the sake of serving others.

God had marriage in mind from the beginning of time. He did not want man to be alone, so he created "them," male and female, in his image and likeness (Gn 1:27). The mystery of divine love would be intertwined forevermore with the mystery of unifying and procreative love. Despite the burdensome weight of sin, Christ would come to the aid of his people. The Church would guarantee the sacredness of the matrimonial covenant sacramentally, for it belongs to the order of creation. Hearing this divine invitation prompts women to pray:

Heavenly Father, the intimacy found in a good marriage is a sign of your sacred call to life and selfless love. You yourself are the "author of marriage"[7] [1603]. Because this vocation comes from your hand, we believe that marriage is more than a human institution. It remains veiled in mystery despite humankind's proclivity to abuse its meaning. However different its celebration is from culture to culture, no change in structures or attitudes can obscure its common, unchangeable character. This institution, so battered in our time, requires your constant care and protection. Restore its dignity. Make its mystery more transparent to eyes blinded by infidelity. Let us reaffirm with Vatican II that "the well-being of the individual person and of both human and Christian society is closely bound up with the healthy state of conjugal and family life"[8] [1603].

By remembering the sacred roots of marriage, people are less likely to take for granted that they are called in and by God's love to become love for one another. This call represents the basic calling of each person on earth, whether she or he is married or single. God is love (1 Jn 4:8). To be made in God's likeness means to be made by, in, and for love. That is why the mutual love of a man and a woman in marriage becomes "an image of the absolute and unfailing love" [1604] with which God loves us.

The union of the two may be blessed, if God so wills, by children and by the work a couple shares to make this world a better place. No longer alone, the two become one another's counterpart, equal and intimate. They are each other's best helpmate, revealing daily the God who is always there for us. When a man leaves his parents and cleaves to his wife, "they become one flesh" (Gn 2:24), not to the loss of their uniqueness but to its communal fulfillment.

Alas, marriage is as vulnerable to the evil around us as any sacrament is. Two people may present a picture of harmony while concealing a dry, smoldering forest of discord below their surface cordiality. Though they promised to be one another's coequals, the temptation to dominate may spoil their relationship. Even when a person falls in love and marries, old habits die hard. Abundant graces, many prayers and sacrifices, are needed to forestall the fires of infidelity, jealousy, bickering, petty competitiveness, and angry conflicts, sometimes so irreconcilable that they end in hatred, suspicion, abuse, and separation. One partner or the other may survive such an ordeal, but not without indelible scars. People who once saw heaven in each other's eyes now feel as if they are living hell on earth.

These draining ordeals are made more or less worse by the circumstances of the marriage or by the culture and time in which the couple live. One thing is certain, as the *Catechism* asserts, marital strife "does seem to have a universal character" [1606].

Broken relationships do not stem from our creation in God's image and likeness, nor from our nature as such, but from sin. What caused a break in our bond with God causes a split in our relationship with one another. The first consequence of the sin of disobedience in the Garden of Eden was—not surprisingly—a "rupture of the original communion between man and woman" [1607]. Words of bitter recrimination marred the picture of their once walking in the garden hand in hand with God (Gn 3:12); lust got the upper hand and distorted love (Gn 2:22); the commands to be fruitful and multiply and to subdue the earth did not disappear, only now these acts would be burdened by the pain of giving birth and having to secure a livelihood by the sweat of one's brow (Gn 1:28; 3:16-19).

Thanks be to God, the story does not end there: God's plan for creation persists despite the impact of sin's wounds. From the beginning, God's love sought also to be healing. We ought to draw always upon the help of grace, for God never refuses to give to those in misery the balm of mercy. Undoubtedly, we cannot find our way alone. We need to seek God's forgiveness to remedy the fatal consequences of sin and its effects on marriage.

Living the Sacrament of Matrimony in the light of the fullness of grace helps spouses to overcome the sins of self-absorption, of egocentric pursuits of power, pleasure, and possession. The promise inherent in marriage is that it can draw one from self-centeredness to self-giving and in so doing to liken one again to God.

In the Books of Ruth and Tobit we receive a glimpse of the elevated relationship of love and loyalty God intends marriage to be. Such love is faithful and tender, a truly enfleshed, inspirited celebration as the Song of Solomon so vividly depicts. Love that reflects God's love is thus as "strong as death," so fecund that "many waters cannot quench" its flow (Song 8:6-7).

Lord, with your coming the meaning of the nuptial covenant between Yahweh and the chosen lights up as a new age dawns. This covenant in time prepares the way for your everlasting union with us, a bond of love sealed with your own body and blood. Single or married, whatever our vocation may be, we are called to be your guests for the wedding feast of the Lamb (Rv 19:7).

Weak as we are, you invite us to rely on your strength, to renounce self-interest and at least try to take up our cross, not by forfeiting our dignity but by meeting its challenges and demands. You are there to grace a marriage beyond what any human efforts can attain. Help husbands, therefore, to love their wives as you love the Church. Let the two become one. Let them be as conjoined with one another as you are joined eternally to the Church (Eph 5:25-26).

Bless the marriages that mirror the New Covenant you have established with us. Bless, too, women and men who freely renounce the good of marriage to follow you alone, who make you

the Bridegroom of their soul by choosing the vocation of virginity
"for the sake of the kingdom of heaven" (Mt 19:12). Their life
sends a powerful signal to the hearts of your people, reminding
them of their need for oneness with you as together we await your
return. What must prevail is our longing for union with you. As
in marriage, so in celibacy, the key to our call must be the confor-
mity of our will to yours in loving intimacy [1612-1620].

The celebration of a marriage during Holy Mass reveals in a special way the link between the love of spouses and the love shown to us by Christ in the Eucharist. The covenant the couple is about to seal by their marriage vows is a reminder of the New Covenant in which Christ united himself to the Church. The offering of their lives to one another is likened to Christ's offering of his life for the Church, for "sacrifice" is the key word when we celebrate the Eucharist. The awesome truth is that, though many, we form but "one body" in Christ (1 Cor 10:17).

A baptized man and woman, after sufficient marital preparation and the reception of the Sacrament of Penance, arrive at the day of their marriage. They are ready to exchange their vows and to receive within the Eucharist the Sacrament of Matrimony. There is much rejoicing on this day, a true festive air, whatever rites are used in the Latin or the Eastern Church [1623]. The liturgy supports the grace and blessing to be bestowed on this new couple. Since their covenant is sealed by the Holy Spirit, they can draw renewed strength from it. They can remember their love on this holy day for the rest of their lives together. A couple thus inspired by the *Catechism* might pray:

Jesus, freed of any constraint or impediment under the law, we consent to be man and wife, to give ourselves to one another in mutual love and care. Bless the consent that binds us to one another on our wedding day, a promise made in time that we believe will last for eternity. Let the consummation of our marriage be a true celebration of who we are as unique persons and who we shall become by the community of love we hope to create. Let our consent be an expression of our will to let one another be all that God intended us to be in an atmosphere of love, not fear, of freedom, not coercion [1625-1627].

On the grounds of this freedom of consent rests the validity or invalidity of a marriage as far as the Church is concerned. That is why, after due process under the guidance of its marriage tribunal, the Church can declare a marriage null and void. Thus discharged from their obligations, either party is free to marry, since no marriage in the eyes of the Church existed between them.

From the start of this event to its fulfillment, the Church considers marriage "an ecclesial reality" [1630]. The consent of the spouses initiates the celebration, a consent blessed by the Church through its priest or deacon in the presence of witnesses. Entered upon here is something much more than a legal agreement or a social gathering. Such may be how the world views marriage, but for the Church it is a sacrament to be celebrated liturgically in the company of supportive family members and friends.

Couples who marry enter into "an ecclesial *order*" [1631], not unlike monks or nuns who enter a religious order. They incur obligations to one another and their children, rights and duties publicly witnessed when they say, "I do." Those two words are a pledge of fidelity, verbalizing again the consent a couple gives in full freedom and responsible love. So much rests on their mature decision that solid preparation and formation for marriage are essential. The process starts with parental example and extends to a variety of modes of pastoral instruction from one's priest and other qualified persons in the Christian community.

So many people these days come from broken homes that the need for a first-class catechetical refresher course speaks for itself. The Church remains a powerful advocate for the dignity of marriage, especially when other voices diminish its importance. The Church is definitely counter-cultural in this regard. It teaches young people to value chastity before marriage and to enter, at a suitable age, upon a courtship that represents an honorable prelude to a wedding, not a substitute for it.

Once a valid marriage takes place, it creates a covenant "knot" between husband and wife that is meant to be "perpetual and exclusive" [1638]. Consecrated to one another by the Sacrament of Matrimony, they pray:

> *Lord, let us feel your hands upon ours as we seal our marital consent before you and all who are present at this ceremony. Help us to uphold each other's life call in full dignity. Let us meet with dedication the daily duties you set before us. May our married love be a shining mirror of your divine love, reflecting the unbreakable bond you established between us from the beginning.*
>
> *We know, Lord Jesus, that you are the wellspring of grace from whence we must draw water continually. It is you whom we encounter in our covenanted love. As spouses, we feel a special sense of oneness with you, Beloved Spouse of the Church. Dwell within us and around us. Give us the strength we need to cross the hurdles of daily encounter and to follow your lead from Calvary to Easter morn. When we fall, be there to help us rise again. Give us the compassion necessary to forgive one another for the hurts that happen in every marriage. Carry our burdens for us when their weight is too much to bear. Show us the true*

meaning of being subject to one another in mutual care and concern, in reverence for your glory in our ordinary lives.

Our love, thanks to you, can be as passionate as it is tender, as fulfilling as it is fruitful. The joy we feel goes beyond gratification and satisfaction. It is transcendent. For this and all the gifts of our life we say, "Thank you, Lord, for allowing us to taste on earth the wedding feast that awaits us in eternity" [1639-1641].

Aimed at a unity that is at once unique and other-centered, "all the elements of the person enter [into conjugal love]—appeal of the body and instinct, power of feeling and affectivity, aspiration of the spirit and of will" [1643]. This most intimate of encounters between a married man and woman is not merely a union of flesh to flesh; it has as its purpose to form one heart and one soul. It calls for the grace of *indissolubility* (versus the "dissolvability" of a casual affair). *Fidelity* (versus the "infidelity" presented almost as the norm by, for example, daytime soap operas) is essential. A true marriage ought also to be a symphony of mutual self-giving, open to the mystery and miracle of *fertility.* How different this is from the birth control-abortion mentality of mastery that tears at the very fabric of a marriage.

All that is good in a relationship ought, therefore, to become better in a sacramental marriage. It embraces not just a portion of a couple's togetherness but the whole of it. Growth for them is not sporadic but continual as God's love itself goes on unbroken.

The Gift of Family

Despite the "double income, no children" mindset that seems to be a fallout of rampant individualism in Western culture, the Church dares to speak with another voice. She states clearly that "by its very nature, the institution of marriage and married love is ordered to the procreation and education of the offspring and it is in them that it finds its crowning glory"[9] [1652].

Openness to building a family is the first fruit of conjugal love. Parents are the best educators of their children, provided they have the courage to hand on the essential elements of their faith tradition. None is more important morally or spiritually than the commitment to what Pope John Paul II has called the "culture of life."

If God does not grant children to a couple, their marriage, though childless, is still conjugal in the deepest sense, for through love there are born the good fruits of charity, hospitality, sacrifice, service, and often a desire to become adoptive and foster parents.

A beautiful image offered to the family in our tradition is that of "the domestic church." Think of the holy family in which Jesus was reared, and the splendor of this image speaks for itself. If the Church, as we believe, is "the family of God" [1655], then those who belong to it are members of one household (Acts 18:8). Just as the first believers "were islands of Christian life in an unbelieving world" [1655], so are families today pioneers of perennial truth in a climate hostile to some of the strongest tenets of our faith: its preferential option for the poor; its pro-life, anti-racist stance; its commitment to protect the elderly from abuse.

A family modeled on the holy family is like a little epiphany radiating faith, hope, and charity by word and deed; encouraging commitment to one's vocational call; and exercising "the *priesthood of the baptized* in a privileged way" [1657]. Together, as members of this domestic church, a family might pray:

> *Lord of life and love, make our home a place of grace where we strive to form one another in your likeness, where human and Christian enrichment are one. Inspire us to persevere in our faith in a world that holds up values alien to the truth of the*

gospel. Help us to endure patiently the differences in one another's personality, not to fight or bicker or call each other names. Teach us, as Joseph taught you, the joy of productive, creative work in and out of the home. Let our love model the fine points of brotherly and sisterly care. As you forgave sinners, soften our hearts so we can forgive the hurts we inflict on each other because of sin. Draw us to worship together, to pray as a family group, and to begin early in life to offer our services at home and to our neighbors.

Let us show the deepest respect for the single members of our own family and for our single friends. Remind them through us of how close they are to your heart, for you were and remained a single person in the world. Let everyone in the Church remember to show singles the affection and solicitude extended also to family members, for all of us belong to the family of the Trinity. This care must be shown especially to people who do not have a family because they are homeless or abandoned. Let us continue to welcome to our door any and all in need of a place to call home. Our arms must be open to embrace them. Give us the grace of generous hearts so no one ever feels alone in this world. Let our homes and churches feel like family to everyone who comes there, hoping to be recognized as the loved persons they are in God's eyes [1657-1658].

The Gift of Sacramentals and Funerals

"Sacramentals" are sacred signs instituted by the Church to respond to special needs, cultural distinctions, and historical changes. Symbols like holy water are used to confer special blessings, to call attention to the liturgy of the sacraments itself, and to show how material things can be seen and used as pointers to the transcendent for the praise of God [1667-1670]. These sacramentals take many different forms: grace before meals, making the sign of the cross, blessing religious assignments as in a monastery, blessing a church, an altar, a sacred vessel. In special cases the Church uses its power of "exorcism" to seek protection from the Evil One or to expel the demonic [1673].

Complementing these forms of sacramental piety are also many popular devotions practiced by the faithful: veneration of relics, pilgrimages, the stations of the cross, and the rosary being a few of these. Devotions never replace, they only extend, the liturgical life of the Church. In her wisdom rests the power of discernment needed to determine if modes of piety are in keeping with doctrine or in danger of deviating from it [1674-1676].

What matters most to the Church is that our entire sacramental life be a pointer toward the "last Passover of the child of God" [1680], our death. Thus it is fitting to end this section with a prayer expressing Christian hope in the life of the world to come.

Lord of life, whose power over death, whose resurrection from the dead, constitutes the core of our faith, in you resides our heart's deepest trust, for we know with the apostle Paul that if we die in you we are "away from the body and at home with the Lord" (2 Cor 5:8). Ready us daily for this final hour. Let it be not only the end of our sacramental life here on earth but the prelude to the new birth begun when we were baptized. There we received the gift of conformity to your image in us. Let this mark of union advance now to its ultimate fulfillment. Grant us the grace in this hour to receive the anointing of your Holy Spirit. Invite us also to the eternal feast prepared by you for us in our reception of the bread of heaven, the only food we need when we pass from this earth. Bestow on us the balm of your divine mercy. Clothe us in the garment of forgiveness. As the Church, like a mother, has borne us in her womb during our pilgrimage on earth, let her

accompany us to the end, offering sacramental solace and sur-
rendering us into the arms of our Father. As children of his grace,
let us feel safe in returning our body to the earth he created,
knowing that in Christ we shall rise again in glory (1 Cor
15:42-44) [1680-1683].

This kind of faith, from the start to the finish of our life, explains why a Christian funeral is a celebration, not only a time to mourn but a time to rejoice. For in the gathering of the community all proclaim their belief in life eternal. Different funeral rites reveal the respect the Church has for tradition. They are ordered so as to sustain the relatives of the deceased and to remind the assembly of one simple truth: the death of this beloved person leaves, as its final legacy, the living of a renewed vision of hope in the risen Lord. For this reason, the Church instructs that "the homily in particular must 'avoid the literary genre of funeral eulogy'[10] and illumine the mystery of Christian death in the light of the risen Christ" [1688]. As on so many other sacramental occasions so, too, on this solemn day the eucharistic sacrifice is the center of the funeral rite. Thus with the whole Church we pray:

Lord, purify your child of his or her sins. Admit the dying to the
fullness of your paschal feast. Let this celebration be a legacy to
your faithful of the joy of falling asleep in the arms of the Lord
only to rise again as living members of his family in heaven.
Remind us daily to pray for the dying and for the souls of the just
in purgatory. They are still part of our family in faith. As we say
farewell to our friend or family member, our hearts ache with
mourning. We will miss their nearness to us, but we are happy we
can commend their souls to so good a God. With the Byzantine
tradition we kiss our deceased good-bye and say: "We sing for
[your] departure from this life and [your] separation from us,

*but also because there is a communion and a reunion. For even
dead, we are not at all separated from one another, because we
all run the same course and we will find one another again in
the same place. We shall never be separated, for we live for Christ,
and now we are united with Christ as we go toward him.... We
shall all be together in Christ"[10] [1690].*

Questions for Reflection and Faith Sharing

1. What is your experience as a Catholic woman of sharing in the "common priesthood of the faithful" [1591]? How does the mission of Christ you have received call for support of the "ministry conferred by the Sacrament of Holy Orders"?

2. If you are married, what does it look like in your family life when you and your husband "love each other with the love with which Christ has loved his Church" [1661]?

3. The Church's teaching on marriage and family life is countercultural in many respects. In what way is your family life in harmony or in conflict with ecclesial norms [1664]?

4. What has been your experience of sacramental blessings [1678]? In what way do they help you bring the sacred into everyday life [1679]?

TEN

Forming Our Character in Imitation of Christ

The Covenant begins with a woman, the "woman" of the Annunciation at Nazareth. Herein lies the absolute originality of the Gospel: many times in the Old Testament, in order to intervene in the history of his people, God addressed himself to women, as in the case of the mothers of Samuel and Samson. However, to make his Covenant with humanity, he addressed himself only to men: *Noah, Abraham, and Moses.* At the beginning of the New Covenant, which is to be eternal and irrevocable, there is a woman: the Virgin of Nazareth. It is a *sign* that points to the fact that in Jesus Christ" *"there is neither male nor female"* (Gal 3:28). In Christ the mutual opposition between man and woman— which is the inheritance of original sin—is essentially overcome.

—Pope John Paul II
Mulieris Dignitatem, 11

∞

This chapter covers Paragraphs 1691-1876 in the *Catechism of the Catholic Church*. It addresses our search for happiness in fidelity to our vocation, the necessity of human freedom and responsibility, the formation of Christian virtue, and the reality of sin. For further insights on the person and society, the call to conversion, and participation in social life in a just and responsible manner that upholds at all times the dignity of the human person [1] [1929], read on your own Paragraphs 1877-1948.

Our call over a lifetime, despite the roadblocks erected by sin, is to grow toward increasing conformation with Christ. Serious choices of the highest moral caliber must be made if we want to regain our union of likeness with God, in whose image we are made. Our liberation is dependent upon our accepting his invitation. Are we willing and ready to cooperate with God's saving plan for our lives? The more we obey, the freer we become.

We are like little words in the Word. The epiphanic light of the Lord that we share mirrors in some small way the resplendent majesty of divine goodness, truth, and beauty. It reveals for all who have eyes to see what we can become by the grace of God.

Sin veils, obscures, dims, and can even erase the light of God in us. Grave sin causes us to fall with the world into what Pope St. Leo the Great called the "power of darkness"[2] [1691]. When this happens, we no longer light our world with the light of Christ, for the dark cloud of sin overshadows us. However, when this happens there is still hope. The process of divine transformation, when interrupted, can begin anew—as soon as we recognize the depth of our divine call and repent of our waywardness. Without repentance, it is impossible to find our way out of the thicket of sin, which snares like thorns on a rosebush and catches us unawares if we are not careful. Christ beckons us to follow the path of lifelong conformation laid out in exquisite detail in his teaching. It is he who untangles sin's knots. It is he who changes the human heart.

When we contemplate the fact that our sins have been forgiven and forgotten by Christ in the ongoing, daily miracle of sanctification, our hearts fill with awe. We see ourselves as endowed by God with marvelous gifts, such as those of physical and spiritual motherhood. But that is not all. These gifts of heart and mind form our characters in imitation of Christ. This same eternal love enables us to uncover them in liturgy, word, and sacrament, and—above all—in prayer [1692]:

> *O my Jesus, you always did what was pleasing to the Father. Enable me to do the same. Let me share humbly in your communion with him. Grant me the grace to live patiently and to persevere prayerfully in his sight. He sees all that I think, feel, and do. Empower me to become perfect as my heavenly Father is perfect, to be compassionate, and to grow in purity of heart [1693].*

As any woman can see, our perfection will never reach its final fulfillment here on earth. The invitation to become "perfect" (Mt 5:48) can only mean that we are on the path to deification by virtue of our participation in the life of the Trinity. To know how to grow in likeness to the Divine, it is wise to look to Mary. She is the best model for human beings of God-guided character formation. Consider for a moment: *Are we in communion with the Father's will? How can we share more and more in the radiance of the Son's love? How can we respond more spontaneously to the guidance of the*

Holy Spirit?

It is false to think that if we push hard enough, we will one day reach perfection here on earth. Nothing could be farther from the truth. The conformation to Christ that the Father asks of us is not the result of our own willpower and the prideful pursuit of worldly or spiritual success. It entails the humble perfection of truly trying. When we do the best we can to live in obedience, to remain open to God's call, to repent, and to seek conversion of heart, we become true imitators of Christ through the power of grace.

God helps women of prayer to grow in this kind of graced and gracious perfection. Whatever height we attain, there will always stretch before us more distance to travel, more unknown lands to traverse, in our homeward trek to heaven. The only thing that counts is that we conform our thoughts, words, and actions to the "mind ... which is yours in Christ Jesus" (Phil 2:5), that we choose as the model of our own formation the example of Jesus and his Mother [1693-1694].

Renewed by the Spirit

The Holy Spirit renews the people of God inwardly day by day. It is the Spirit who teaches us how to pray in and with Jesus and Mary to the Father. The question is this: Do we allow our Lord and Savior to heal the wounds of our sin? Do we act in response to the fruits of the Spirit, pursuing, despite every roadblock and obstacle, "all that is good and right and true" (Eph 5:8-9) [1695]? Challenging us to this kind of radical response, St. John Eudes says:

> *I ask you to consider that our Lord Jesus Christ is your true head, and that you are one of his members. He belongs to you as the head belongs to its members; all that is his is yours: his spirit, his heart, his body and soul, and all his faculties. You must make use*

of all these as of your own, to serve, praise, love, and glorify God. You belong to him, as members belong to their head. And so he longs for you to use all that is in you, as if it were his own, for the service and glory of the Father[3] [1698].

A woman's life, lived in the Spirit of Jesus, fulfills her supreme call as a human being. This call culminates in the grace of transformation in Christ. It draws her day and night to heartfelt prayer:

Lord, I thank you for helping me to grow in strength of character, in courage and compassion, in competence and care. I realize I must accept responsibility for the choices of my will: to conform or not to conform to the good promised to me by your Beatitudes. You guide me with a special gift, the compass of conscience. It warns me when my life is veering off course, when wrong choices erode the dignity you ordained for me. How profoundly you respect the inner nobility of my wounded human existence. You ask me to follow the way to interior conversion.

Spirit of light and love, teach me to read Holy Scripture and the writings of the spiritual masters as guides to Christ-centered reformation. Inspire me to turn my whole sentient and spiritual life into a means of holy maturation. How can I ever thank you enough for the floodgates of grace you release to me day by day? You make it possible for me to grow in virtue and to avoid sin. And when I fall, you are there to lift me up. Help me to entrust myself to the mercy of my Father in heaven, as did Mary Magdalene and the Prodigal Son. Let me share in the perfection of your charity, which I in my womanhood am called to image with increasing clarity. Let me glimpse "as in a mirror darkly" something of my eternal deification and everlasting participation in the life of the Triune God I love [1700].

Restoration of Our Divine Image and Likeness

Christ, our Redeemer and Savior, restored to its original beauty God's divine image in us, which we reflected before the sin of our first parents led to its deformation. He ennobled us anew by the grace of his mercy [1701]. Every man, woman, and child carries in their soul this image of the invincible God. It shines forth in the solidarity of human persons and in every act of charity. Though our communion with the Trinity is marred by sin, no lack of love, however severe, can detract from our being made in the image and likeness of God (Gn 1:27).

God endowed each of us with a spiritual and immortal soul. Therefore, as human persons, we are the only creatures on earth whom he willed for our own sake. From conception to death, we are destined by God for eternal beatitude [1702-1703].

Through the power of reason, we are capable of understanding the order of things established by our Creator. Our free will, guided by the light and power of the Holy Spirit, enables us to direct ourselves toward the good, just as our reason prompts us to pursue the truth [1704].

Our soul, with its spiritual powers of intellect and will, endows us with the gift of freedom. Human freedom, however limited, is a true sign of our imaging the Divine [1705]. It is by virtue of our freedom that we can recognize God's voice, do what is good and avoid what is evil, obey his law. God's voice makes itself heard in our conscience whenever we hear him asking us: *Do you fulfill my law out of love for your neighbor and me? Are you trying your best to live a moral life? Do you uphold your own and others' dignity, despite the cost of the cross [1706]?*

We are often hampered in making moral choices due to human pride and weakness. Other times we are influenced by the presence of the "Prince of this world," the Evil One, the demonic [1707]. At the beginning of human history, Adam and Eve were enticed by the devil. They chose to forfeit the freedom God gave them when they succumbed to his temptation. Disobedience prevailed over humble submission to God's will. Instead they overruled by their own willfulness the command not to eat of the fruit of the tree of the knowledge of good and evil, lest they die.

Our nature bears the wound of this original sin. Sheer observation reveals that there is in us an evil despite the fact that we desire the good. So often we feel divided in mind and heart, hearing the voice of God from within yet finding it muffled by the noise of a demanding world operating contrary to God's law. Our lives are seldom smooth sailing. Struggle, betrayal, and disappointment make for stormy days. We often experience a tug of war inside us, a veritable battlefield between good and evil, light and darkness. This battle affects every facet of our existence, for, in truth, we are inclined by original sin "to evil and subject to error" [1707].

By his Passion, Death, and Resurrection, Christ delivered us individually and as a people from Satan. He released us from the imprisoning power of sin, meriting for us new life in the Holy Spirit. However, so devious are the wiles of the devil and the ways of sin that prayer is ever on our lips:

Lord, restore in us what sin and its evil consequences have done to your daughters and sons [1708]. Bestow anew the gift of filial adoption. Transform us in your image and likeness. Enable us as women of the Church to follow your example and meet its every challenge with grace and favor. Help us to walk humbly and act justly, to do what is good under all circumstances. In union with you, Beloved Savior, let us attain to that perfection of charity, which is holiness. Show us through the power of the Holy Spirit how to mature in grace. Let our lives singly and in community be an epiphany on earth until that day when we come to enjoy with you and all the holy ones of God the glory of heaven [1709].

Roots of Christian Character Formation

The roots or sources of Christian character formation are given to us by divine teaching in the Sermon on the Mount. These blessings fulfill the promises of God made to the Chosen People but in new and surprising ways. The Old Testament foretellings, like the prophecy made to Abraham, seemed to center mainly on the gaining and possessing of earthly territory in the land of Israel. For the followers of Christ, these promises refer to the kingdom of God, as expressed with simplicity and great power in the Beatitudes:

Blessed are the poor in spirit, for theirs is the kingdom of heaven.

Blessed are those who mourn, for they shall be comforted.

Blessed are the meek, for they shall inherit the earth.

Blessed are those who hunger and thirst for righteousness, for they shall be satisfied.

Blessed are the merciful, for they shall obtain mercy.

Blessed are the pure in heart, for they shall see God.

Blessed are the peacemakers, for they shall be called sons [and daughters] of God.

Blessed are those who are persecuted for righteousness' sake, for theirs is the kingdom of heaven.

Blessed are you when men revile you and persecute you and utter all kinds of evil against you falsely on my account.

Rejoice and be glad, for your reward is great in heaven[4] [1716].

These blessings give priority not to territorial acquisition but to faith, hope, and love, to justice, peace, and mercy. Such dispositions give form to Jesus' own human and divine character. Voiced in these proclamations are not only foretellings of future glory but also commitments that will lead him ultimately to his Passion, Death, and Resurrection.

The Beatitudes express the character traits that shine in our own countenance when we develop a virtuous character in imitation of Christ. In them we find the attitudes and actions that ought to typify our Christian life.

The promises inherent in the Beatitudes sustain hope in the midst of tribulation. They proclaim rewards already secured, however dimly, for us as disciples of Jesus. Just as these divine directives bore full fruit in the lives of the Virgin Mary and all the saints [1717], so we hope they will come to fruition in us if we trust in their truths.

The Desire for Happiness and Christian Beatitude

God places in every woman's heart the natural desire for happiness, though it is he alone who can fulfill it. As St. Augustine said:

> We all want to live happily; in the whole human race there is no one who does not assent to this proposition, even before it is fully articulated.[5]
>
> How is it, then, that I seek you, Lord? Since in seeking you, my God, I seek a happy life, let me seek you so that my soul may live, for my body draws life from my soul and my soul draws life from you[6] [1718].

The Beatitudes respond to this desire. They can be understood as invitations to inner purification as well as promises of profound transformation. The road to happiness is not paved in gold. It is covered with cobblestones, the ones over which Jesus trod when he dragged his cross to Golgotha. But the way leads to entrance to the glory of Christ, to the joy of the Trinitarian life.

The eternal beatitude, promised by Jesus, requires us to purify our hearts, our characters, our personalities in their entirety. We must seek the love of God above all else. True happiness cannot be found in any other way, not in riches or well-being, not in fame or power, not in any human achievement, only in conformity to Christ.

The Meaning of Human Freedom

God created humans as rational beings, and granted us the freedom to initiate and control our own actions. It is our human freedom, lived in conformity with God's call for us, that steers the course of our spiritual unfolding. Our freedom to adhere obediently yet creatively to the life God intended for us can only be perfected when it is directed toward the Divine.

Freedom is not without its burdens. It makes us responsible for our actions [1732]. Every time we make the right choice, we enter more fully into the freedom and wholeness God wants for us. The converse is also true—every time we choose wrongly, we dig our way more deeply in a kind of spiritual "rut." This makes it increasingly difficult for us to choose the good.

The fact that we are endowed with free will does not mean that we are the masters of our destiny. We must grow in the capacity to choose wisely and to act virtuously until it becomes almost second nature. Then it seems as if we come to recognize right away the paths of goodness. We find them through prayerful discernment and detachment from anything that deviates from God's plan. In this way we begin to conform *all* our actions to the revealed will of God. This truly is the goal of mature Christian character formation.

Lord of light and love, grant us the courage to seek your will always as the ground of our free choice and consent. How tiresome it is to grope in the darkness of sin, oblivious to our true transcendent destiny. Give us the gifts of wise appraisal and decision by making us more attentive, patient, and resistant to sin. Save us from doubt and lack of discretion.

Lord of mercy and forgiveness, keep before us the vision of what you would have us do to protect and foster the spiritual and human rights you entrusted to your people by law and example. Help us to fulfill with compassion the duty to direct our life's journey in the light of your revelation. Save us from the pitfalls of divisiveness. Bring peace to our relationships with all people. Help us to give loving expression to your inspiration [1731-1738].

Growth in Virtue

Virtues are Christian dispositions at the core of our heart and matching character. They are the stabilizing forces that help us to think and act in all situations as Christ would do. Like guards standing at attention, virtues sustain a woman's disposition to do the best she can to follow God, even when the going gets tough! The model to whom she looks for the fullest evidence of the virtuous life is Mary. Her strength and valor made her the handmaiden of the Lord.

Virtues shore up our determination to choose good over evil. They spur us on to meet the demands Holy Providence places before us in the modern world. Trials and errors notwithstanding, dispositions to pursue the good invite us in the diverse and demanding situations of life to ask: *Am I doing the best I can to serve my God [1803]?*

The virtues that comprise our characters help us to cope with tragedy or to meet a challenge, to thank God for his help or to ask humbly for a more appreciative outlook. They become in time stable, firm, and continuous forces in our personality [1804]. From this central anchor of our existence, we learn to attune our passions and emotions, our thinking and willing, to the graces of ongoing transformation. We try to attend with care to our own and others' well-being. Once we reach the age of reason we are expected to take responsibility for our actions.

Four Pillars of Virtuous Formation

The virtues of prudence, justice, fortitude, and temperance are not acquired solely by human effort; they represent the culmination of many graces. Combined with them are the infused gifts of faith, hope, and charity. These dispose us to stay in communion with the love of God that is the wellspring of our peace and joy. Against this background of goodness, we bind our characters to the four cardinal virtues that comprise the cornerstone of a virtuous life [1805]. As the Book of Wisdom declares: "If anyone loves righteousness, [Wisdom's] labors are virtues; for she teaches temperance and prudence, justice, and courage" (Wis 8:7).

Prudence guides a woman's judgment of conscience. To the degree that she develops a prudent character, she will be able to appraise habitually, in her family and in the world, all sides of a life situation. She will then determine the best course of action and direct her attention to pursuing it in the light of her practical reason. Her prudent character thus enables her to attune her judgment to the finer details of everyday living.

The virtue of prudence also instills in her the courage to stand up for her faith. It prevents her from caving in at the first sign of trouble. Instead of pressing the panic button, she strives to act in a wise and balanced way. And she is not afraid to witness to her convictions, even at the risk of being misunderstood.

Because prudence is a cardinal virtue, it is like the conductor of an orchestra, who directs the whole ensemble. All virtues are formed in the light of prudent gifts of appraisal and judgment [1806].

Justice is the second pillar upholding the edifice of a woman's

Christian character. It stands on the foundation of an unwavering will. It honors the commitment to give to others what belongs rightly to them. In justice, women of faith insist that all people be treated with dignity, that they receive what is their due [1807].

Fortitude grants a woman the courage to continue to care for others even when she does not feel appreciated. It helps her to carry on despite the obstacles she meets in an unjust society. Fortitude enables her to pursue charity and to show respect for all people. In materialistic self-centered civilizations, this virtue is often sorely lacking. Fortitude empowers a woman to "outrun" fears and temptation, trials and persecutions, name-calling and slander [1808].

Temperance prompts a Christ-centered woman to keep a close watch on her instincts, passions, volatile emotions, and desires. She strives to rein these in before they run away with her. Temperance helps her to heed the directives of reason and will as enlightened by the commands of God and the teaching of the Church. She listens to her own divinely guided life call and to the inspirations of the Holy Spirit. About temperance and the other cardinal virtues of our character, St. Augustine had this to say:

> *To live well is nothing other than to love God with all one's heart, with all one's soul and with all one's efforts; from this it comes about that love is kept whole and uncorrupted (through temperance). No misfortune can disturb it (and this is fortitude). It obeys only [God] (and this is justice), and is careful in discerning things, so as not to be surprised by deceit or trickery (and this is prudence)[7] [1809].*

Wounded as we are by original sin and its consequences, we are prone to sidestep the path of virtue. That why we beseech God to purify our hearts and to elevate our wills to do good by divine grace [1810]. Christ offers us the gift of redemption, but we must want to convert our wayward reluctance to be his disciples.

To live prudent, just, strong, and sober lives with the right balance of patience and persistence is not a goal we can accomplish on our own. We rely on God's help, but we must never take for granted "Christ's gift of salvation" [1811]. Prayer to the Holy Spirit, our companion on the long road to a virtuous existence, readies us to receive the light and strength we need to run the race to the finish.

The Theological Virtues

The theological virtues of faith, hope, and charity are woven into the same tapestry of character formation as the four cardinal virtues . The Church designates them as "theological" because they transform every aspect of our nature in such a way that we are enabled to participate in the divine nature. These three infused virtues make it possible for us to meet God in an encounter of utmost intimacy [1812].

Faith, hope, and charity, in other words, besoul our deepest "I," endowing each act a woman does with a divine character. All moral virtues are given divine life and light by the theological or God-oriented virtues the Holy Trinity infuses in our souls. They prompt us to pray:

Thank you, Triune God, for the infusion of your own infinite life into our limited existence. By your divine transformation of our wounded souls, you enabled us to become your beloved daughters. Overwhelming is the love you lavished upon us. By enduring excruciating suffering for us, you merited our entrance into eternal life. Your limitless generosity did not leave our frail nature to fend for itself in its lowliness and weakness. You transfigured our human spirit by the presence and action of your Holy Spirit. How can we ever praise and thank you enough for giving us this foundational triad of faith, hope, and charity [1813]?

Faith is the theological virtue that points us at the same time in two directions. It is both God-originated and God-oriented. Faith thus infused by the Spirit moves us to believe in God's existence and goodness. It enables us to say that we assent freely to the revelation, to Holy Scripture, Tradition, and Church doctrine [1814]:

Father, we praise you and thank you for your intimate presence in each of us by virtue of our belief in your divine revelation. How immensely this gift of faith, undeservedly granted to us, enriches the shadowy light of human reason, already in us by virtue of our creation. Your infusion of faith illumines our minds and strengthens our weak and wayward hearts. Through faith you ready us time and again to commit our lives to you alone, our eternal, living, and true God.

Through the treasury of our faith tradition, your Holy Spirit inspires us to hold fast to what we believe, also with hope and love. Only through this sacred threesome can we be united fully with your Son, Jesus Christ. Transform each of us tenderly into a living cell of his Body. Pour into us and all believers the firmness to stand up for the treasures of faith you implant in our Christ-formed character. Enable us to bear witness to our faith with courage and wisdom. Deepen especially our Spirit-guided sensitivity for teachable moments. Make us aware of appropriate and providential times and situations when our faith commitment, through your grace, will not hurt and estrange but heal and unite the thirsty souls and hungry hearts of people created for your love and entrusted to your care [1815-1816].

Hope instills in human hearts a longing for the kingdom of heaven. It lifts us from this valley of tears to the anticipation of life eternal, where with the saints we shall be welcomed to the banquet God has prepared. A woman's hope-saturated trust is not rooted in her own performances but in the promises of Christ. Her reliance on the grace of the Holy Spirit helps to keep her hopeful in the midst of adversity and near despair. Sin's hold weakens each time she reads, "Let us hold fast the confession of our hope without wavering, for he who promised is faithful" (Heb 10:23) [1817]. Knowing that all believers are by the grace of Jesus Christ heirs to the "hope of eternal life" (Ti 3:6-7), she prays:

Father, I praise and thank you for putting within my womanly heart the aspiration for happiness. By the generous overflow of your mercy, you filled this created aspiration of mine with the transforming power of hope. This gift of heaven-sent hope fills me with newly found dynamism, a godly energy at the heart of my personality. It continues to inspire and purify my ability to receive and give life. How lovingly you save me by hope from discouragement. Your gift buoys me up in the face of sin and misery.

Fill my heart, too, with the inspired sentiments of your glorious bride and Doctor of the Church, St. Teresa of Avila, who says: "Hope, O my soul, hope. You know neither the day nor the hour. Watch carefully, for everything passes quickly, even though your impatience makes doubtful what is certain, and turns a very short time into a long one. Dream that the more you struggle, the more you prove the love that you bear your God, and the more you will rejoice one day with your Beloved, in a happiness and rapture that can never end"[8] [1821].

Charity is the definite and conclusive theological virtue granted to true believers [1822]. This divine gift illumines every other virtue in our character. It creates in women of faith a capacity for the deepest possible love of God, self, and neighbor. No one can develop love of this depth and intimacy by human means alone. It is infused in our hearts directly by God. It enriches us with a special generosity and sensitivity for the defenseless and all who suffer. When women express this divine love in their hearts, in some mysterious way it divinizes them.

From the beginning of time, God gifted us generously with the ability to receive and to give love. Infused charity upholds and elevates this dynamic striving of our will. Our created yearning for love is empowered by the new commandment Jesus gives us [1823] and the fruits of the Spirit it produces [1824].

Animated by charity, a woman's character becomes more childlike and joyous. No longer does she serve God out of fear of punishment. Her character is more like that of a person who responds in love to love—to Christ who "died out of love for us" [1825].

The fruits of a divinized loving character include an increase in the virtues of joy, peace, and mercy. As St. Augustine says, "Love is itself the fulfillment of all our works. There is the goal; that is why we run: we run toward it, and once we reach it, in it we shall find rest"[9] [1829]. With the spiritual freedom granted to the children of God [1828], we pray:

We love you, Jesus, for transforming us by your new commandment of charity. We praise you daily for modeling this love for us so vividly in your own life. You died a horrifying death out of sheer love for us. Grant us the grace to imprint the apostle Paul's description of charity on our heart. For, in his words: "[Charity] is patient and kind; [charity] is not jealous or boastful; it is not arrogant or rude. [Charity] does not insist on its own way; it is not irritable or resentful; it does not rejoice at wrong, but rejoices in the right. [Charity] bears all things, believes all things, hopes all things, endures all things" (1 Cor 13:4-7).

Gifts and Fruits of the Holy Spirit

The transformation of a woman's Christian character is the outcome of God's enlightening gifts to her graced mind and will. These gifts enable her to maintain and expand her Christian presence in family, community, and society.

By no means does a life of virtue put a lively and spontaneous woman in a straitjacket. On the contrary, it makes her open, flexible, and dynamic. The Holy Spirit grants truly Christian women permanent character dispositions that form the lasting core or heart of their feminine personality. These dispositions literally "dispose" us to be more pliable and eagerly open to divine inspirations [1830].

The seven gifts of the Holy Spirit—wisdom, understanding, counsel, fortitude, knowledge, piety, and fear of the Lord—endow us with the inner lights we need to hear and do the will of the Lord with daring obedience. They help us to fulfill the inspirations of an increasingly Christ-formed personality.

Added to these seven gifts are the twelve fruits of the Holy Spirit. These are offered to us as the first harvest of what it means to radiate our dignity in Christ. They provide a foretaste of our eternally glorified characters in heaven. These fruits are, to cite Galatians 5:22-23, "love [charity], joy, peace, patience, kindness, goodness, generosity, gentleness, faithfulness, modesty, self-control, chastity" [1832].

The Deviation of Sin and
the Call of Continual Reformation

The formation of a truly Christian character is nothing we dare take for granted. We must watch vigilantly for any deviation that makes us vulnerable to sin. The Spirit of truth reveals—at times suddenly, at other times slowly—how our character needs to be changed. Our willingness to listen may grow into a conviction that we should try to reform our hearts, no matter how difficult this turnaround may seem to us. One thing is certain: if we try our best to respond to the call to continual reformation, the Holy Spirit will grant us a still deeper grace: that of transformation in Christ.

Grace heals the wounds of sin. It transfigures a woman's mind, will, heart, and character. The Spirit of truth opens us to the voice of our conscience as well as to our need for purification and redemption through the mercy of Jesus (see Romans 5:21).

Sin is an offense against God [1849]. As Psalm 51:4 puts it: "Against thee, thee alone have I sinned, and done that which is evil in thy sight." When sin turns our hearts from God's love, self-love gains the upper hand. Idolized selfhood generates vices as grim as merciless competition, violence, inordinate passions for pleasure and possession, rampant individualism, and cruelty to defenseless people. Christ crucified was the victim of such evils. Unbelief in the face of truth, mean depreciation, a hatred that instigated people gripped by envy and jealousy—all such forces converged to murder this innocent Healer of suffering humanity. He was a threat, as were his followers, to the inordinate competition for power by the religious leaders of that time. They attacked, shunned, and mocked a "newcomer" like Jesus, who threatened their authority.

Think of the streak of cowardice in Pilate's character, the sadistic bent of the soldiers who scourged Jesus, crowned him with thorns, and nailed him to the cross. Add to this the betrayal by Judas, whose mercenary character was deformed by lust for money. Finally, Peter's denial and the way his friends abandoned Jesus in his final hour are the bitter fruits of their weakness of character.

In the end only grace could eradicate their cowardice. The Holy Spirit had to descend upon the apostles at Pentecost. Out of the depths of his saving grace, Jesus gives us this same Spirit. We must be reminded, lest we forget, that Jesus suffered for our sake the brunt of our sinful nature—a suffering inflicted not only by the people torturing him but by all people in history, ourselves included [1851].

The root of sin resides in our free will, its inclination in our heart, its expression in our characters. Any one of us is more than capable of rejecting what is right and good in the eyes of God. As our Lord teaches: "For out of the heart come evil thoughts, murder, adultery, fornication, theft, false witness, slander. These are what defile a [person]" (Mt 15:19-20). Our hearts are at once a pool of sinfulness and a possibility for good, but all is not lost. Conversion of heart is always possible with the grace of God. Consider the wondrous change that occurred in a woman like Mary Magdalene. She who had been a sinner became a saint. Her character, like ours, was washed clean by the blood of Jesus. We can make a new start at any time. Such is the merciful response of God to a repentant heart wounded by sin but open to redemption [1853].

A woman's will and character affect her response to divine love. This love directs her steadily to its supreme end, who is God. She kills this divine orientation whenever she makes choices that are incompatible with the divine love directing her heart toward the good. If she does so with full knowledge and free consent, then she commits a grave sin [1854]. She can no longer cooperate in God's loving transformation of her personality. By idolizing the sinful object of her choice over and against God, she drives him out of her life. The consequences of such sin are, in a word, fatal or mortal

[1855-1861]. But not all sins are mortal. There are smaller, venial sins that lessen our intimacy with God but do not cut us off from his presence and the unmitigated generosity of his grace.

Our will to change may itself be weakened by sin. In small but corrosive and depleting ways, the solidity of our Christian character can be slowly whittled away. An example might be a tendency to judge harshly the everyday imperfections in people around us. As women of faith, we must pray for the grace to rise above all sin, and, without a doubt, above all mortal sin.

In the end each of us is responsible for the consequences of sin. Only in and through the saving grace of Jesus Christ can we hope to be liberated from its bondage. Only in his light and through his love can we fulfill the worldwide mission he has given us: to offer light and hope, peace and compassion to all in need.

Questions for Reflection and Faith Sharing

1. In what ways can we encourage our children to value the dignity of all persons? To teach them that we are all created in the image and likeness of God [1700]?

2. "The more one does what is good, the freer one becomes" [1733]. How do you understand this teaching in light of your own life experience?

3. The great contrast between God's holiness and our sinfulness can be overwhelming. How have you sensed God's mercy and love in your life, despite your imperfection [1870]?

4. In moments of quiet reflection, what sins do you feel the Lord is asking you to submit to his divine forgiveness? What holds you back from releasing these attributes and habits into the Lord's care?

ELEVEN
∾

Sharing in Divine Salvation

The hour is coming, in fact has come, when the vocation of women is being acknowledged in its fullness, the hour in which women acquire in the world an influence, an effect and a power never hitherto achieved. That is why, at this moment when the human race is undergoing so deep a transformation, women imbued with a spirit of the Gospel can do so much to aid humanity in not falling.

—*Pope John Paul II*
Mulieris Dignitatem, 1
(Citing the Second Vatican Council's
Message to Women, December 8, 1965)

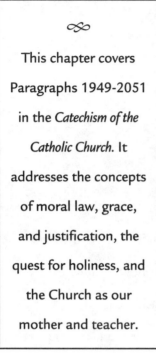

This chapter covers

Paragraphs 1949-2051

in the *Catechism of the*

Catholic Church. It

addresses the concepts

of moral law, grace,

and justification, the

quest for holiness, and

the Church as our

mother and teacher.

Living the Beatitudes transforms our earthly loneliness of soul into everlasting intimacy with the Trinitarian mystery. Time and again, due to our woundedness by sin, we get lost on the perilous passage to our homeland in the Lord. We need a guide to help us skirt the many obstacles that obstruct our way. This map is the moral law. It is the compass given to us by God that puts us on the right course to Jesus' kingdom of peace and joy.

Our basic woundedness makes it impossible for us to live in perfect fidelity to our call. Thus the Lord accompanies us with his guiding law and an abundance of undeserved graces, without which our vulnerable ship would surely sink. On our passage through the muddied waters of the world, the Scriptures also clear the way. The apostle Paul does not mince words when he declares: "Work out your own salvation with fear and trembling; for God is at work in you, both to will and to work for his good pleasure" (Phil 2:12-13) [1949].

The Forming Power of the Moral Law

The moral law is an eternal, ultimate source of truth and goodness, subtle in its elegance, direct in its commands. Its truth is revealed to us in different ways. The eternal law sourced in God is the basis of all natural moral law. Its two foundations are the Old Law in the Hebrew Scriptures and the New Law or the Law of the Gospel.

Other laws, civil and ecclesiastical, assure our specific adherence to what promotes the common good and rights of our citizens [1952]. These various branches or codes of law do not exist in isolation from one another; they are completely interconnected. They comprise a bright mosaic intended by Love Eternal for our life direction.

The moral law finds its fullest expression in Christ, who is the perfect embodiment of eternal wisdom. We celebrate the wisdom of God in all laws that are in tune with his will. Christ is not only the great exemplar of God's laws; he is also their final end. Only Christ lives to the full, only he bestows on us, the justice of God: "For Christ is the end of the law, that every one who has faith may be justified" (Rom 10:4) [1953].

Formation in Christ does not happen all at once; it is a tale of gradual, graced unfolding. During a woman's lifetime the Holy Spirit writes in her heart the chapters of this story. Her Beloved releases bit by bit the secrets of God's eternal plan for her. From one day to the next, the Spirit discloses how her life can reflect the wisdom and goodness of God. Slowly, by the patient and persistent repetition of good acts, her character is bound to the heart of Christ. His law of love is grafted onto her very nature [1954].

Justification and Sanctification

Thanks to the grace-filled revelation and guidance of the Holy Spirit, a woman of spirit may be able during the course of her life to turn away from whatever separates her from Jesus. More and more she feels ready to share his life to the full. Through the power of the Holy Spirit, she is cleansed from her sins (sanctified) and released from their bondage (justified) by faith. She receives "the righteousness of God through faith in Jesus Christ" and through Baptism. In the words of the apostle Paul:

> *But if we have died with Christ, we believe that we shall also live with him. For we know that Christ being raised from the dead will never die again; death no longer has dominion over him. The death he died he died to sin, once for all, but the life he lives he lives to God. So you also must consider yourselves as dead to sin and alive to God in Christ Jesus (Rom 6:8-11) [1987].*

Dying to sin and becoming alive to God in Christ is not an event that only happens inwardly. This process affects our life as a whole. Such enlivening is only possible when, by virtue of our Baptism, we become truly and lastingly Christ-formed [1987]. Through the power of the Holy Spirit, we participate in Christ's Passion, Death, and Resurrection. We are given the grace we need not only to die to sin inwardly but also to detach ourselves from the sinful "holds" of our prideful self-sufficiency and of that in our culture which operates contrary to God. Christ redeems and reforms, if we let him, the myth that we can do it alone, the greed that causes selfish consumers to ignore the poor, the prejudice that kills peaceful harmony between the sexes, races, and religions. With humble and contrite hearts, we come to see ourselves and others as members of Christ's body. We are the branches grafted into the Vine, which is Christ himself (see 1 Corinthians 12; John 15:1-4).

Such grace cannot be merited. It is a free gift granted to receptive hearts by a generous God. Grace enables us who seek salvation to partake of the divine nature as daughters and sons adopted into the family of the Trinity [1996].

Whether we are baptized as infants or adults, this sacrament gives us our initial taste of the grace of Christ. We share through Baptism in the transforming effects of this new life as members of his Body. Thus, it is by grace and only by grace that we can call God "Father." Now it is our privilege to share by adoption in the eternal, generative formation of the Son by the Father, even as the Holy Spirit breathes his love into the very fiber of our Christian character. This conversion never occurs autonomously; it is an event that happens in and with the Church [1997]. The older we get, the more we realize that everything in us is a result of God's initiative [1998]. Christian virtues are a good example.

The roots of Christian character formation grow in the soil of the virtues. They are the finest fruit of sanctifying grace. Rightly understood as a miracle of gratuitous love, this grace does not lie dormant, buried, as it were, in the depths of our soul; it is a dynamic, divine power rendering us capable of loosening the bonds of sin and restoring our likeness to God. Sanctifying everything in us, it wells up from the very nucleus of our existence. It renews our character from its inmost core to its every expression. Just as practice makes perfect in any endeavor, so, too, as we practice the virtues, we experience a certain ease in living and acting in fidelity to our call and vocation, both seen as originating in the sacred [1999]. We understand and accept that we have been preordained by grace to collaborate with the mercy of God already at work in us. God always brings to completion in us what he has begun. St. Augustine sheds light on this mystery by explaining:

> *Indeed we also work, but we are only collaborating with God who works, for his mercy has gone before us. It has gone before us so that we may be healed, and follows us so that once healed, we may be given life; it goes before us so that we may be called, and follows us so that we may be glorified; it goes before us so that we may live devoutly, and follows us so that we may always live with God: for without him we can do nothing*[1] *[2001].*

Only God can move our hearts decisively and directly to follow his way. However, our response to the gift of God-likeness is free. We can say *yes* or *no* to the divine initiative. We can either accept or refuse God's offer to know him more clearly, to love him more dearly. Divine truth and goodness will not coerce us. It frees us to fulfill our desire for happiness in a limited way here on earth, and fully, beyond our wildest imagining, in eternity [2002].

Graces as Gifts of the Spirit

Once awakened to our new life in the Spirit, it is natural for us to want to open our hearts to others in loving concern. To care in and with Christ for humanity and the world is a great privilege many women share. Even in this endeavor we do not operate alone. The same Spirit is already at work in the world. He waits there to enlist us with our gifts to work for the salvation of others and to nurture their growth as members of the Body of Christ, his Church.

It is this graced sense of working in collaboration with the Spirit that makes women characteristically effective in the areas of Christian healing and social care, spiritual guidance and religious education and formation. Since these works should be Spirit-inspired and guided, God grants his ministers specific graces. The *Catechism* highlights three of these: sacramental graces, special graces, and graces of state.

Sacramental graces refer to the gifts proper to the different sacraments [2003]. For instance, the graces afforded by the Sacrament of Matrimony enable spouses to collaborate with the Spirit in the Christian formation of each other and of their children. These sacramental graces make them also more effective in ways of family management, thus enhancing the Christian witness their "domestic Church" may give to the world.

Special graces are also designated *charisms* in the *Catechism*. These comprise "favor[s]," "gratuitous gift[s]," "benefit[s]" [2003] that reveal just how a person or group may be called to serve in a distinctive way the needs of a particular human community in conformity to Christ and the gospel. As mothers of a family, as single parents, as spiritual guides and teachers, we can count on special charisms to fortify our naturally good characteristics and to strengthen us for the tasks we undertake for the good of the Church and the world. Charisms are thus not intended for the isolated growth of one person only but for the common good.

Graces of state refer to the fact that a woman's state of life places demands upon her. She may be assigned special responsibilities and ministries within the Church. She has to manage these prayerfully and efficiently along with her Christian commitments in the world. In this case she can count on the Spirit to endow her with special graces, aptly called the "graces of state." Of them the apostle Paul says:

> *Having gifts that differ according to the grace given to us, let us use them: if prophecy, in proportion to our faith; if service, in our serving; he who teaches, in his teaching; he who exhorts, in his exhortation; he who contributes, in liberality; he who gives aid, with zeal; he who does acts of mercy, with cheerfulness (Rom 12:6-8) [2004].*

Effects of Grace

Women touched by grace seek new depths of faith formation. We may find ourselves drawn to social action while growing in trustful surrender to God's mercy. The efficacy of grace eludes our grasp. It is a supernatural mystery no human mind can fathom. That is why no one but God knows with absolute certainty what precise state of grace we may be in.

Suppose a woman makes every effort to develop her Christian character and personality in cooperation with sanctifying grace, in fidelity to her charisms, and in obedience to directives inspired by the Holy Spirit and upheld by the Church. Now, what if something goes wrong? From living the moral law, she falls into mortal sin, loses the state of grace, does not go to confession, and instead of repenting keeps living in sin? Neither her character nor her personality will change overnight. People who do not know the truth of her fall from grace may still be inspired by her dedication to good causes. They see lingering traces of the outer nobility of her character. Their expressions of gratitude may have the counter effect of causing her to rely on her own feelings or works for fulfillment while she persists in her sin. She may falsely conclude that she is still justified and saved. What she fails to realize is that the Christian dispositions that together comprise her character were and are a fruit of grace. They may still be used by God to inspire others, even if she herself is no longer living in sanctifying grace.

God alone can judge the ultimate guilt or innocence of our souls, or know for certain the absence or presence of grace in our lives. Even St. Joan of Arc, when asked by her ecclesiastical judges if she knew if she was in God's grace, had to reply, "If I am not, may it please God to put me in it; if I am, may it please God to keep me there"[2] [2005].

Merit in Christian Living

The question of merit and meritorious acts falls within the parameters of the virtue of justice, commonly understood as a principle of equality, "this for that" [2006]. The idea of merit in Christian life differs, however, from this general notion. Between God and us there is not equality as we understand this term to apply between people in society. On the contrary, what characterizes our relation to

God is an immeasurable inequality. Everything we are and have comes from God as a gift. No person, therefore, has a strict right to claim any merit [2007].

God did not have to engage us in the work of salvation. Our sanctification was and is due totally to his free initiative. Indeed the source of any merit in our relation to God lies in God alone. We may consent to or refuse the divine call to follow God's commands and inspirations. We can choose to cooperate with grace, or we can resist its abundant, unmerited outpouring.

Merit is not about me but about what God does in and with and for me. Only in a secondary way do merits flow from the good works I do. Let us always remember that our good actions, along with the ensuing virtues they promote, spring from the help we receive from the Holy Spirit.

In other words, true merits are a result of God's gratuitous justice. As partakers by grace in his own divine nature, we are the recipients of new rights bestowed on us by God. Among these are to be "coheirs" with Christ; to be found worthy to acquire "the promised inheritance of eternal life"[3] [2009]; and to recognize that any merits emanating from actions, including Christian character virtues, are gifts of God's goodness. Above all, as the *Catechism* emphasizes, *"No one can merit the initial grace* of forgiveness and justification" [2010]. No amount of education, not even years of disciplined self-exertion, merit our receiving this unfathomable storehouse of grace and revelation. All we can say is that to the degree that we are moved by the Holy Spirit and divine charity, we can merit for ourselves and others the graces needed to live a sanctified life. We can pray for an increase of Christlike love and the fruits that flow from it. We may even request temporal goods like education, health, adequate living standards, friendship, and the like, in accordance with God's will and plan for our lives. Not to be overlooked is the request we make of God for the favor of attaining eternal life. With the familiarity afforded his intimates, women of faith can converse thusly with the Holy:

You are pleased, Father in heaven, are you not, when I ask you for what I need to fulfill your call in my life? I trust that my hopes will come true in your own good time. No matter what happens, I know you will always be there to hear my cry. I sense you at my side. No genuine prayer will pass you by without a hearing. Loving me as you do, you grant my prayers the power to draw down from on high the graces I need for meritorious actions and the humble crafting of truly Christian virtues [2011].

Holy Spirit, keep the flame of love Christ enkindled burning brightly in me. This love is the source of any merits you may see. Eternal Father, your grace unites my heart, my acts, my virtues to your Son, Jesus. It clothes them in and through him with the resplendent garments of supernatural nobility. It transfigures the smallest expressions of charity into sources of true merit before God and for his people. How well St. Thérèse of Lisieux understood the ultimate purpose of life when she said: "After earth's exile, I hope to go and enjoy you in the fatherland, but I do not want to lay up merits for heaven. I want to work for your love alone.... In the evening of this life, I shall appear before you with empty hands, for I do not ask you, Lord, to count my works. All our justice is blemished in your eyes. I wish, then, to be clothed in your own justice and to receive from your love the eternal possession of yourself"[4] [2011].

Christian Holiness

The *Catechism* reiterates the teaching of Vatican Council II that all Christians in any state or walk of life are called to the fullness of Christian discipleship and to the perfection of charity. Christ himself invites us to "be perfect, as your heavenly Father is perfect" (Mt 5:48). In the words of St. Gregory of Nyssa, this means that "Christian perfection has but one limit, that of having none"[5] [2028]. As women of faith we glorify the Father not only by the quality of our interior life but also by our mirroring his divine attributes in the virtues governing our personalities.

In the throes of spiritual warfare [2015], we may doubt at times that we are called to holiness. Our hesitation could deepen still further when we hear of the sublime graces and extraordinary signs of the mystical life with which certain saints were blessed.

The truth is that holiness cannot be equated only with heroic feats and ecstatic experiences; it consists mainly of inconspicuous, everyday fidelity to Christ who lives within us. Our heart, quite simply, belongs to God. This oneness or intimate union with him is called "mystical," meaning that it represents a person's participation in his own love-will. The common ways of faith deepening in our tradition that foster such participation are liturgy, word, and sacrament [2016]. The sacraments are called "holy mysteries." They open us to the possibility of mystical union promised to us since Baptism. The question is: Are we ready to receive the divine messages contained in them?

Extraordinary graces, such as sublime visions and locutions, are granted to some mystics for the sake of manifesting the openness to a deeper life of prayer granted to all of us by our gracious God, at least potentially. Elevating our character and personality to conformation to Christ calls for a lifelong response to grace and a continual refinement of our sensitivity to God's call. Repentance, humility, obedience, faith, trust, and love are the lasting dispositions of a heart or character enriched by grace with charisms and Christlike virtues.

The Church, Our Mother and Teacher

Our moral life has an inner guide, and that is our conscience, as formed and informed by the teachings of the Church. Conscience formation is not the result of memorizing a list of do's and don'ts; it is above all an expression of our spiritual growth in and with the *ecclesia*. Our body, soul, will, heart, character, and personality are transformed in the light of the everyday sacrifices it takes to remain lovingly obedient to the law of Christ. The lifelong process of becoming another Christ finds its source and summit in the eucharistic sacrifice, nourished by the liturgy and the celebration of the sacraments [2031].

The highest truth of faith formation comes directly from God; its source is divine revelation. The Church is the "pillar and bulwark of the truth"[6] [2032]. She received it from the apostles along with the solemn command of Christ to announce his saving message (1 Tm 3:15). The principles of moral life and of spiritual transformation are never our own subjective invention. They must be proclaimed authoritatively by Christ's Church and implemented faithfully in her preaching, teaching, and practice.

Such authoritative teaching represents the ordinary ways in which the *Magisterium* of the Church stands firm amidst whirlwinds of change. The task of pastors and lay people responsible for catechesizing the faithful is to teach the *Catechism* while taking into account the works of recognized theologians and spiritual authors. Sustained in their efforts by grace, teachers are called to reflect this truth in their own lives. This is the most persuasive way of teaching the gospel [2033].

It is not enough merely to say we believe. Our responsibility is to put faith into practice at all levels of decision and action. Submission in peace and joy to the *Magisterium* enables laity, religious, priests, and bishops to work together for the betterment of the Church. This kind of collaboration offers a powerful witness to Christ's way in a world where self-fulfillment all too often takes precedence over any sense of sacrifice [2034].

The doctrine of *infallibility* expresses and guarantees the supreme degree in which the Holy Father shares in the authority of Christ himself [2035]. His infallibility extends not only to the deposit of divine revelation; it covers also those elements of doctrine, including morals, without which the saving and transforming truths of the faith "cannot be preserved, explained, or observed"[7] [2035]. Under the umbrella of infallibility fall also the specific precepts of the natural law, such as that which forbids the killing of an enemy other than in self-defense. Such precepts are to be revered and observed by every believer. This law is written by our Creator in the hearts of all people and affirmed by revelation as the Fifth Commandment of the Decalogue confirms.

Putting into practice the enlightening message of faith on a daily basis is an overwhelming task. It is impossible to achieve without unceasing prayer. Beyond the teaching roles of pastors and theologians, the Church needs a laity well trained in catechetical and formational theology to help in the spiritual guidance of parish and family life and to inspire people of good will in all professions to grow in the faith. Graced themselves with the experience of new life "in Christ," women may be able to nourish others hungering for God. The Most High delights in using the humble of this world to inspire and transform the learned and the powerful [2038]. Women pray for the chance to serve Christ in traditional ways and to break new ground under the guidance of the Church:

We thank you, Lord, for calling us to the ministry of transformation of ourselves and others. Spirit of Jesus, enable us to exercise this ministry in humble service to our brothers and sisters. Insofar as possible, illumine our conscience so that we may honor your moral law, both natural and revealed, and other sources of Christian transformation, notably the Beatitudes.

Holy Spirit, guard us against the temptation to abuse our personal conscience and reason by allowing it to oppose your moral law or the Magisterium of your Church [2039]. Grant us and those entrusted to our care the virtue of a true filial spirit. Let this spirit be the flower of the baptismal grace, which has made us members of the Body of Christ.

Heavenly Father, teach us to appreciate the motherly care of our Church shown to the fullest extent in your mercy. Forgiveness prevails over forgetfulness of sin. It is especially at work in the Sacrament of Reconciliation. With a mother's foresight, your Church lavishes on us, day after day, in liturgy, word, and sacrament, the nourishment we need. May we always be worthy to approach the eucharistic table of the Lord [2040].

The Precepts of the Church and Her Mission in the World

The Church has decreed by her pastoral authority certain laws to be obligatory [2041]. Therefore, every member of the Church has to do at least the following: 1) attend Mass on Sundays and holy days of obligation; 2) confess his or her sins at least once a year; 3) receive Holy Communion, at least during the Easter season; 4) observe the holy days of obligation; and 5) conform to prescribed times of fasting and abstinence. Added to these five precepts is the duty of providing for the material needs of the Church, each according to their own ability [2042-2043].

The test of authentic Christian character does not confine itself to the interior life alone. Neither ought it to restrict itself to the care of people in our immediate circle. Our vision of Church ought to be much wider than that. We are to involve ourselves in her mission in the world. In this endeavor women of faith can lead the way, doing what has to be done to build up the Church and to hasten the coming of God's reign. Let us draw others to the Lord by the witness of our Christian lives, by the constancy of our convictions, by our moral faithfulness, and by our conformity to Christ [2044-2046].

Questions for Reflection and Faith Sharing

1. "The entire Law of the Gospel is contained in the '*new commandment*' of Jesus, to love one another as he has loved us"[8] [1970]. Why do you think God chose this new commandment as a way to transform our hearts?

2. Why is it so important for young people to understand that the "natural law is a participation in God's wisdom and goodness," that it "expresses the dignity of the human person," that it upholds "fundamental rights and duties" [1978]? How might reminders like this offset the fear of violence and the sense of hopelessness gripping young hearts today?

3. When are you most aware of God's grace at work in your life [see 2017-2021]? How do you see divine grace and personal freedom operating hand in hand in your life?

4. Why is it so important for Catholics to understand and stand up for the Magisterium [2049] and its infallibility in doctrinal matters [2051]? What are you doing in your sphere of influence to preserve, expound, and observe the saving truths of our faith?

TWELVE

∞

Transforming Our Lives Through the First Three Commandments

The Council has confirmed that, unless one looks to the Mother of God, it is impossible to understand the mystery of the Church, her reality, her essential vitality. Indirectly we find here a reference to the biblical exemplar of the "woman" which is already clearly outlined in the description of the "beginning" (Gn 3:15) and which proceeds from creation, through sin to the Redemption. In this way there is a confirmation of the profound union between what is human and what constitutes the divine economy of salvation in human history. The Bible convinces us of the fact that one can have no adequate hermeneutic of man, or of what is "human," without appropriate reference to what is "feminine." There is an analogy in God's salvific economy: if we wish to understand it fully in relation to the whole of human history, we cannot omit, in the perspective of our faith, the mystery of "woman": virgin-mother-spouse.

—Pope John Paul II
Mulieris Dignitatem, 22

This chapter covers Paragraphs 2052-2195 in the *Catechism of the Catholic Church*. In it we begin the first of four chapters on the Ten Commandments. This one considers the adoration of God alone, the veneration of his name, and the remembrance of the Sabbath.

"Teacher, what good deed must I do to have eternal life?" the young man asks Jesus in Matthew's Gospel (19:16-19). We, too, ask this question in our hearts. We sense that life is supposed to have a deeper meaning—both here and now as well as in the hereafter. God created us for divine union, yet so often we feel the pain of being born in original sin and weakened by personal sinfulness.

Jesus answers this query by proclaiming how necessary it is to acknowledge God as the One who is good. God asks that we allow his divine goodness to permeate our lives. Prayerful attention and free consent to the commandments of God open us to this blessing, on one condition: that we do everything in our power to counteract the forces that separate us from God.

Pride prevents us from accepting that, on our own, we can do nothing, that God alone is the source of any transcendent good. But the more we embrace our nothingness, the more the Spirit reminds us of our "allness" in the mind and heart of God. It is in this first, precious caress by the Spirit that we are empowered to will wholeheartedly what Jesus tells us: "If you would enter life, keep the commandments."

It is our Beloved who inspires us to mellow our hardened hearts; he who reveals the precepts that will free us from self-obsession. It is he who shows us how to live in the light of the Decalogue: "You shall not kill; you shall not commit adultery; you shall not steal; you shall not bear false witness; honor your father and mother." In due time Jesus consolidated the Ten Commandments into two basic Christian virtues: love of God and love of neighbor [2052]. For the grace to keep this Great Commandment, women ask Jesus:

> *Master, what must we do to gain a life of intimacy with you? Our everyday routines can seem so empty, boring, and tedious. At our best moments your Holy Spirit whispers to us that there is far more to our existence here on earth than we may realize here and now. We should not be content with this or that success nor upset unduly by this or that failure. Your Spirit inspires in us a longing for transformation. Thank you, Jesus, for the grace of insight you give us into our nothingness and your allness. Draw our aloof and distant minds closer to your truth. Enliven our listless will. Soften our stony heart. Show us how to choose life abundantly through the gateway of your Commandments [2052].*

Jesus added another directive for the young man seeking liberation: "If you would be perfect, go, sell what you possess and give to the poor, and you will have treasure in heaven; and come, follow me" (Mt 19:21). Do we not find in this text the basis for growth in the life of any Christian? It is not enough merely to follow the letter of the law. We must come to know its spirit through the life and teachings of Jesus. That is why the Commandments are inseparable from the Beatitudes. We find that the Beatitudes reveal the virtues that provide a point of reference for us who seek to live a life of obedience to God's commands [2053].

The Law of Moses, the Old Covenant, was not abolished but fulfilled in the New Covenant (Mt 5:17). That is why Christ preached a "righteousness [that] exceeds that of the scribes and Pharisees" (Mt 5:20).

He laid bare the hidden depths of obedience, poverty, and chastity embedded in the demands of the Commandments. "You have heard that it was said to the men of old, 'You shall not kill.' ... But I say to you that every one who is angry with his brother shall be liable to judgment" (Mt 5:21-22) [2054].

When Jesus was questioned, "Which commandment in the law is the greatest?" (Mt 22:36, NAB), he replied: "You shall love the Lord your God with all your heart, and with all your soul, and with all your mind. This is the great and first commandment. And a second is like it, you shall love your neighbor as yourself. On these two commandments depend all the law and the prophets" (Mt 22:37-40; Dt 6:5; Lv 19:18). In response to these New Testament commands, women might share their inner thoughts with Jesus, saying:

How can we raise our self-sacrificing abandonment to the Father to new heights, dear Lord? How can the commandments of the Old Covenant sustain and expand our Christian womanhood and manhood? Their solidity protects us from being blown hither and yon by the gusty winds of false doctrines and empty promises. May they awaken in our souls an eternal flame of sober yet fervent holiness as we combine the power of the Commandments with the poverty of the Beatitudes [2055].

The Decalogue in Sacred Scripture

God did not create us, then leave us to our own devices. Rather, our Creator continues to form, reform, and transform us over a lifetime. The Commandments given by God in some way are known already by us, no matter how veiled and obscure our commitment to live them may be. They are written by God in all human hearts. The weakness of our fallen race makes it difficult for us to read the manuscript of right living etched on every God-illumined heart.

Therefore, through Moses, God revealed his eternal Law in the Decalogue. These "ten words" frame the Old Testament (Dt 31:9-24), though only in the New Covenant does God reveal their full meaning [2056]. They summarize the conditions of a soul freed from slavery to sin, just as God liberated the chosen people from servitude in Egypt.

The Decalogue is no abstract list of do's and don'ts. It presents a fundamental, vibrant way to craft an authentic human and Christian character [2059]. The Decalogue is God's divine legacy. It is best understood within the context of the covenant as a whole. Consent to this divine initiative (our response) is at the same time an invitation (God's call) to cooperate freely with the plan God has in mind for each person. Within this design, each population, family member, and individual has to disclose and realize his or her own call to purifying formation, illuminating reformation, and unifying transformation.

The revelation of the "ten words" on Mount Sinai represents a watershed in God's telling of our earthly story of loss and gain, of damnation and salvation. Notice that these divine communications come to us in the first person ("I am the Lord"). They are addressed to another personal subject ("you"). The *Catechism* makes clear that in all these Commandments, the *singular* personal is used to designate the recipient of the message. God makes his will known to each woman and man in particular. At the same time he makes it known to the whole people [2063].

The Decalogue in the Church s Tradition, Its Unity and Obligations

In her tradition of spiritual direction, the Church treasures the Decalogue as a captain does the compass on his ship. It occupies a privileged place in her catechesis [2064-2066]. The first three commandments concern the love of God, the following seven the love of neighbor.

Every God-fearing person is bound to keep the Commandments. They are the very building blocks of a fully human, fully Christian life of faith and good works [2068]. The Commandments are intertwined, from first to last; their messages about the love of God and neighbor are inseparable. To break one of them is to fracture all of them. To obey any single directive is to advance the integration of one's life as a whole [2069].

The Ten Commandments teach us the true meaning of our character makeup. Not only do they highlight the essential obligations placed upon us by God, they also point indirectly to the basic rights inherent in the unique life call and dignity that is God's gift to women and men from the beginning [2070].

When our hearts are illumined by the Commandments, our actions will give rise to more virtuous characteristics. For this reason to obey the Commandments entails *grave* obligations just as to disobey them entails *grave consequences*. No one can change arbitrarily what God has inscribed in the human heart. We are unremittingly pursued, even at times hounded, by these dictates and directives, which always and everywhere oblige us to choose and do what is right [2072-2073].

What Jesus asks is nothing less than all of who we are and all of what we do. We are to worship God over and beyond any idol of our own making. The First Commandment intends to awaken in us a powerful attraction to the God of the Old and New Testaments. It makes us want to respond more worthily to God's offer of temporal and eternal intimacy. Our wholehearted consent to this command unlocks the door to happiness we hope to pass through.

THE FIRST COMMANDMENT

I am the LORD your God, who brought you out of the land of Egypt, out of the house of bondage. You shall have no other gods before me. You shall not make for yourself a graven image, or any likeness of anything that is in heaven above, or that is in the earth beneath, or that is in the water under the earth; you shall not bow down to them or serve them (Ex 20:2-5; Dt 5:6-9).

It is written, "You shall worship the Lord your God and him only shall you serve" (Mt 4:10).

Lord, to hear your voice in these commanding words
is to behold in one adoring glance
your loving interventions
in our wounded world.
It is to delight in the rescue of your people
out of Egypt's house of bondage [2084].

Your revelation foreshadows our liberation
from sin's encapsulation.
Mightily it prefigures our release
from a culture that refuses to worship you.
Bowing our heads in prayer, we praise and thank you
for the mercy you have poured
upon our wounded lives.
Thank you for hearing our cry for help,
for disclosing the true course of the river
of our own destiny [2085].

Your First Commandment embraces
what shall be made known to us
as the ground of faith, hope, and charity [2086].
Our moral life and our mortality
have no other source than thee, O Trinity.
Let us sink into your embrace,
adore your lovely face,
its endless trace of peace and grace.

Let us guard our faithfulness
with prudence and vigilance [2088].
Rescue us from deadly temptations,
from the confusing intonations
of doubt and incredulity,
of schism, heresy, apostasy [2089],
leading to the fatal decision
of self-excision
from the Body of Christ.
Do not let the edge of disobedience
cut us off from our holy mother, the Church.

Fill us, O merciful majesty,
with a springtide of joyous hope.
Pour into us the capacity
to meet everyone in your healing way.
We pray:
Guide our actions so that we, too, may
give form to the virtues
that align our womanly personality
with your commandment of charity [2090].
Crown this hope of ours with the uplifting
anticipation of your everlasting regeneration,

with the final expectation
of the Beatific Vision we are awaiting.
Spare us the scourge of either a despairing
or a presumptuous heart [2091-2092].
Grant us faith in your boundless affection,
faith deep enough to make us respond
beyond the world's fascination
by loving you and all creation
in you, for you, and because of your inspiration
*   (see Deuteronomy 6:4-5) [2093].*

Let your gift of hope instill
in our vacillating will
the virtue of holy fear
to insult your invitations
by indifference or repulsion,
ingratitude or lukewarmness,
spiritual sloth or hatred of God [2094].

Living and Praying in Faith, Hope, and Charity

The theological virtues of faith, hope, and charity are like the trunk of the tree of virtues that comprise our Christian character. The stem that springs from charity is the *virtue of religion [2095]*, the first act of which is adoration. As women we have the example of Mary, Jesus' mother, who taught us to praise God with our whole heart: "[God] has done great things ... and holy is his name" (Lk 1:49) [2097].

The First Commandment calls us to prayer and adoration of the Most High. It brings us to our knees in humility. We pray first of all for the grace to obey the Commandments. We ask for the wisdom to follow the Spirit's direction to "always ... to pray and not lose heart" (Lk 18:1) [2098]. Somehow we know that the ongoing sanctification of our womanhood is best served when we turn the daily things we do and experience into holy acts of simple sacrifice. Every time we adore God in self-forgetful awe and wonder, our actions become acceptable to him and our outward sacrifices make life better for our neighbor [2100]. In this way, we unite our simple efforts with God's perfect sacrifice of love. We would not think of placing other gods before him when nothing but God suffices.

Keeping Promises and Vows

The First Commandment calls upon us to cultivate not only the virtue of adoration but the virtue of fidelity. With the help of grace, we pledge to keep all the promises we've made or will make before God and the Church at Baptism, at Confirmation, during renewal rituals at Easter and other occasions by married or single people, by priests and religious. Here promises of fidelity become lifelong commitments. The capacity to maintain such "I do's" is only possible when we keep the Lord our God at the center of our concern rather than any selfish motives. How we fulfill these commitments must, of course, be in tune with our life call, our talents, limitations, temperament, personal tasks, and avocations.

Commitments raised to the level of consecration may result in the vows taken in religious life or during a marriage ceremony. Vows once made in accordance with the laws of the Church are binding except when dispensations or annulments are granted by lawful authority [2103]. Most familiar to us are the vows religious make to practice the *evangelical counsels* of poverty, chastity, and obedience, though all women—married, single, and in the sisterhood—strive "to conform [their lives] more fully to the obedient Christ"[1] [2103].

The requirement of charity has to prevail under all circumstances as a validation of our loving obedience to God. This pledge of fidelity extends obviously to people who share our convictions, but the Church also urges us "to treat with love, prudence and patience those who are in error or ignorance with regard to the faith"[2] [2104]. No one should be forced to act against her convictions or contrary to what her informed and faithful conscience dictates. This right to choose according to one's conscience is inherent in the nature of persons. It "continues to exist even in those who do not live up to their obligation of seeking the truth and adhering to it"[3] [2106].

Have No Other Gods Before Me [nor] Make for Yourself a Graven Image

The First Commandment forbids the Chosen to honor "gods" other than the one true Creator of all [2110]. It is not easy to unmask the "false gods" of the present age, where personal pleasure overrides care for the poor, where killing pretends to heal, where idolatry of power and possession takes precedence over humility and charity. We pray with all women of faith for enlightenment:

Lord, do not let us drift away from your truth into superstition and idolatry [2111-2112]. Help us to recognize religiosity and self-centered devotions. Prevent us from falling into the trap of ascribing the effectiveness of prayers or sacramental signs to external performances disconnected from the inner dispositions they require [2113-2114].

Save us especially from divinizing anything as a substitute for you, our one and only God. Warn us in time if we begin to idolize power, possessions, career, status, money, food, sexuality, pleasure, sports, our race, our ancestors, the state, gods, or demons. Protect us against all forms of divination, such as recourse to

Satan or witchcraft or conjuring up the dead. Extinguish in us any desire for power over time, history, and other human beings. Do not let us swerve from the honor, reverence, and awe we owe to you alone, almighty Master of heaven, universe, and humanity [2115-2116].

Stop us when we are tempted to practice magic or sorcery, or to place ourselves under occult powers to gain a supernatural hold over others. Let us realize before it is too late that such prideful attempts to gain godlike glory are serious deformations of the virtue of religion [2117]. Save us from the main sins of irreligion: tempting God in words or deeds, sacrilege, and simony, the buying or selling of spiritual things [2118-2122]. Remind us that any form of atheism, agnosticism, or indifferentism is incompatible with the First Commandment and with the virtues it requires [2123-2128]. Let us not place any image before you, "the author of all beauty" (Wis 13:3). Help us to find the fine line between "respectful veneration" and idolatrous adoration [2129-2132]. Let all holy icons be pointers toward the transcendent God, who is more than any image is or can be.

THE SECOND COMMANDMENT

You shall not take the name of the Lord your God in vain (Ex 20:7; Dt 5:11).

You have heard that it was said to the men of old, "You shall not swear falsely." ... But I say to you, Do not swear at all (Mt 5:33-34).

The Second Commandment, like the first, belongs to the virtue of religion because it, too, guides our awe-filled, humble relationship to God and contributes significantly to the makeup of our

Judeo-Christian character. God reminds us that a good relationship requires respect for the name of the Lord and by extension the proper use of speech in sacred matters [2142]. Among all the words of revelation, none ought more to be revered than the name of God. By guarding and protecting its integrity in speech, we acknowledge the mystery enshrined in this holy utterance:

> *Like a sturdy bridge over the infinite abyss between creature and Creator, you gave us your name to honor, O Lord. May it be our firm intention to bless, praise, and worship—both inwardly and outwardly—this epiphany of your love and glory [2143-2145]. Extend our respect for holy names to the Virgin Mary and all the saints [2146]. Grant that we may never forfeit the gift of your grace by the grave sin of blasphemy [2148]!*

The virtue of religion, so beautifully unveiled in the first three commandments, gives us a *sense of the sacred*. Sacred names evoke wonder. They prompt us to praise and thank God with grateful hearts [2144]. That is why the Second Commandment forbids irreverence in any form, including the taking of false oaths [2149]. This means that we invoke the truthfulness of God as evidence that what we say is true. That is why this Commandment prohibits the practice of promising something under oath with no intention of keeping your word, or pledging under oath to execute or support a deed that is evil. Both acts discredit the holiness of the divine name [2152].

In the Sermon on the Mount, Jesus explains the Second Commandment in an even fuller way: "You have heard that it was said to the men of old, 'You shall not swear falsely, but shall perform to the Lord what you have sworn.' But I say to you, Do not swear at all.... Let what you say be simply 'Yes' or 'No'; anything more than this comes from evil" (Mt 5:33-34, 37). Jesus urges his disciples, as he does us, to say what we mean and to mean what we say! Anytime we swear about this or that, we may deviate, however slightly, from the truth. The risk of defacing God's name makes it advisable that we do not swear at all. Such discretion can only become second nature to us when we grow in prayerful awareness of the holiness of God's name [2153]:

> *What a grace above all graces it is, dear Lord, to be baptized "in the name of the Father and of the Son and of the Holy Spirit" (Mt 28:19). Your name transforms and sanctifies saint and sinner alike. You gift each of us with our own name, that special designation that may place us under the protection of our patron saint [2156]. Naming is more than a social need. It signifies to us in faith that we are called and chosen. Thus, in daily commemoration of our Baptism, the Church teaches us to begin our day, all our prayers and actions, with the Sign of the Cross. This sign strengthens us in temptation. It makes every difficulty more bearable [2157]. Let our name be holy as your name is!*

THE THIRD COMMANDMENT

Remember the sabbath day, to keep it holy. Six days you shall labor, and do all your work; but the seventh day is a sabbath to the Lord your God; in it you shall not do any work (Ex 20:8-10; Dt 5:12-15).

The sabbath was made for man, not man for the sabbath; so the Son of man is lord even of the sabbath (Mk 2:27-28).

Scripture describes the Sabbath as a celebration of the seventh day of creation, the day on which our Creator rested [2169]. Would that we in the modern world followed his example! God intended the Sabbath to be a day of respite from the accumulated tension of labor; a joyous interruption of the threat of enslavement to work; a period given over to the worship of God beyond the "golden calf" of human performance, success, and money making [2172]. On this day devoted to wise and balanced relaxation, we should be free from anxious rigidity. In the words of Scripture: "The seventh day is a sabbath of solemn rest, holy to the Lord" (Ex 31:15).

The Lord s Day

On the first day of the week, "Jesus rose from the dead." This day in the New Testament is a symbol of our being made a new creation. Christ's Resurrection initiated this new beginning and its Sunday celebration. This day is for us the first day of all. It is the Lord's Day—Sunday.

Think of your Sundays, if you can, as days of inner nourishment, days to replenish your energy, days to ready you anew for effective service, for charitable sacrifices.

From the urgent, faith-filled beginnings of the apostolic age, Sunday was set apart for the celebration of the Paschal Mystery. As members of the universal Church, we observe Sunday as the foremost holy day of obligation. There we gather with our parish community to celebrate liturgy, word, and sacrament. There we praise and thank God for our faith in the setting of our shared liturgical life. Already St. John Chrysostom counseled the faithful of his time: "...Come to Church early, approach the Lord, and confess your sins, repent in prayer.... Be present at the sacred and divine liturgy, conclude its prayer and do not leave before the dismissal...."[4] [2178].

The Sunday Eucharist is meant to be a celebration, not a routine event. It is the source and center of our graced efforts to place our life in family and society under Christ. The graces of the Eucharist can nourish our spiritual life for the rest of the week if we take to heart the Third Commandment and truly honor the Lord's Day.

The Church obliges us to participate in the Eucharist also on holy days of obligation. By their example mothers and fathers can set the tone for worship. Modes of appeal instead of coercion, joyful celebration instead of fear of punishment, may encourage children to love the Mass. One may be excused for a serious reason, such as illness or the care of infants, but to deliberately fail this obligation without a valid reason is to fall into error and grave sin [2180-2183].

Women realize that to keep holy the Lord's Day helps us to enjoy precious time with our Beloved. In his presence we come to a wise and balanced recovery of our often overstretched lives. The Lord's Day offers us not only the joyous relief of relaxation and rest but the leisure to pray and contemplate. It is the best preparation for creative work when we remember to ask:

Free us, Lord, from the stress that exhausts us so often during the week. Remind us, when we are tempted to overwork, that Sunday offers us a chance for restoration. The Lord's Day creates room to cultivate warm and attentive times with our family, to enjoy cultural and social events, and above all, to deepen our spiritual life [2184]. Prevent us from robbing ourselves of appropriate relaxations of mind and body. Imprint on our hungry heart the sound advice of St. Augustine: "The charity of truth seeks holy leisure; the necessity of charity accepts just work"[25] *[2185].*

Questions for Reflection
and Faith Sharing

1. What episode in Jesus' life comes first to your mind when you recall how "by his life and by his preaching Jesus attested to the permanent validity of the Decalogue" [2076]?

2. How do you fulfill your duty "to offer God authentic worship ... both as an individual and as a social being" [2136]?

3. What can you as a Christian woman do to prevent the improper use of God's name in society today [2162]? What do you see as viable ways in your familial and professional circles to halt blasphemous language?

4. Is Sunday observed in your home "as the foremost holy day of obligation in the universal Church"[6] [2192]? Are you aware of the need "to abstain from those labors and business concerns which impede the worship to be rendered to God ... or the proper relaxation of mind and body"[7] [2193]?

THIRTEEN

Affirming Respect for Life: the Fourth and Fifth Commandments

Wherever the work of education is called for, we can note that women are ever ready and willing to give themselves generously to others, especially in serving the weakest and most defenseless. In this work they exhibit a kind of affective, cultural and spiritual motherhood which has inestimable value for the development of individuals and the future of society.

—Pope John Paul II

Letter to Women, 9

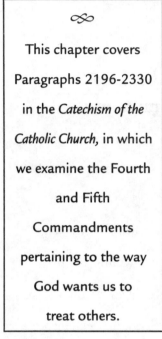

This chapter covers

Paragraphs 2196-2330

in the *Catechism of the*

Catholic Church, in which

we examine the Fourth

and Fifth

Commandments

pertaining to the way

God wants us to

treat others.

These Commandments turn our attention to what a God-oriented life looks like as we begin to relate to one another in the light of the divine law. Demands are made—to honor our elders, not to kill, nor to be unfaithful—but the outcome of obedience is good for everyone concerned. The Commandments build respectful, loving, faithful relationships. They showcase the Catholic principle of respect for life. We need to listen to them for the sake of our aged, our children, our spouses. As women who often fulfill the role of caregivers, we mourn for the loss of a sense of honor. We weep when the streets of our city become killing fields. We suffer when vows are broken. These Commandments may sound harsh to some, but to a believer's ears they are full of compassion.

THE FOURTH COMMANDMENT

Honor your father and your mother, that your days may be long in the land which the Lord your God gives you (Ex 20:12; Dt 5:16).

He ... was obedient to them (Lk 2:51).

The Fourth Commandment opens the second tablet of the Decalogue. It reveals the virtues of Christian character formation that give priority to charity for our neighbor [2196]. Honoring our parents is a directive meant to guide not only immediate family relations; it also extends care to the wider community of elders and those in authority over us—to teachers, employers, government officials, and similar people who deserve our respect [2197-2200].

The Family in God s Plan and in Society

A man and a woman united in marriage, together with their children, form a family whose deepest source and origin is God. The Christian family is where we first learn what it means to be part of the family of God. That is why the family is and should be called a *domestic church.* At its best, the Christian family can reflect the sanctifying work of the Trinity and the sacrificial life of Jesus [2204]. Daily devotions strengthen a family in charity and give it a heart that is open to reaching out to others through evangelism [2205].

The family is, therefore, a privileged community. Respect for one another creates an atmosphere of affinity and affection that enables parents to work together in their children's upbringing and to share in each other's unique life journey [2206].

The Fourth Commandment sheds light on other relationships in society as well. It helps us to see every person as a son or daughter of the one true God. Good family experiences teach us that each child of God is endowed with dignity and full membership in the human community [2212-2213]. For this reason, the vocation of marriage and parenthood is an unparalleled privilege, a holy calling.

The Duties of Parents and Children

God intended that each family, at every stage of life, mirror the never-ending mutuality and fellowship of the Trinity. "With all your heart honor your father," we read in the Book of Sirach, "and do not forget the birth pangs of your mother. Remember that through your parents you were born; what can you give back to them that equals their gift to you?" (Sir 7:27-28). Our parents deserve to be honored and respected, especially in their elderly years. They ought to be allowed to run their own lives without unnecessary interference from grown-up children [2215].

By the same token, parents must treat their daughters and sons as children of God, endowed with their own vocational call [2222]. The home parents provide should be a good place in which to grow up and be educated, a safe space to learn the virtues that build Christian character [2223].

Raising children in gospel values is a demanding task under *any* circumstances. Through the graces bestowed by the Sacrament of Matrimony, parents accept the responsibility and privilege of evangelizing their children in the light of biblical truth and in obedience to the Commandments [2225]. By their efforts and example, by the witness of their mutual respect, they see to it that their children learn the meaning of commitment. It is from the parents that children learn how to follow Jesus [2232], how to accept "the invitation to belong to *God's family*" [2233].

Authority in Civil Society

Christ looks with compassion on the sufferings of his children—suffering that is often inflicted upon them by the misuse of authority and the condoning of cruel discrimination. Jesus looks to women of faith to help him inspire people in authority to be servant leaders who realize that their first duty is to care for all God's children in justice and charity [2235]. He enlists us in the battle against indifference and arrogance. Such attitudes destroy the harmony Christ wants to see between women and men in family life and society. As a result, we may resist in Christ's name any regulations in society that unjustly elevate the interests of the powerful at the expense of the oppressed, the abused, and the exploited. Governments, schools, and social institutions must be brought to this awareness so that they do not set "personal interest against that of the community"[1] [2236]. The gospel calls those in political power to respect the fundamental rights of women and children. Nonviolent protest or recourse to some other form of action is first of all an expression of your citizenship in a free country. It becomes your serious duty when police, courts, or other public authorities usurp, without legitimate reason, the human dispensation of justice that is your due [2237]. The right and duty to support properly appointed and executed authority or to withhold support have to be exercised in all cases where the dignity of persons is at stake [2238].

Duties of Citizens

The obligation to serve the well-being of society is one we should gladly accept out of gratitude for what our country has done for us and to set a good example for others. In spite of the unjust exploitation often suffered by women, hope is not lost for a better tomorrow [2239]. The defense of women's rights extends in a special way to immigrants who come to this country seeking a better life. For them and their families, for all parents living under oppressed conditions, we may pray:

Jesus, compassionate friend of all who suffer, give us a share in your unbounded love for men, women, and children seeking to relieve the hardships that weigh so heavily on their family life.

Grant us the grace to uphold the rights of oppressed people longing to be free. Help us to see them not as foreigners but as friends. Many among them have been treated ruthlessly in the lands of their birth. You know how hungry they are for security from deadly threats, for the chance to make a decent living.

Spirit of fire and light, instill in us profound empathy for those who have been exploited. Give us the courage to end the debasement of so many because of the greed of a few. Arouse in those who come to our shores a love for their new land and a desire to honor its laws. Inspire them to do their part to carry its burdens to pay taxes, to vote, to support the economy, and to be ready and willing to defend its shores [2240-2241].

When all is said and done, the only objective and ultimate touch-stone for decision-making by people in authority has to be the authority of God. When this is lacking, people of faith cannot assent to attitudes that undermine the basic rights of the defenseless. We are called to join the chorus of voices that proclaim, "We must obey God rather than men"[2] [2242].

Women may suffer oppression—explicitly or implicitly, inside or outside democratic institutions, and even at certain periods in the history of the Church herself. The institutional reality of the Church can betray at moments her own humanness, for none of us is immune to sin. Still, women can look to the Church as the God-given sign and protector of the transcendent character of the human person and therewith of oppressed women everywhere [2245]. She who has been persecuted and despised over the ages knows from experience what women have had to endure. Therefore, her daughters should insist that it belongs to the mission of the Church to pass moral judgment whenever and wherever the basic rights of human beings are threatened or the salvation of souls is at stake [2245-2246].

THE FIFTH COMMANDMENT

You shall not kill (Ex 20:13; Dt 5:17).

You have heard that it was said to the men of old, "You shall not kill; and whoever kills shall be liable to judgment." But I say to you that every one who is angry with his brother shall be liable to judgment (Mt 5:21-22).

This commandment states in a few words a mighty message. The reason *human life is sacred* is that "from its beginning it involves the creative action of God.... God alone is the Lord of life from its beginning until its end: no one can under any circumstance claim ... the right directly to destroy an innocent human being"[3] [2258]. Deliberate murder is gravely contrary to the dignity and value of human life created by God. Killing violates the Golden Rule and the holiness God intends for our happiness. "The law forbidding it is universally valid: it obliges each and everyone, always and everywhere" [2261].

Legitimate Defense

Christ tells us to "love our enemies" (Mt 5:44) and to sheath our swords (Mt 26:52). His command notwithstanding, the *Catechism* makes clear that legitimate defense has its place in life [2262]. St. Thomas Aquinas sheds light on this difficult issue by distinguishing between two outcomes of self-defense. One effect is the preservation of one's life, the other is the death of the aggressor. The saint adds this crucial clarification: While saving one's own life was intended, the death of one's assailant was not [2263].

A woman may be forced to defend her life against a rapist. Her aim is not to take undue risks but to save herself using whatever methods of self-protection she has at her disposal in the heat of the crime. What if she finds herself in a "kill or be killed" situation? Once more St. Thomas has the answer: "Nor is it necessary for salvation that [one] omit the act of moderate self-defense to avoid killing the other ... since one is bound to take more care of one's own life than of another's"[4] [2264]. Legitimate defense can actually be the grave duty of a person who would otherwise be a victim of violence and in danger of death. A person in such a dilemma is also responsible for the safety of others when life and virtue are at stake [2265].

The Church acknowledges, therefore, the right and obligation of legitimate public authority to punish criminals. The penalty should fit the gravity of a crime. The *Catechism* states explicitly that in cases of extreme gravity the death penalty ought not to be excluded in states electing to mandate it under conditions that rigorously uphold the dignity of victims and the humane treatment of prisoners [2266-2267]. Of course, the Fifth Commandment forbids direct and intentional killing. Murder is a heinous crime. Less drastic means of protecting a population may be preferable to capital punishment or life imprisonment, but punishment ought to be at least commensurate with the crime for justice to be served [2268].

The Fifth Commandment also forbids doing anything to another human being with the intention of *indirectly* bringing about his or her death. Refusing reasonable assistance to people in mortal danger is a serious sin, at once cowardly and irresponsible [2269]. Many women die in cases of domestic violence because there is no one willing to "interfere" when help and protection is most needed. Their fate must be seen as a wake-up call to an increasingly indifferent society. At the heart of a transformed city there must be transformed hearts. For the grace of conversion we pray:

Eternal Father, spread your mantle of protection over women who live in fear and mortal danger. Jesus, be a woman's rock and shield, the hidden power she can lean on to resist aggressors who would reduce her to a victim of their cruelty. Spirit of wisdom, enlighten the minds of brave women when they must defend their personal dignity, life, and virtue. Be with them when they have to deal defensively with an oppressor or protect their life from an assailant.

Trinity Divine, inspire and strengthen us as courageous and compassionate members of Christ's mystical body to help our sisters and brothers, especially when they are in mortal danger.

Mother of our Redeemer and all virgin martyrs, save us from indifference. Watch over the most vulnerable among us, especially anyone in danger of death.

Defending Life from Abortion, Euthanasia, and Suicide

As women of faith, we should be the first to insist that people respect and protect human life from the moment of conception [2270]. From its most pristine beginnings, a new human being is entitled to all the rights of personhood, including the inviolable right to life. He or she is not a possession of the parents whose life can be planned or taken at will but a gift of God. The pro-life stance and doctrine of the Church is not new. Since the first century she has taught that every intentional abortion is a grave contradiction of the moral law [2271]. This teaching has not changed over the ages because it is by definition unchangeable.

The Church's condemnation of abortion as an horrific affront to the Fifth Commandment is a doctrine we as Catholic women must uphold completely.

By the same token, the Church extends a compassionate invitation to women who have had abortions to seek forgiveness and reconciliation. At the time they acted, these women may not have been aware of the gravity of their actions. Under severe pressure, their consciences may not have guided them to make the right choice. Later, perhaps years later, they may find themselves mourning for their loss. Tears of repentance are always a sign of grace. The Church may condemn the sin, but never the sinner. Women in this position are not alone. They remind the rest of us of the need for ongoing individual and social repentance and for heartfelt prayer:

> *God of justice and compassion, accept our prayers of reparation for taking the precious life you entrusted to the safety of a mother's womb. Thank you for giving your Church the courage to name abortion a heinous crime and a grave offense. Grant sinners the courage to repent and seek reconciliation for this life-denying act. You are waiting with open arms, Lord of mercy, to forgive anyone who offends you by taking the life you lovingly created or who assisted in this crime. Welcome for all eternity helpless little victims you invested with such awesome, now never to be realized, potentials [2272].*

God gave our life to us on the day of our birth. No matter how old or sick we are, God has determined the day and the hour of our death as well. Taking our life in our own hands offends our divine Master. God alone sets the time of our final good-bye. It must not be subject to our haughty manipulation by a crime like euthanasia. The *Catechism* mentions various circumstances, such as serious psychological disturbances or torture, that can diminish the responsibility of people who do take their life [2282]. It also tells us that God, in ways we cannot know, may grant a last opportunity for repentance to persons who decide to commit suicide and sadly succeed. The motherly care of our Church, manifested in the prayers said for victims of self-destruction, reminds us of the merciful face of God.

Respecting Our Health

Women often find themselves in advocacy positions when it comes to protecting the right to decent and equitable health care on the part of all people [2288]. Our body is a gift from God to be treated with respect and solicitude at all times, in sickness and in health. This does not mean that we ought to be drawn into a "body cult" that promotes physical perfection as an end in itself [2289]. The Holy Spirit guides us to care for our lives as a whole, as a means to a higher call. Reasonable concern for our bodily well-being, good nutrition, and exercise can enhance our lives without causing us to lose the balance between love of self and love for God and neighbor. The virtue of temperance reminds us to avoid every kind of excess. It helps us to be on guard against over-exertion (or under-exertion); against eating and drinking too much; against misusing drugs or medications [2290]. Such abuse erodes our own dignity. It damages our ability to express our gratitude to God for making us who we are uniquely called to be.

Respect for the Person and Scientific Research

Scientific research can either serve the dignity of human personhood or offend against it. We find ourselves at a crucial juncture of history in this matter [2292]. Almost daily, science reports new breakthroughs that can enhance or harm the unique dignity of the person. Neither age nor circumstance may matter in unscrupulous hands. We find ourselves praying with the Church that respect will prevail over the potential disrespect involved in immoral applications of science:

Thank you, Lord, for giving human beings dominion over your creation, for generously enabling your people to grow in insight. Over the centuries you illumined minds with new waves of understanding, making it possible for people to discover the precious resources of science and technology.

We beg you to remind us in the throes of discovery that the results of scientific research by themselves alone—cut off from moral teachings—can be more destructive than creative. Simply because we have the technological means to do something does not mean that we should do it.

Heavenly Majesty, you are the source of both our moral wisdom and our scientific and technological advances. Fill us and all humanity with the firm conviction that certain God-guided principles must be at work in the application of our findings.

Let us look first of all to the Commandments you have written in our hearts and clarified through your Church. Teach us that the marvels of our functional knowledge and skill have as their purpose to serve the dignity and well-being of all human persons, in conformity with your loving will for every man, woman, and child on earth [2296].

Respecting Bodily Integrity

A quick scan of the headlines reveals the terrible consequences of kidnapping, hostage taking, terrorism, and torture; clearly, these actions are morally wrong. Directly intended amputations, mutilations, and sterilizations performed on innocent persons for other than strictly therapeutic, medical reasons violate this law of God [2297].

The respect due to human dignity extends not only to the living but also to the dead and dying. All possible attention and care should be given to assist the dying in their last decisive moments to pass from this life in dignity and peace. As responsible caregivers women are often the ones who try to make sure that the prayers and sacraments of the Church are available to their loved ones in their final moments [2299].

Our respect for the living and the dead is a reflection of our faith and hope in the resurrection. We believe that every baptized person is a temple of the Holy Spirit. We see it as a corporal work of mercy to bury the dead. Remembrance of the dying as temples of the living God deepens our respect. We insist on the dignified treatment of their remains [2300-2301], on memorial services that celebrate their passage from this life to the next.

Safeguarding Peace

Along with respect for life, the Fifth Commandment upholds our desire to live in peace and harmony with one another. St. Augustine calls peace "the tranquillity of order"[5] [2304]. To obey this aspect of God's Law is to stem the tide of murderous anger and hatred, of every form of violence blighting the earth [2302-2303]. If we allow anger to grow unchecked in our heart, it may spawn the seeds of resentment. Rancor, vengefulness, and vindictiveness make it impossible for us to maintain inner peace, let alone to make peace with others.

The best safeguards for peace are free and forthright communication among people and respect for individual dignity. Two virtues that make this possible are justice and charity [2304]. These are exactly the gifts absent in any country devastated by war. With hearts full of compassion for war-torn sisters and brothers, we pray:

Prince of peace, bring harmony to our planet. Reconcile your people to one another and to our Father in heaven. Keep inspiring your Church to preach a gospel of peace. Bring her people to her altars to receive the sacrament of unity, your own body given up for us [2305].

Jesus, you know that our hearts long for peace in this world,
even if it seems impossible, humanly speaking, to guarantee it.
Still our trust in you does not waver. Help us to renounce violence
and bloodshed, to defend the weak, to show charity to all who seek
a gentle touch, a caring word. Let our voices rise together to sing
a new melody of harmony within the heart of the Trinity [2306].

Peace, Not War, Is Christ s Way

How desperate and powerless women feel when they and their children are caught in war. Mothers know from painful experience that the time to change our hateful ways is not tomorrow but today. The moment to proclaim peace, not war, is now. As women of spirit, we beg God to heal the breach between people. How can charity and justice prevail when violence presents itself as a solution to conflict? We want Christ's own virtues of mercy, gentleness, and reconciliation to be central in public and private life. We ask the Lord to help us to serve each other in love, to call us "to prayer and to action so that the divine Goodness may free us from the ancient bondage of war"[6] [2307]. As mothers and educators, we try to instill in the hearts and characters of the young virtues that will dispose them later in life to choose peace over anger and revenge.

If, despite every effort to make peace, a just war erupts, it does not banish the moral law engraved by God in the human heart to preserve human dignity and decency, both on and off the battlefield [2310-2314].

Prompted by charity, wisdom, and social concern, some women may seek with like-minded people to find ways to limit the production and sale of arms and to address the root causes of bearing them [2315-2316]. Women come forward in countries around the world to raise their concern for social injustice, excessive economic inequality, envy, distrust, and the devastating consequences of self-

centered pride. When such life-denying attitudes and power struggles predominate, leaders may see war as a solution to their problems, rather than its evil consequences. That is why women's voices
form a chorus to end war even as we pray for its innocent victims:

> *Prince of peace, enable all nations and peoples to do all they can
> to diminish the threat of war, armed conflict, and destruction.
> Let the balm of your loving heart, wounded by our prideful and
> quarrelsome humanity, soften hostility everywhere. Fill our wom-
> anly spirits with the sacrificial love that is our best defense
> against life-threatening hatred.*
>
> *Spirit of wisdom and truth, arouse our sense of compunction
> for the personal and social sins that ultimately evoke the catastro-
> phe of annihilating violence.*
>
> *Jesus and Mary, save us from the willful stubbornness that
> ruins humanity's chances for the good life you promise. Grant us
> the graces we need to transform our hardened hearts into
> Christlike mirrors of mercy, "building up peace and avoiding
> war" [2317].*
>
> *Inspired by the words of your prophet Isaiah, let us pray that
> his vision may come to fruition in our lifetime: "They shall beat
> their swords into plowshares, and their spears into pruning hooks;
> nation shall not lift up sword against nation, neither shall they
> learn war any more" (Is 2:4).*

Questions for Reflection and Faith Sharing

1. What do you think you can do to foster in young people a respect for the elder generation, "parents and those whom [God] has vested with authority for our good" [2248]? By the same token how can you help parents and elders to understand the responsibility they bear to educate children "in the faith, prayer, and all the virtues" [2252]?

2. As a parent (biological or spiritual) are you committed to encouraging children to follow their own life call and vocation, or is there in you a tendency to impose on them your choice for their direction? Are you as respectful of the vocation to the single life, to the priesthood and religious life, as you are of the vocation to marriage? Do you assiduously teach your children "that the first calling of the Christian is to follow Jesus" [2253]?

3. Why do you think the "culture of death" (murder, abortion, euthanasia, suicide) has invaded society to such a degree that many no longer believe that "every human life, from the moment of conception until death, is sacred because the human person has been willed for its own sake in the image and likeness of the living and holy God" [2319]?

4. Why may women have a special role to play in the area of peace-making? Can you suggest some ways to overcome the bellicose dispositions that fuel table-side battles as well as the "evils and injustices ... all war brings" [2327]?

FOURTEEN

Healing Relationships by Observing the Sixth and Seventh Commandments

Human beings are not the same thing as the images proposed in advertising and shown by the modern mass media. They are much more in their physical and psychic unity, as composites of soul and body, as persons. They are much more because of their vocation to love, which introduces them as male and female into the realm of the great mystery.

Mary was the first to enter this realm, and she introduced her husband Joseph into it. Thus they became the first models of that fairest love which the church continually implores for young people, husbands and wives and families.

—Pope John Paul II
Letter to Families, 20

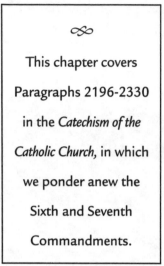

This chapter covers

Paragraphs 2196-2330

in the *Catechism of the*

Catholic Church, in which

we ponder anew the

Sixth and Seventh

Commandments.

Two sublime expressions of God's love for us are the bond of love between a man and woman in marriage and the bond of trust—not lying or betrayal—that ought to exist between us as friends in Christ. This complementary call to fidelity and honesty is taught by the Sixth and Seventh Commandments. They teach us the healing power God's law effects in human relationships [2331].

THE SIXTH COMMANDMENT

You shall not commit adultery (Ex 20:14; Dt 5:18).

You have heard that it was said, "You shall not commit adultery." But I say to you that every one who looks at a woman lustfully has already committed adultery with her in his heart (Mt 5:27-28).

The gift of unitive love between spouses (their marital spirituality) finds itself immensely deepened by the gift of procreative love (their marital sexuality). In body and soul the two become one. Their sexuality touches every aspect of their relationship: their capacity to give and receive love as well as their openness to building a family [2332].

Male and female sexual identity is the blessed consequence of divine creation (Gn 1:27; 5:1-2). Both men and women are equal in dignity. Both are called to transformation in the image and likeness of the God who blessed them and told them, "Be fruitful and multiply" (Gn 1:28). This mutual support of husband and wife causes family life to flourish and contributes to the good of society at large [2333].

Marriage celebrates the *union of a man and woman* who pledge to revere one another in a spirit-to-spirit bonding [2335]. "Therefore a man leaves his father and his mother and cleaves to his wife, and they become one flesh" (Gn 2:24). This togetherness in love enables husband and wife to become a more striking image of the power and tenderness of God. Different as their sexual identity is, it does not detract from their dignity in the eyes of God nor from their ability to image God's goodness in the domestic church they promise to establish when they marry.

This ideal of responsible marital love includes openness to the procreation and rearing of children, though many today struggle with the practical implications of the Church's teachings on fertility and contraception. An ideal is never easy to live because all of our actions since the Fall have been overshadowed by sin and infidelity to God's plan. That is why it is inspiring to see how many couples do rise to the challenge of living out the laws of the Church in these areas of married life. Our courage to do so comes from the fact that we believe that "Jesus came to restore creation to the purity of its origins" [2336]. In the Sermon on the Mount, he offers a deeper interpretation of the divine law. He teaches us how to subordinate our sexual life to the life of the spirit and in this submission to come to the fullness of our purpose: to integrate our sexuality and our spirituality in responsible unitive and procreative love. In the light of Jesus' teaching, the Church understands the Sixth Commandment "as encompassing the whole of human sexuality" [2336].

The Call to Chaste Love

Sexual maturation in inner chastity "involves the integrity of the person and the integrality of the gift" [2337]. It entails, in other words, the integration of body, mind, will, heart, and imagination. Our vital sexuality becomes distinctively human when we connect it with the spiritual dimension of our personality. The result is a chaste relationship for married and single people alike. One expression of such chaste, respectful love comes to fruition in the lifelong, mutual self-gift of a man and a woman in marriage as well as in the chastening togetherness of spiritual friendships. Shining through our care and concern is always the transforming mystery of Trinitarian love.

The virtue of chastity enables women and men to live lives of moral integrity, free from the bonds of lust. Its fruit is the freedom to enjoy authentic relationships marked by honesty and respect.

The Integrity of the Person

As women of spirit, we know how important it is to keep all dimensions of our lives in tune with our Christ-formed feminine character and personality. This *apprenticeship in self-mastery* means that we have to learn: "... to act out of conscious and free choice, as moved and drawn in a personal way from within, and not by blind impulses ... or by mere external constraint"[1] [2339]. For the grace of reaching this goal we pray:

Teach us, Lord, how to remain faithful to the promises of our Baptism. Be our shield and our strength when we are assailed by temptations against chastity. Be our forgiving shepherd when we fail in our struggles to retain our integrity. Grant us the humility we need to acknowledge our weaknesses and to rally our defenses in tempting situations. Grant us a taste of the original unity you intended for us before our lives were fragmented by sin [2340].

None of us ought to underestimate the long and exacting work of reforming our heart. Nor should we assume that the virtue of chastity can be mastered once and for all. The effort required to be chaste can be more intense in certain phases of life, for example, in adolescence. Here young people experience the awakening of sexual impulses that may leave them temporarily bewildered and embattled [2342]. Here, too, prayer is the best teacher and protector of the free decisions we make. Even relatively young in life, it is not too early to pray to remain both Christ-centered and chaste:

> *Chastity is your gift, dear Lord, but I need the help of grace to live it. Keep me ever mindful of my initial purification from sin in the waters of Baptism. You granted me this gift of being made new by your own suffering and death for my sake. Help me to imitate your own purity (see 1 Jn 3:3) by bestowing on me the strength I need to follow your commands. Lest I succumb to discouragement, allow me, in your own good time, to see the fruits of my commitment [2344-2345].*

The Integrity of the Gift of Self

In our struggles to live a life of chaste, respectful love, we learn much about the weaknesses and strengths of our personality. The courage to be chaste prepares us, among other things, for the gift of *spiritual friendship*. It creates optimum conditions for self-giving love since it puts the good of the other before all else. Chaste friendships foster transcendent intimacy. They enable us to emulate the friendship Jesus felt (see Jn 15:15) [2347]. He is the model of the chaste life style we seek for ourselves and look for in others.

Those who are *engaged to marry* go through a special "time of testing" [2350]. Their growth in chastity ought to be marked by a mutual courageous effort to practice this virtue. Expressions of affection that are appropriate only for the married need to be held in check. Otherwise the passions behind even seemingly innocent exchanges may lead to a loss of chastity. Before long the continent style of loving demanded by God in the Sixth Commandment is compromised, often with unhappy consequences.

Keeping this commandment before marriage is the best preparation for conjugal chastity in marriage. By practicing continence before wedlock, an engaged couple discovers the key to harmony and respect after the honeymoon is over! It is to live in fidelity to God's law for each other's sake, which makes it possible for them to be faithful to God for his own sake [2350].

Offenses against Chastity

One of the most devastating faces of sin is lust. Sadly, women and children are often vulnerable to being abused by those who sever sexual pleasure from marital love [2351]. But the reverse may also be true. In our day women may come across as being as lust-prone as men. Sadly, too, abuse may work both ways.

Lust takes many forms in the human condition. Those who feel lonely and frustrated may be tempted to relieve themselves by means of *masturbation*. Circumstances notwithstanding, the moral teaching of the Church states that this kind of sexual pleasure, which is sought outside the marital relationship, is contrary to its purpose and is therefore "gravely disordered"[2] [2352]. Likewise, *fornication* debases the full beauty and value of human sexuality. When fornication involves the corruption of minors, the results are not only devastating; they are aggravated by scandal [2353].

Pornography detaches real or fantasized sexual acts from the intimacy and responsibility legitimate love demands. "Celluloid" sex has nothing to do with the intimate giving of spouses to each other; it debases the dignity of anyone who cooperates in its production and spread [2354].

In much the same way, *prostitution* destroys the unique dignity of those who offer their bodies for sale to clients seeking acts of loveless satisfaction. Most tragically, young children, especially those stricken by poverty, are easily victimized by this abomination. Prostitution endangers marriages, leads to the spread of infectious diseases, and gives free rein to promiscuous behavior [2355].

When one person forcibly violates the sexual intimacy of another, the crime committed is *rape*. The freedom, dignity, self-respect, and integrity of a woman so injured can never be the same. This intrinsically evil act, if perpetrated on children by their parents, constitutes the gross sin of *incest*. The wound such a betrayal of trust inflicts on the young defies any semblance of morality [2356]. This and all offenses against the Sixth Commandment call for vigilance of heart and faith-filled prayer:

Jesus, we need to feel your presence in our hurting lives. Heal our loneliness. Lessen our frustrations. Give us the grace to try in faith, hope, and love to grow beyond the uncontrolled impulses of lust. Enable us to avoid passing relationships that steal our peace and joy.

Blessed Trinity, protect your little flock from the effects of sexual perversion. Offer compassionate consolation to all parents and children whose integrity has been violated by pornographers, prostitution, rape, and incest. Make the perpetrators of these heinous crimes aware of your justice. Be there to judge and forgive them if they ask for the grace of conversion. Befriend survivors gently, oh Lord. Help them to move forward on the long journey to reclaim their inmost souls.

Chastity and Homosexuality

The Sixth Commandment counsels chastity and fidelity for all people, regardless of their sexual orientation. The Church, in accordance with the Scriptures (Gn 19:1-29; Rom 1:24-27; 1 Cor 6:9-10; 1 Tm 1:10), holds that "homosexual acts are intrinsically disordered,"[3] and that such acts are incompatible with the natural law since they totally exclude the gift of life [2357]. By the same token, discrimination against a person based on his or her sexual identity is strictly forbidden by this Commandment. Always compassion and charity must prevail. We need to help each other to carry the cross of Christ whatever our condition may be. Together in his love, we can walk toward the joy of Christian perfection [2359]. For this grace women pray:

Jesus, you lived in our world. You know full well how much the world around us can affect our own struggle for chastity. Teach us to respect and foster every person's right to receive the education and spiritual formation they need to live in chaste and chastened love, whatever their sexual orientation may be [2358].

The Love of Husband and Wife

Genuine love for God and neighbor is the basis of a healthy society. It animates and invigorates the lives and actions of all people. Women are the chief guardians of this love. It is in the family that we first learn to love. Seeing a good marriage at work is the best preparation young adults can receive to enter into a committed life of conjugal love until death [2360-2361].

Sexuality and the sexual act in marriage are a source of joy and pleasure for husbands and wives. Openness to procreation reveals the depth of generosity and self-giving each act of love symbolizes. To live together for a lifetime requires wisdom and an abundance of care and respect for each other's feelings and desires [2362].

Conjugal love characterized by fidelity and fecundity is a beautiful witness to gospel values in today's world. These dispositions reflect "the twofold end of marriage: the good of the spouses themselves and the transmission of life" [2363]. These aims cannot be separated from one another. The spiritual life of a couple begins to deteriorate when either end ceases to be of concern. The future of marriage and family life today may well depend on women of faith who pray:

Loving Creator, you call the family to be the cornerstone of society. Let couples to whom you entrust the privilege of parenting uphold the nobility of family life. Let this vision begin with a courtship enlightened and deepened by chaste affection. Crown it with a marriage that always upholds the true meaning of human sexuality. Let it be lived as a divine gift of family love, not merely as a source of gratification. The hunger of our inmost being is for transformation by the indwelling Trinity. It is this sweet longing that inspires spouses to seek the pleasures and enjoyments you bless. Let each sharing of their marital intimacy be open to the noble calling to bring new life into your world.

Conjugal Fidelity

In marriage a man and woman are called to an intimate partnership of love for life. Theirs is a sacred bond instituted by God. When a man and a woman freely give themselves to one another in body and spirit, their decision is irrevocable. "What therefore God has joined together, let not man put asunder" (Mk 10:9; Mt 19:3-12; 1 Cor 7:10-11) [2364].

To maintain the fidelity demanded by the Sixth Commandment is especially hard in times of matrimonial discord, family crisis, sickness, and economic adversity. The preservation of marital fidelity is impossible without the help of a higher power. Christian couples can draw strength in this regard from Christ's fidelity to his Church, for it is a sign of his fidelity to them. As they bear witness to the mystery and grace of conjugal love, they might do well to meditate on the words of St. John Chrysostom, who advises young husbands to say to their wives:

> I have taken you in my arms, and I love you, and I prefer you to my life itself. For the present life is nothing, and my most ardent dream is to spend it with you in such a way that we may be assured of not being separated in the life reserved for us.... I place your love above all things, and nothing would be more bitter or painful to me than to be of a different mind than you[4] [2365].

Conjugal fidelity extends not only to one's marriage partner but to potential members of the family as well. By remaining open to the possibility of children, married couples are prevented from barricading themselves behind the walls of self-centeredness and individualism. Couples making a deliberate decision not to have children may become wholly self-serving and gradually cut themselves off from the community of the family and of Christ's body, the Church. That is why she teaches that "each and every marriage act must remain open to the transmission of life"[5] [2366]. Mindful of the need for openness to the call to bring life into the world and the challenge to do so in the context of one's own Church's teaching on the regulation of birth, women pray:

> *Eternal Father, never let our marriage slip into the tight trap of self-absorption. Body of Christ, burn deeply into our human spirit the sacred conviction that each conceived child, once born*

and baptized, is called to enhance your mystical presence on earth and in heaven. Spirit of love, give our children the fortitude to remain faithful to their baptismal justification.

Help us as parents to avoid techniques of coercion and control that are immoral in your sight. Fill us with awe for the sacred rhythms guiding conception you initiated in the bodies of women as life-givers. Give husbands and fathers the grace to grow in chaste self-control. Liberate women everywhere through your gift of conjugal chastity and tender care [2370-2373].

The Gift of a Child

A child is not owned by his or her mother and father. That child is a gift of God, indeed the supreme gift of their conjugal love. Nobody has a "right to a child." That is why techniques that "dissociate the sexual act from the procreative act," for example, artificial insemination or surrogate motherhood, are held to be "gravely immoral" by the Church [2376-2377]. From the moment of conception, a child has the right to be cared for and respected as is deserving of every human person [2378].

What of the case where a loving and faithful couple cannot have children? The Church empathizes profoundly with their pain but tries to give it a deeper meaning. The disappointment of physical sterility need not mark the absolute end of their generative intentions. If infertility persists after legitimate medical procedures to examine its cause have been investigated, a couple may bring the difficult reality of their situation to God and ask him to help them to focus on, what now? Within their marital vocation theirs may be a call to spiritual generativity in union with Christ for the sake of suffering humanity. Perhaps God wants them to be adoptive parents of children who would otherwise be abandoned. Maybe they will be drawn to charitable services for the disadvantaged and needy

[2379]. Of this they can be certain: God's love will be generated through them in ways beyond their imagining. All he asks is their fidelity.

Offenses against the Dignity of Marriage

The capital sin of adultery, which the Sixth Commandment explicitly condemns and forbids, is not only deeply hurtful to the betrayed spouse, it is a grave infraction of justice [2380]. When a married person has sexual relations—even transient ones—with another party, great injury is done to the marriage, to the children, and to anyone else who relies on their stable union [2381]. Infidelity, under whatever circumstances it occurs, is a tragic occurrence. The injured party feels hurt, betrayed, angry, and confused about what to do next. If separation in the end is the only answer, it can be legitimate in certain cases provided for by canon law [2383], but first every effort must be made to seek reconciliation and to uphold the indissolubility of the marriage bond [2382-2383].

Other grave offenses against marriage and family life in Catholic teaching are divorce [2384-2386]; polygamy [2387]; incest or intimate relations between relatives or in-laws [2388]; sexual abuse of children or adolescents [2389]; so-called free sexual union without judicial and public approbation [2390]; and trial marriages [2391]. All such offenses against the Sixth Commandment threaten the divine institution of marriage and call for the proper legal recourse as well as for compassionate pastoral care. We must as always submit our faults and failings to God's forgiveness in repentance and prayer:

> *Lord Jesus, protect us from the plague invading a society that defiantly predicts the breakup of marriages, treats adultery with soap opera superficiality, and tries to convince the young that a life of immorality has no bad consequences. Protect us from these*

despicable lies and the destruction they inflict on society. Keep our lives in tune with your moral law, for only in its light can we know true happiness on earth.

THE SEVENTH COMMANDMENT

You shall not steal (Ex 20:15; Deut 5:19; Mt 19:18).

The free formation of our Christian personality and family life implies "respect for the right to private property" and the guarding of one's privacy. It also calls for a commitment "to order this world's goods to God and to fraternal charity" [2401]. That is why the Seventh Commandment assures the protection of our material, educational, and environmental resources. We need these goods for our survival and development. For many women, some kind of private ownership is the only security they have in the face of poverty and the threat of violence [2402]. So uncaring has the world become in this matter of respect for property and the sharing of goods we feel sometimes like crying aloud to heaven:

We implore you, Holy Spirit, to endow all people of good will with the courage to sacrifice what is necessary in service of the well-being of all members of the human family. Grant people the necessary property and resources they need to guard their health, happiness, and mutual harmony. Do not let us destroy ourselves by greed and envy. Give us what we need to live decent and holy lives.

Jesus, Mary, and Joseph, help us to resist the temptation to separate our families from others in self-righteous satisfaction. Make us generous sharers in the hardships and tribulations of our neighbors, whether poor or wealthy. Do not let us take what does not belong to us, but teach us to treat everyone as equal in

dignity in your eyes. Grant us the virtue of temperance in the use
of earthly goods that are our own and of generosity toward those
in need. Let justice prevail over greed [2404-2407].

Economic Activity and Social Justice

Women have a stake in the economy. We care for the well-being of
our families, our neighbors, and the disadvantaged among us. We
are involved in supplying the everyday needs of our immediate families, and perhaps even our parents. All these factors make us sensitive
to the social needs that are impacted by social policies. We reject,
therefore, any tendency to look at the economy as only a money
matter or a way to augment production and to enlarge profit or
power. For women who live by the gospel, the economy should be
directed first of all by concern for human beings. For that reason,
money making and spending must be guided by the principles of
social justice and be in tune with God's loving plan for the ongoing
formation of humanity [2426].

Work in and outside the home enables women to express the
unique gifts and talents God gives them. Hard as work is, it is also
rewarding. Think of Jesus. He traveled, taught, preached, and
labored day after day to spread God's word. His reward was Calvary,
yet the cross was not the end of his story. Think of Mary. She
worked to make ends meet as an immigrant mother in Egypt, as a
simple carpenter's wife in Nazareth, as a coredemptive woman
standing with her crucified Son. We, too, share in the work of
redemption so beautifully lived by Jesus and Mary. Our work done
in and for the Lord becomes a means of sanctification, a daily sacrifice of praise and thanksgiving to our Triune God [2427].

In and through our labors, we use our God-given gifts to provide
for our own and others' needs. There is no question but that we
should be paid a just wage and have access to benefits such as health

care, pension plans, and maternity leave [2428].

The *Catechism* acknowledges that "*economic life* brings into play different interests, often opposed to one another" [2430]. Conflicts arise as a result of this interplay of opposing forces. One source of conflict is the just demand that women enjoy equal rights in pay and promotion. It is right for us to call attention to inequities and, whether through negotiation or compromise, to work toward ensuring the full equality of rights and opportunities of all those in the workplace [2430].

Justice and Solidarity among Nations

When we witness the sufferings of mothers, fathers, and children in underdeveloped countries, our compassion urges us to respond to the insistence of the Church on justice and solidarity among nations. In her love for the poor she laments the unfair distribution of resources over the globe. She deplores the real "gap" between populations. Rich nations advance while countless families in underdeveloped countries miss out on the bare necessities of life. They pile up debts that sink them deeper into the misery that begs for relief [2437]. Who but another woman can really feel in her heart what it must mean for a mother to see her baby starve to death? How devastating it must be for her not to have sufficient medicines, doctors, and nurses available to heal her children and relieve their helpless plight!

What can we do to halt the suffering of God's people in less fortunate circumstances? The answer is, we must do what we can. This may seem to be pitifully little in the face of such massive calamities as hunger and homelessness. Yet each effort to live the gospel helps to dismantle the "perverse mechanisms" that hold up the processes of development in less advanced countries as well as our own [2438].

Undoubtedly, a common effort on the part of all nations should be to mobilize the resources by which poorer nations can begin the slow climb to prosperity so as to meet their own obligation to charity. People in authority must take seriously their responsibility to alleviate the low standards of living found among the very poor. Lack of opportunity may make it impossible for people to attain sufficient education to foster a rise in living standards. Those in power need to convert their hearts to help alleviate the plight of poverty and not succumb to greed [2439].

While the administration of financial aid may be necessary in times of natural disasters and other catastrophic events, such handouts do not provide an adequate and enduring answer to a less advanced country's deep-seated financial problems. The *Catechism* suggests that challenges of such a magnitude may call for the reform of international economic and financial *institutions*. Then equitable relations with less advanced nations may become more of a reality than a distant dream [2440]. The commitment to fight demeaning poverty, sickness, and illiteracy and the courage to resist exploitation call for a sense of our shared origin in the one God and Father of all. This sense of the sacred, more than mere material donations, "makes for growth in respect for cultural identities and openness to the transcendent"[6] [2441].

A woman's Christian vocation includes her willingness to address, together with other citizens, social issues and actions pertinent to the complex arena of public life. On the local, national, and international scene, the role of the laity in the mind of the Church is "to animate temporal realities with Christian commitment, by which they show that they are witnesses and agents of peace and justice"[7] [2442].

Love for the Poor

Holy Scripture admonishes us repeatedly to come to the aid of the poor: "Give to him who begs from you, and do not refuse him who would borrow from you.... You received without paying, give without pay" (Mt 5:42; 10:8). Jesus recognizes his disciples by what they have done for the poor in their midst (see Mt 25:31-36). When the poor have the good news preached to them by loving people, it is the sign of Christ's presence (Mt 11:5; Lk 4:18) [2443].

What inspires the constant tradition of the Church's love for the "least of these" is the Beatitudes, the poverty of Jesus himself, and his unwavering concern for the spiritually poor of the earth, for all who are physically and materially impoverished (Lk 6:20-22; Mt 8:20; Mk 12:41-44). The cry of the poor for help and mercy does not go unheeded by the women of the world whose prayers reach heaven's portals:

Lord, Jesus, let the poor of this earth see in our eyes the unfathomable depths of your mercy. Let them sense in our touch your own healing hands. Spirit of love, let everything in us become an expression of your care for the spiritual and bodily needs of our neighbors. Keep us open to the specific tasks for which we are to be responsible—to such spiritual works of mercy as teaching, writing, advising, counseling, educating, forming, consoling, and comforting as well as to such corporal works of mercy as feeding the hungry, sheltering the homeless, clothing the naked, and visiting the sick and imprisoned (see Mt 25:31-46) [2447].

Mary, our Mother, grant us a portion of your own courage and compassion. Teach us to bear joyously the great blessing of sharing in the misunderstanding that marked the life of your Son Jesus. Let us always be moved, dear Lord, by the preferential love with which you inspired your Church to seek out for special attention persons oppressed by any kind of poverty [2448]. Help us to recognize as St. Rose of Lima did that "when we serve the poor and the sick, we serve Jesus. We must not fail to help our neighbors, because in them we serve Jesus"[8] [2449].

Questions for Reflection and Faith Sharing

1. Given your state of life as a married or single woman, what inner and outer conditions facilitate your following Christ as the "model of chastity" [2394]? If there was one thing you could say to a young person about the importance of remaining chaste before marriage, what would it be?

2. What do you see as the main causes of infidelity in a marriage? Is there a necessary link between fecundity understood as "a good, a gift and an end of marriage" [2398] and fidelity understood as upholding the "dignity of marriage" [2400]?

3. How do you strike a balance in your life between the "right to private property" and the "universal destination of goods" [2452]? When this balance is lost, what violations against the Seventh Commandment are likely to occur? Who are the people most victimized by unscrupulous greed?

4. Do you see Lazarus, the hungry beggar in the parable told in Luke 16:19-31, "in the multitude of human beings without bread, a roof or a place to stay" [2463], or have you become somewhat indifferent to the cry of the poor? What can women do to focus the attention of society on "the least of these" (Mt 25:45)?

FIFTEEN

Telling the Truth in Obedience to the Eighth, Ninth, and Tenth Commandments

God's work in forming his people is revealed and fulfilled in Jesus Christ the Teacher, and reaches to the depths of every individual's heart as a result of the living presence of the Spirit. Mother Church is called to take part in the divine work of formation, both through a sharing of her very life, and through her various pronouncements and actions. It is thus that the lay faithful are formed by the Church and in the Church in a mutual communion and collaboration of all her members: clergy, religious and lay faithful. Thus the whole ecclesial community, in its diverse members, receives the fruitfulness of the Spirit and actively cooperates towards that end. With this in mind Methodius of Olympo wrote: "Those not yet perfected are carried and formed by those more perfect, as in the womb of a mother, until the time they are generated and brought forth for the greatness and beauty of virtue."

—Pope John Paul II
Christifideles Laici, 61

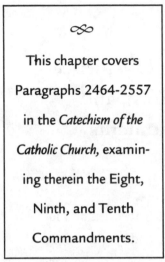

This chapter covers

Paragraphs 2464-2557

in the *Catechism of the*

Catholic Church, examin-

ing therein the Eight,

Ninth, and Tenth

Commandments.

Holy women are called to bear witness to God, the source of all truth, whose "faithfulness endures to all generations" (Ps 119:90). Understood in this light, any offense against the truth is an expression of infidelity to God. The choice before us is unambiguous: if we misrepresent the truth, we bear no witness to God; if we commit ourselves to candid truthfulness, the truth will set us free [2464].

THE EIGHTH COMMANDMENT

You shall not bear false witness against your neighbor (Ex 20:16; Dt 5:20).

It was said to the men of old, "You shall not swear falsely, but shall perform to the Lord what you have sworn" (Mt 5:33).

Women who have a biblical view of life "live in the truth" [2470]. Truth is the cornerstone of our relationships in the world, in our marriages, family circles, and friendships. We know and love the Lord Jesus Christ in whom "the whole of God's truth has been made manifest" [2466]. Sincerity in speech and action flow from the character virtue of truthfulness. It encourages us to be persons who are "true in deeds and truthful in words" [2468].

Since God is "true" (Rom 3:4), the members of his Body, all the baptized, need to strive to live in the truth and most especially to model their lives on Jesus. That our lives may witness to "the unconditional love of truth" [2466], we pray:

Thank you, Lord Jesus. Thank you, Blessed Lady, for sharing so deeply and uniquely in the treasures of Jesus' grace and truth. Jesus, you came among us as the Epiphany of epiphanies to bring light to a world darkened by deceit (Jn 1:14; 8:12). How merciful it is of you to lift those who believe in you out of the darkness into your own wonderful light (Jn 12:46).

Enable us as loving disciples to live in obedience to your word. Make us spokeswomen for the truth that we are and do. To follow you, we must live in "the Spirit of truth," whom the Father sends to us in Jesus' name and who leads us "into all the truth" (Jn 16:13).

To live in the truth of a life conformed to Christ is to show others what it means to shun deception and to walk in the light. Turn our confused existence, darkened by untruth, into a disciplined existence, alight with Jesus' every word and example [2470].

Offenses Against Truth

As disciples of a most truthful Master, we must "put away all malice and all guile and insincerity and envy and all slander" (1 Pt 2:1; Eph 42:5). To serve this lofty aim requires vigilance of heart and unceasing prayer:

Holy Spirit, help us to hold our tongue if we are tempted to commit the sins of false witness or perjury [2476]. Gracious Lord, grant us a renewal of mutual appreciation. Help us to guard against judging too harshly our own or others' failings. Reform our tendency toward flattery and people-pleasing—attitudes that mock the forthrightness of your own speech, O Lord [2480]. Equally harmful is boasting or bragging, and the malicious caricaturing of someone's behavior or personality [2481]. Let us use

*the gift of speech you grant us to communicate to others the truth
we know, to proclaim it, not to profane it by lying. Holy Trinity,
help us to repair, not tear apart, "the fabric of social relationships" [2486]. And if we are guilty of such an offense, give us the
courage we need to make reparation, to do what it takes to right
this wrong [2487].*

Respect for the Truth

Untruth divides; truth unites a humanity called to grow in solidarity.
Within the limits of propriety, each of us has a right to know the
truth. Such appropriate limits are set for us Christians by the gospel.
Framing these limits are the precepts of brotherly and sisterly love.
It is our responsibility as God-fearing people to discern whether or
not to disclose the truth to a person who asks for it [2488].
Conscious of the need to protect the well-being and security of
others, sensitive to the common good, and respectful of the right to
privacy, we pray:

*Spirit of truth, inspire in us respect for the privacy of all people.
Silence any word on our lips that would disclose to people what
they have no right to know about another or what would cause
scandal [2489]. Grant us the discretion we need to keep a confidence and never to disclose to any other person professional secrets
entrusted to us [2490]. By the same token, do not let our curiosity
get the best of us. Grant us the virtue of appropriate reserve when
it comes to what belongs to the inner sphere of any human existence [2492].*

THE NINTH COMMANDMENT

You shall not covet your neighbor's house; you shall not covet your neighbor's wife, or his manservant, or his maidservant, or his ox, or his ass, or anything that is your neighbor's (Ex 20:17).

Every one who looks at a woman lustfully has already committed adultery with her in his heart (Mt 5:28).

To walk the path of generous, unenvious living laid out by the Ninth Commandment, we must all purify our hearts and practice temperance [2517]. As the Beatitude proclaims, "Blessed are the pure in heart, for they shall see God" (Mt 5:8).

This purification requires a single-minded commitment. As we read in the Gospel of Matthew, "Out of the heart come evil thoughts, murder, adultery, fornication" (Mt 15:19). To be "pure in heart," we must attune our intellects and wills, our hearts and imaginations, to God's appeal to holiness. A life of genuine sanctity manifests itself in the virtues of charity, chastity, love of truth, and orthodoxy of faith.

With charity we show our love for God and neighbor (2 Tim 2:22). Chastity expresses itself in the living of a morally and spiritually upright sexual life (1 Thes 4:7; Col 3:5; Eph 4:19) and in the love of truth, especially the truth of faith [2518]. Taken together, these virtues make it possible for us already here on earth to see in some way what awaits us in eternity [2519].

Liberate us, O Lord, from disordered desires. Help us to love women and men, girls and boys, with an undivided heart. Jesus and Mary, let the grace of chastity grow in us more and more abundantly in a world besieged by pornography. Ask the Father

to bestow on us a purity of intention that makes us seek and ful-
fill the splendid mission of Christian womanhood and manhood
in a wayward world. Let us be guided by your divine will in
everything (see Romans 12:2; Colossians 1:10).

Teach us to discipline our feelings and imagination, our needs
and passionate yearnings. They may spring up overwhelmingly
at moments of loneliness, when we feel misunderstood by friends
and family members. Grant us the strength of will not to give in
to impure thoughts and fantasies. Inspire us to pray with St.
Augustine: "I thought that continence arose from one's own pow-
ers, which I did not recognize in myself. I was foolish enough not
to know ... that no one can be continent unless you grant it. For
you would surely have granted it if my inner groaning had
reached your ears and I with firm faith had cast my cares on
you"[1] [2520].

Purity demands modesty. Modesty preserves the gift of a
woman's mystery. It enables her to be patient and moderate in her
search for intimacy. It protects her chastity, whatever her choice of
vocation may be. Mindful of her Beloved's gaze, she prays:

Your infusion of modesty illumines my choice of dress and
apparel. It nourishes my feminine discretion. You guide my
silence and my speaking, my reserve and my spontaneous self-
expression. Your presence enables me to resist the allure of fashion
and the pressure of false ideologies [2522-2524]. You help me to
witness to purity in a social climate that in the name of freedom
parades indecency [2525-2526]. How blessed I am to be the
recipient of your word. It fortifies, completes, and restores me to
spread the good news of tasteful Christian modesty [2527].

THE TENTH COMMANDMENT

You shall not covet ... anything that is your neighbor's.... You shall not desire your neighbor's house, his field, or his manservant, or his maidservant, his ox, or his ass, or anything that is your neighbor's (Ex 20:17; Dt 5:21).

For where your treasure is, there will your heart be also (Mt 6:21).

As women of the Church, we care generously for the bodily and spiritual welfare of our families and of the communities we serve as married or single persons. Not coveting another's goods is the best defense we have against the greed that threatens to destroy justice and charity [2534].

Disordered Desires

Loving God and following what is good will keep us on course with the Tenth Commandment. What harms our progress are disordered desires that cause us to succumb to *greed* ("the desire to amass earthly goods") and *avarice* ("a passion for riches and their attendant power") [2536].

The covetousness forbidden by the Tenth Commandment is the root cause of the theft, robbery, and fraud forbidden by the Seventh. This vice endangers the kind of contentment that puts the gospel first. It presses people to amass more and more things. Their unjust yearning for possessions becomes a thirst that can never be quenched [2537]. The Tenth Commandment points to another sin as well—envy, which St. Augustine saw as "*the* diabolical sin"[2] [2539]. With the same keen awareness, St. John Chrysostom remarks: "Would you like to see God glorified by you? Then rejoice in your brother's [your sister's] progress and you will immediately give glory to God. Because his servant could conquer envy by rejoicing in the merits of others, God will be praised"[3] [2540].

Turn our hearts, Spirit of love, completely away from these devouring desires of greed, avarice, and envy. Cleanse our inmost being of covetousness so as to unite us with the immaculate heart of your holy mother. Her heart was spotless from the beginning. Help us, we pray, to heal the consumeristic tendency to replace heavenly goods by earthly gains, as if things alone can make us happy.

Our Lady of Epiphany, help us to follow the longings that alone can satisfy our ultimate hunger for God [2541-2543].

Spirit of holy poverty, liberate us from an adherence to riches that puts us at odds with simplicity and humility of a life lived wholly for Jesus. Let us always heed his Beatitudes and the beauty of divine vision they promise. St. Augustine, you summarize our true desire: "Let the proud seek and love earthly kingdoms, but blessed are the poor in spirit for theirs is the Kingdom of heaven"[4] [2547].

Questions for Reflection
and Faith Sharing

1. Have you ever been the victim of "duplicity, dissimulation, and hypocrisy" [2505]? How are you able to keep true to yourself and God in deeds and words when others appear to doubt your character?

2. Have you ever put respect for your reputation and honor above the truth of your faith [2506-2507]? Have you experienced the humbling yet redemptive process of making amends to those you may have hurt with lies or broken confidences [2511]?

3. Are you conscious of actually practicing purity of heart by controlling your fantasy and imagination, by modifying your curiosity, by guarding your eyes [2531-2533]? What makes such practice so difficult today?

4. When and under what circumstances are you aware of feeling envious of another person, literally sad at the sight of her goods, and immoderately desiring to have them for yourself [2553]? Do you agree with the teaching that "detachment from riches is necessary for entering the Kingdom of heaven" [2556]? What does this detachment look like in your life here and now since you surely hope one day to see God?

SIXTEEN

Entering into the Heart of Prayer

The Church sees in Mary the highest expression of the "feminine genius" and she finds in her a source of constant inspiration. Mary called herself the "handmaid of the Lord" (Lk 1:38). Through obedience to the Word of God she accepted her lofty yet not easy vocation as wife and mother in the family of Nazareth. Putting herself at God's service, she also put herself at the service of others: a service of love. Precisely through this service Mary was able to experience in her life a mysterious, but authentic "reign." It is not by chance that she is invoked as "Queen of heaven and earth." The entire community of believers thus invokes her; many nations and peoples call upon her as their "Queen." For her, "to reign" is to serve! Her service is "to reign!"

—Pope John Paul II
Letter to Women, 10

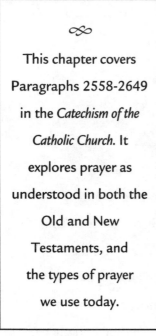

This chapter covers Paragraphs 2558-2649 in the *Catechism of the Catholic Church*. It explores prayer as understood in both the Old and New Testaments, and the types of prayer we use today.

"Great is the mystery of the faith!" [2558]. We profess this mystery in the Creed. We celebrate it in the liturgy. The faith we believe, celebrate, and live draws us into a dynamic relationship with God, who is living and true. "This relationship is prayer" [2558].

Notice that God puts a requirement upon us. It is not something legalistic; it is invitational and appealing. It calls us to companionship, to encounter, to intimate conversation, to communion. Our response to this call is prayer. In the words of St. Thérèse of Lisieux, "Prayer is a surge of the heart; it is a simple look turned toward heaven, it is a cry of recognition and of love, embracing both trial and joy"[1] [2558].

What a perfect definition of prayer hers is! The initiative to pray is not our own doing; it is a nudging by the Holy Spirit, a "surge of the heart," a gentle yet urgent stirring.

St. Thérèse's favorite two-word prayer was "Draw me!" Her response to God's wooing of her heart was a simple gaze of love, a wordless moment of wonder, a silence that contains all words. In God's embrace it was hard for her to tell where trial ends and joy begins, so absorbed was she in the mind and heart of God. Thus it is that willfulness disappears. Pride crumbles, and we acknowledge with humility that we do not yet know how to pray as we ought (see Romans 8:26).

Defining Prayer

Prayer is not something we do for God. It is first and foremost God's gift to us. Difficult as it may be for us to believe, God thirsts for us as much as we thirst for God [2560].

The *Catechism* invites women at this juncture of spiritual maturity to stand still, to stop searching for answers hither and yon, to return to their tradition, where prayer is both a gift and a covenant. "According to Scripture, it is the *heart* that prays. If our heart is far from God, the words of prayer are in vain" [2562].

In the inmost center of our being, in a heart-to-Heart relationship of covenant love, God calls, and we respond. Prayer is the union of the human spirit with "the thrice-holy God" [2565].

Prayer does not take us out of this world; rather, it places our feet on the firm bedrock of faith. It leads us to rediscover the depths of the divine initiative. It assures us of "communion with Christ and extends throughout the Church, which is his Body" [2565]. Christ is *the* source of prayer, *the* teacher of prayer, *the* One whom our hearts seek.

What Is Prayer?

Whether we are professional theologians, expert catechists, or people in the pew, few of us can help but ponder the opening question posed in Part Four of the *Catechism*: "What is prayer?" There are as many replies to this question as there are people who pray. Yet underneath a symphony of experiences runs the same motif. Women pray because they have no choice. Whether we realize it or not, the initiative for prayer, the impetus to pray, is not our own doing. Whether our hearts are contrite or uplifted, burdened by sorrow or enlivened by joy, they at once long for and await a real encounter with Christ.

Discerning women realize that prayer is not something they do, an action they schedule, or a technique they master. It is a gift they receive. The initiative for prayer is neither theirs to command nor to control; it is both call and response, pursuit and surrender.

You who are thirsty seek water from the well. Christ will fill your cup. He will give you drink as he gave living water to the Samaritan woman (see John 4:10). He will teach you what it means to worship in spirit and in truth. Prayer is your humble response to the unmerited gift of redemption you have received from the living God. It is the reply of your grateful heart to Jesus' thirst for your love.

The heart is a symbol for the whole of womanhood. We may say prayers with our lips. We may meditate on their meaning with our minds, but "if our heart is far from God, the words of prayer are in vain" [2562].

Faith Revealed in the Covenant

The initiative for prayer comes not from us but from God. God calls us first. We respond because we are disciples attentive to our divine Master. Like a lover, Christ woos a woman's heart. Sinners though we are, and foolish though we may have been, he goes in search of us. He initiates the covenant drama by which we are saved [2567].

Humankind suffers under a veil of forgetfulness of the God who made every man, woman, and child on earth. We choose to lurk in the dark; God calls us into the light. The indifference women witness to the sacred in our time is as startling as the spiritual hunger many claim to feel. As a result they swing from low-grade depression to frenzied action, from the solutions offered by popular psychology to the gnostic trends of new-age spirituality. They erect idols one day. They accuse the Holy of having abandoned them the next.

However forgetful or selfish we are, God never tires of calling us home to prayer. From the creation to the time of Noah, every activity that happens in relation to God occurs in the context of prayer. When Abel offers the firstborn of his flock, he prays. When Enoch invokes the divine name, he prays. When Noah walks with God, he prays [2569].

Four witnesses to the life of prayer shine in these Old Testament accounts. From each of them, women and men, on the way to faith deepening, can learn a powerful lesson. Abraham, our Father in faith, teaches us that submissiveness and obedience are essential to prayer. Abraham's heart is both docile and attentive to the call of God. He hears the command to go forth, and he does "as the Lord had told him" (Gn 12:4). Asked to sacrifice his only son, Isaac, he does not waver in his obedience. Tested sorely, his faith does not weaken. Abraham teaches us that prayer is "a battle of faith and ... the triumph of perseverance"[2] [2573].

Moses, the mediator between God's saving power and a stubborn people, shows us that essential to prayer of the heart are humility and meekness. God forms a nation by lifting up a God-molded man more humble than anyone else on the face of the earth (see Numbers 12:3, 7-8). Moses witnesses to the power of intercessory prayer, a style of beseeching that reaches perfection in the priestly prayer of Jesus. Servant though he is, Moses is not afraid to also practice his faith with boldness. He meets God face to face and contemplates the totality of his love. He agrees to be his messenger despite the misunderstanding he is bound to incur. Nothing can deter him from his mission as long as Moses draws strength from God, who "cannot forsake this people that bears his name" [2577].

David, the shepherd-king, learned, as did his predecessors, that first one must listen to God and only then act according to his will. David did not always obey, but he surely knew how to repent, and God loved him for that. David prays, and so must we, with unshakable confidence in the mercy of God. He never doubts God's longing to forgive our sins. Essential to prayer is something of David's abandoned and joyful trust in God [2579], his confidence that our prayers will be heard, though in ways we cannot fathom. The question is: Does your heart belong wholly and entirely to him [2580]?

Elijah, the prophet, calls us to conversion. True prayer, he warns with fiery splendor, must resist the dangers of empty ritualism and external worship if it is to remain powerful and effective (see James 5:16b-18). Elijah learned to purify prayer of human expectations during his own sojourns in the desert. Later he taught a widow to pray so ardently that God brought her child back to life (see 1 Kings 17:17-24). His life reveals that prayer is not a flight from an unfaithful world but a constant alertness to God's presence in human hearts. His mission was to call a wayward world to convert to God.

Obedience, intercession, trust, and conversion—these four dispositions are made concrete in the lives of Abraham, Moses, David, and Elijah. Abraham models faith professed; Moses reveals faith celebrated; David demonstrates faith lived; and Elijah shows us faith prayed. Faith professed is inconceivable without obedience; faith celebrated, without intercession; faith lived, without trust; and faith prayed, without conversion of heart.

Be it an argument or a complaint, a song of praise or a plea for forgiveness, prayer presumes the intervention of God in history and prepares us for his final coming. There is thus an urgency to our prayer as well as a willingness to wait upon the mystery as we prepare "for the intervention of the Savior God, the Lord of history"[3] [2584].

The crowning masterpiece of the Old Testament's teaching on prayer is the Psalter or "praises." This collection of chants, songs, and meditations both nourishes and expresses the prayer of God's people wherever believers assemble [2585-2587].

In the psalms God's word becomes the prayer of God's people as they recall the saving events of the past and praise the Lord for promises fulfilled. Whether they are old or young, people turn to the psalms to voice their past woes, their present experiences, their hopes for the future. The psalms possess such direct expressions of lamentation and longing that they can be prayed by people under any and all circumstances.

Jesus Prays, Teaches Us How to Pray, and Hears Our Prayers

In his quiet moments away from the crowd and throughout his public ministry, Jesus prays (see Mark 1:35; 6:46; Luke 5:16). He turns to the Father in prayer before the decisive moments of his mission, during his Baptism and Transfiguration, and before his Passion (Lk 3:21; 9:28; 22:41-44). When he calls the twelve, Jesus asks that Peter might not fail the test (Lk 6:12). Before the events leading to his Crucifixion, Jesus begs for the strength to place his human will entirely at his Father's disposal. He remains in prayer when he performs miracles as well as when he instructs his disciples. "His words and works are the visible manifestation of his prayer in secret" [2602].

Two prayers from Christ's public ministry exemplify his teaching on the simultaneous need for contemplation and action, for child-like trust and unwavering confidence. Both begin with thanksgiving. In the first, Jesus thanks the Father for hiding the mystery of revelation from the learned of this world while opening it to mere infants (Mt 11:25-27; Lk 10:21-23), who contemplate God's power and act, as he does, out of pure obedience. "The whole prayer of Jesus is contained in this loving adherence of his human heart to the mystery of the will of the Father"[4] [2603].

The second prayer occurs before the raising of Lazarus. Jesus thanks the Father in advance for having heard his prayer, saying with the simplicity of a trusting son, "I know that you always hear me" (Jn 11:41-42, NAB). Only then does he perform his awesome miracle, bringing life out of death. We learn from this remarkable episode to persevere in prayer. God, who is the Giver of all gifts, will not withhold from us whatever he knows to be life-giving.

From the beginning of his life to its final hour, Jesus teaches women and men to overcome fear and to place their lives in God's hands with the faith of children who cry, "Abba, Father." Despite the imprisoning power of sin and death, we enjoy the blessed assurance that in the praying Christ our redemption has been brought to completion and that not one of our prayers will go unanswered in God's good time.

Mary Prays

What better teacher of prayer could women turn to than Mary? In her bold yet docile faith, God finds "the acceptance he had awaited from the beginning of time" [2617]. Mary's *"fiat"* is the foremost example of Christian prayer. Her words, her life, her powers of intercession, convince us that we can "be wholly God's, because he is wholly ours" [2617].

Mary's own song of thanksgiving, her *Magnificat*, ought to dispel any doubt we may have about how God responds to the cry of the poor. She witnesses to the truth that from age to age God continues to fulfill the promises he made to our ancestors, "to Abraham and to his posterity for ever" [2619].

Prayer in the Age of the Church

From the Day of Pentecost until now, the prayer of the Church is "founded on the apostolic faith; authenticated by charity; nourished in the Eucharist" [2624]. Under the guidance of the Holy Spirit, certain "common ways" of faith deepening, certain forms of prayer, become concrete in our liturgical and spiritual traditions, in the

Scriptures, especially the psalms, and above all, in the sacraments and mission of the Church.

Two types of Christian prayer are blessing and adoration. When we are blessed, we experience the descent of God to us through the power of the Spirit. When we pay homage to the Lord, the movement is one of ascent. We go to God in awe and adoration, singing songs of praise or sitting still in silent adoration.

These two movements underpin the four expressions of prayer the *Catechism* names. Briefly, when we pray in Jesus' name, we ask, intercede, give thanks, and offer praise.

Prayer of Petition

Lord, I entreat your help and support in this difficult situation. Without your help there is no help for me. I confess my weakness. I consign myself to your strength and mercy. I pray for the coming of your reign in my life and world. I ask now for the grace to accept what you ask of me [2632]. I ask also for the courage to respond to your leading and for the wisdom to accept the guidance I receive. As I grow in spiritual maturity, help me to see that my every need can become the object of petition and that, as a result, I can pray at all times [2629-2633].

Prayer of Intercession

Lord, I ask you in Jesus' name for the salvation of all people, especially sinners. I beseech you on behalf of those for whom I pray to respond to their needs. I know you want all of us to share in the redeeming mission of the Trinity. I commend those who cannot ask for themselves to your care, O Lord. Let them break through the boundaries that hold them to false hopes. Let them trust in the boundless wonder of your love for all people [2634-2636].

Prayer of Thanksgiving

Lord, I come before you with a grateful heart, conscious at every moment of your saving love. Thank you for helping me to see "people, events, and things with your eyes. Thank you for the gifts of grace I receive without ceasing. Continue to draw me into a life of prayer and thanksgiving (see 1 Thessalonians 5:18; Colossians 4:2) [2637-2638].

Prayer of Praise

Lord, I praise you in purity of heart because you are the center of my life. You are worthy of receiving all my love, not only because of what you have done for me but because of who you are. I praise you because I am your child by virtue of adoption (see Romans 8:16). Father, you call me to glorify you in the Son through the Holy Spirit to such a degree that my "faith is pure praise" [2642]. Since praise draws me toward you, the source and goal of every prayer, it embraces petition, intercession, and thanksgiving. In praising you I rediscover how infinitely praiseworthy I am in the Father's eyes [2639-2643].

Questions for Reflection
and Faith Sharing

1. Do you sense God calling you to a mysterious encounter with him when you pray [2591]? In the words of Thérèse of Lisieux, have you ever experienced prayer as "a surge of the heart"?

2. Which of the psalms is your personal favorite? What does it say to you of trust in God's faithfulness and loving guidance [2592-2597]?

3. Are you able to pray as Jesus taught his disciples to pray, "with a purified heart, with lively and persevering faith, with filial boldness" [2621]?

4. What convinces you from your own prayer experience that God hears your petitions and intercessions, your words of thanksgiving and praise [2644]? Have you reached the point in your life of being able to "give thanks in all circumstances" (1 Thes 5:18)?

SEVENTEEN

Renewing the Heart of Praying Persons

Perhaps more than men, women acknowledge the person, because they see persons with their hearts. They see them independently of various ideological or political systems. They see others in their greatness and limitations; they try to go out to them and help them. In this way the basic plan of the Creator takes flesh in the history of humanity and there is constantly revealed, in the variety of vocations, that beauty—not merely physical, but above all spiritual—which God bestowed from the very beginning on all, and in a particular way on women.

—Pope John Paul II
Letter to Women, 12

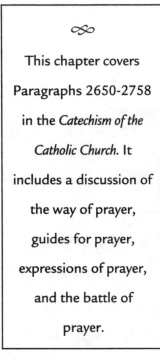

This chapter covers Paragraphs 2650-2758 in the *Catechism of the Catholic Church*. It includes a discussion of the way of prayer, guides for prayer, expressions of prayer, and the battle of prayer.

In Paul's first letter to the Corinthians, he reveals to us the difference between an intellectual comprehension of the will of God (knowing the law) and a heartfelt understanding (knowing God). Of this difference he writes: "Knowledge inflates with pride, but love builds up. If anyone supposes he knows something, he does not yet know as he ought to know. But if one loves God, one is known by him" (1 Cor 8:1-3, NAB).

In the same way, it is not knowing what the Scriptures reveal *about* prayer that satisfies a woman's heart. We must pray with tender longing in response to God's call, thereby inviting this intimacy in accordance with our fidelity to the Church and our receptivity of the guidance of the Holy Spirit. Then together with the Church as the Body of Christ, we can help to teach "the children of God how to pray" [2650]. Of course, *the* source and wellspring of Christian prayer is our Lord Jesus Christ. When we pray, we do so in the Spirit of Jesus, for our thirst for God can only be quenched by living water (Jn 4:14).

St. John of the Cross gives us in a few words what the heart of a praying person looks like. He says: "Seek in reading and you will find in meditating; knock in mental prayer and it will be opened to you by contemplation"[1] [2654]. To ourselves we say: Read the Scripture as frequently as possible in a formative way. This slakes your thirst. Let prayer of the heart accompany your reading of the Word of God. Converse intimately with God as with your best friend. Hear his call and respond.

Reading Scripture, frequently sharing the liturgy, receiving the sacraments—these are the common ways that bring prayer to life, that draw us into communion with the Trinity [2655]. We enter into the Church's sacramental life and its liturgy through "the narrow gate of *faith*" [2656]. Living liturgically in expectation of Christ's return "teaches us to pray in *hope*" [2657]. And "hope does not disappoint us, because God's *love* has been poured into our hearts through the Holy Spirit which has been given to us" (Rom 5:5) [2658]. These three theological virtues of faith, hope, and love really release the floodgates of prayer.

Faith expresses the firm commitment we make as women who believe to hear, trust, and keep God's word. Only eyes of faith can see signs of God's presence everywhere. To pray is to say, "I believe even if I do not see."

Hope nourishes our expectation that Christ, who has died and risen, will come again. Hope assures us that what is impossible for us is possible for God. Hope in the promise of the Beloved does not, will not, disappoint us. We abound in hope, even in the face of what, humanly speaking, seems hopeless.

Love is the spring whence our prayer overflows. "Prayer, formed by the liturgical life, draws everything into the love by which we are loved in Christ ... whoever draws from it reaches the summit of prayer" [2658].

When life becomes a living prayer, when a woman of spirit prays not because she has to but because she knows she will die spiritually if she does not, then every minute of every day counts for her. Nothing about her stays the same. In her here and now situation, she hears the voice of the Lord. He becomes her dearest companion in her single or married life. Her sensitivity heightens like finely tuned radar to the role she plays in his Paschal Mystery. She wants more than anything to be faithful to her divine life call.

A hospital chaplain prays the Lord's Prayer with a dying woman.

A mother begs God to save her child from drugs. Two parents hug each other and weep for joy when an organ donor is found for their child. There is no human situation where prayer is not appropriate if we heed the psalmist's words: "O that *today* you would hearken to his voice! Harden not your hearts" (Ps 95:7-8) [2659].

Women pray for the coming of the kingdom of justice, peace, and mercy. In appreciative abandonment to God, we let go of our sorrow about yesterday (sins confessed are forgiven) and our worry about tomorrow (today has enough cares of its own). We sense, as faithful people everywhere do, the divine embrace that gathers the events of each day and every grace-filled moment of our lives under the canopy of Holy Providence.

Ways of Prayer

Diverse as personal expressions of prayer may be in Christian life, underlying all of them is the Trinitarian structure. Applied to prayer, this means that "the sacred humanity of Jesus is ... the way by which the Holy Spirit teaches us to pray to God our Father" [2664].

We pray to Jesus by invoking his sacred name (Son of God, Word of God, Savior, Good Shepherd). The name of Jesus, according to the churches of the East and the West, contains "the whole economy of creation and salvation" [2666]. Simply put, "The invocation of the holy name of Jesus is the simplest way of praying always" [2668].

We pray to the Holy Spirit, our Comforter and Advocate, for "no one can say 'Jesus is Lord' except by the Holy Spirit" (1 Cor 12:3). In hymns and antiphons, we say from the heart, "Come, Holy Spirit, fill the hearts of your faithful and enkindle in them the fire of your love"[2] [2671]. However many ways of prayer there are, the same Spirit is acting in, with, and through them all, for "the Holy

Spirit, whose anointing permeates our whole being, is the interior Master of Christian prayer" [2672]. In communion with the Spirit, the prayer of Christians becomes the prayer of the Church.

It is our Mother, Mary, who shows us the way to Jesus and "is herself 'the Sign' of [this] way" [2674]. Her consent in faith to the Annunciation at the beginning of her life, her decision to be with her Son to the end, her capacity for self-giving love, draws us who pray with her and to her into full communion with the Church. Mary's way of prayer—obedient, chaste, poor in spirit—has to become our way if we want to approach the culminating point of our formation journey—the mature faith she lived.

In Mary women witness the power of prayer emanating from seeming powerlessness. They see strength welling up from surrender to the will of God. In her lowliness, God filled her with grace. May he not do the same for all women if we entrust our supplications to him through her who is blessed among women?

Prayer Guides

The saints and spiritual masters are powerful witnesses to intense prayer and its efficacy in their hearts and for the whole world. Different schools of spirituality (Augustinian, Benedictine, Carmelite, Franciscan, Dominican, Ignatian, Spiritan) teach the foundations of Christian prayer. Each has a unique style that appeals to particular liturgical and theological currents, as well as to the given missions of the communities to which they belong. "In their rich diversity they are refractions of the one pure light of the Holy Spirit" [2684].

In the family we receive our first real taste of prayer. Then, over a lifetime, these seeds can be tended patiently by the Spirit until Holy Providence is ready to bring them to full bloom.

Women have a tremendous role to play in teaching the life of prayer. We can introduce children to the saints, teach them to pray to their guardian angel and the blessed in heaven, and to ask God's mercy on the souls in purgatory. As parents, teachers, and lay workers, we can work with priests and religious to develop excellent catechetical programs, small faith sharing groups, and ongoing formation sessions. We can seek the training we need to become qualified spiritual directors and retreat facilitators. We can encourage attention to the importance of symbolic places, such as prayer corners, retreat centers, and pilgrimage sites, that remind us of the living God. Above all, we can continue to tell the story of God's love, written in human hearts, by the witness of our own faithful lives. Prayer then becomes not only something we do but an authentic expression of who we are [2685-2691].

Becoming Living Prayer

Prayer is meant to animate every moment of our life, for as St. Gregory of Nazianzus says, "We must remember God more often than we draw breath"[3] [2697], praying with intensity and duration when we are moved to do so as well as when we feel spiritually dry. Following rhythms of praying while working is a good way to nourish continual prayer. We can also say grace before and after meals; attend, when possible, the Liturgy of the Hours; prepare thoughtfully for the Sunday celebration of the Eucharist; and follow the cycle of the liturgical year and the readings and symbols associated with it [2698]. These attitudes of prayerfulness begin to feel like second nature when we keep God's word and abide, in awe-filled attentiveness, with the divine presence permeating every facet of our life and world.

Praying Vocally

Praying aloud depends, according to St. John Chrysostom, "... not on the number of words [we say], but on the fervor of our souls"[4] [2700]. Vocal prayer is an essential component of Christian life. Jesus himself taught us how to pray by giving us the Our Father. He prayed aloud the liturgical prayers of the synagogue. He prayed his experiences—from exultant blessings of the Father to deep groanings during his agony in the garden.

Voiced prayer links our senses to interior prayer. It reminds us in songs and sighs that we are embodied beings, not pure spirits. Living prayer is an expression of the body-mind-spirit unity to which we are being led by grace. When it is divinely directed, vocal prayer is not only on our lips; it arises from the depths of our soul. It is an expression of faith accessible to fervent seekers—not an end in itself but a doorway to meditative and contemplative prayer [2704].

Praying Meditatively

The attentiveness that meditation demands is not easy to attain in a world increasingly dominated by noise, technology, and television. A woman who wants to deepen her faith has to be willing to mobilize her thoughts, direct her imagination, quiet her emotions, and abide with the word.

Meditative spiritual reading, particularly of Scripture and the masters, helps us to connect what we read with the here and now, with who we are, and with what the Lord wants us to do [2706]. We taste and savor the richness of the text. We take its meaning to heart.

Meditation strengthens our determination to follow Christ. It engages our thoughts, imaginations, emotions, and desires; it deepens our faith and hastens the conversion of our hearts [2708]. Whatever method we use (formative reading, devotions, the rosary), our prayer is to be guided by the Holy Spirit. Our goal is Jesus. He is *the* way of prayer for us.

Praying Contemplatively

St. Teresa of Avila describes contemplative prayer as "a close sharing between friends; it means taking time frequently to be alone with him who we know loves us"[5] [2709]. She teaches us to fix our gaze on the Lord whom we love, and to trust that he knows the secrets of our heart.

While formal meditation may elude us in times of trial or dryness, we can always enter into inner prayer of the heart, into the prayer of simple union, the prayer of presence. Whatever the condition of our health, work, or emotional state, we can follow the example of St. Teresa and place our whole being at the disposal of "his Majesty." We can depend on our Beloved for everything. Such is the secret of the saints. Teresa trusted that God waited upon her as much as she awaited his coming. When she least expected it, her heart was uplifted. With her and women of faith everywhere, we come to understand that "the heart is the place of this quest and encounter, in poverty and in faith" [2710].

Contemplative prayer is not an esoteric practice for the spiritually elite. Guided by the Holy Spirit, we go to the God who awaits us, as parents stand by the window, waiting hour by hour until their child comes home. We pray as women forgiven and fearless, who experience what it is like to receive a new heart, reformed and renewed, by their relationship with God. Such communion with the Trinity awes us. Such grace conforms us to Christ and enhances our likeness of God [2713].

Contemplative prayer is the prayer of people who take off the mask of self-sufficiency and offer themselves to God in poverty of spirit to be transformed. To enter into contemplation is to recollect our scattered lives around Christ as our center. It means to gather our heart together. It is to go to God with undivided attention. It is to abide with the mystery in awe-filled wonder as when, for example, we bring our whole selves into the sacrifice and celebration of the eucharistic liturgy [2711], praying fervently:

> *Jesus, you who dwell in our inmost being through faith (Eph 3:17), send us the grace to gaze contemplatively upon you. Grant that we may forget ourselves entirely, if only for this brief duration. Let us be one with you in contemplation. Never let us give in to the temptation not to pray, however dry our inner desert may be. Even when we feel like dust, teach us to offer to you the prayer of our dryness. Combine with our loving commitment to you the unconditional acceptance of your will when joy and sorrow invade our lives [2714-2718].*

With the grace of God, contemplative prayer, grounded in love, may draw us into a vision of pure faith, fixed on Jesus. In contemplative silence, listening intently to God's word, we renounce all that stands in the way of total surrender. We want to participate in the mystery of Christ's own prayer life, even if this means living in the darkness of not knowing or feeling the consolations of God while still believing completely in the God who consoles.

Women of prayer want the "Yes, Father" of Jesus and the "Be it done unto me" of Mary to become the core of their contemplative life and the key to their commitment to serve God in this world. In the darkness of faith, or at its dawning, contemplative prayer invites us to keep watch with the Lord as we await our consummation with him in his risen glory [2719].

Struggling to Pray

Prayer is not a practice we can take for granted. It is our determined response to the grace of God. It involves a constant struggle against our sinful, forgetful self and against the wiles of the Tempter [2725].

To be victorious in this battle, we need, first of all, to lift up to God the objections to prayer we face in ourselves. We must free our minds from erroneous notions of prayer, which only complicate our spiritual struggle. Some of these might be that prayer is simply a psychological activity, like voiding our minds when they are overloaded. We may treat prayer as an effort of concentration or a form or relaxation rather than a graced event that is life-transforming.

It is equally mistaken to think that prayer is an occupation incompatible with all that we have to do. Rather, it is the wellspring of anything worthwhile we might hope to accomplish. Prayer comes from the Holy Spirit in response to our own receptivity to grace and our renewed commitment to pray as if we had all the time in the world [2726].

Prayer is our openness to a covenant relationship with the Trinity. Such love surpasses understanding. We pray because we must. We do not pray to divorce ourselves from the real world but to enter into the ultimate meaning of its existence [2727].

When spiritual dryness comes, and at times it will; when disappointment overtakes us, and at times it will, we must not cease to pray; rather we must enter more deeply into the process of prayer, allowing the Holy Spirit to pray in us. Though we may think we have failed to pray, God sees our meager efforts and blesses even those. With humility, trust, and perseverance, we can overcome dejection, discouragement, and disappointment.

One common difficulty is distraction. That is why vigilance of heart is so important. Like a plague of locusts, buzzing thoughts, words, and images disturb our prayers. The tendency is to try to drive these distractions away, when instead we ought to turn to God, who is the object of our adoration or intercession. Otherwise we may end up being distracted by our battle with distractions! The culprit we must really contend with is our dominating self-will, our attachment to something less than God. Now is the time to seek his face (Ps 27:8), to return to the text we are meditating upon or to the psalm we are praying.

Distractions are part of the struggle to develop a mature life of prayer. So, too, is dryness. Now prayer begins to ripen as we say:

It feels as if my heart is separated from you, O God. I cannot think. I have no feelings, "even spiritual ones" [2731]. Rather than fighting this sensation directly, or worrying excessively about it, help me to see it as an inner movement, an invitation to turn to Jesus in sheer faith. Don't let me get lost in the idle expectation that I will be able to overcome these difficulties in prayer by my own power. Test my faith in these times of tribulation, but never leave me.

Obstacles to Prayer

Distractions are but one of the many obstacles to a rich and fruitful prayer life. The *Catechism* tells us that "the most common yet most hidden temptation [not to pray] is our *lack of faith*" [2732]. If we wish to cultivate true intimacy with God in our hearts, we must ask ourselves some probing questions that may reveal our inner intention. As we read in the Gospel of Matthew: "For where your treasure is, there will your heart be" (Mt 6:21).

Consider for a moment: *Where is my heart? Whom have I made my highest priority in life? What do I truly believe? Have I cultivated a humble, expectant spirit? Do I trust Jesus' words that "apart from me you can do nothing" (Jn 15:5)?*

Another obstacle to be considered is the tendency to apathy or "spiritual sloth" (*acedia*) [2733]. The sins of pride and presumption can block the flow of grace and lead to discouragement, depression, lack of self-discipline, decreasing vigilance—for "the spirit indeed is willing, but the flesh is weak" (Mt 26:41).

Once again in the face of such onslaughts, women must hold fast to the Lord. Faith proves itself in tribulations [2734]. It is difficult to cling to Jesus, especially if it seems as if prayers of petition or intercession are not being heard. Then what? The answer offered by the *Catechism* comes in the form of two questions. Ask yourself:

(1) Why do I think my prayers are not reaching God's ears?

(2) When and how is my prayer efficacious?

It may seem to women of faith that—despite our attempts to praise God, give thanks, walk with Jesus, and practice the spiritual disciplines—nothing is happening. The problem may not be that God is not listening but that we may be praying with a divided heart. We say in the Our Father, for example, "Thy will be done," and secretly we want to hand God the script! We may even be asking for something God cannot give us because it does not conform to what he desires for our overall well-being. Paradoxically, God's apparent lack of response may be the answer we need most.

Childlike confidence and a sense of flowing with the providential unfolding of God's care are sure marks that our prayers are effective in God's sight. This trust is founded on the power of the Spirit praying in us. It is a reflection of the faithful love of the Father for us and his gift of the Son to us.

The heart that prays undergoes a profound transformation. It is configured to the heart of Jesus, and it expresses itself in matching character and personality traits, in a life of virtue [2740].

Since the heart of the Son seeks only what is pleasing to the Father, it behooves us to center our prayers not so much on the gifts we receive from God as on God, the Giver. Then our prayers unite resolutely with Jesus' intercessions to the Father (Heb 5:7; 7:25; 9:24). Under the sign of his cross, we obtain all that we ask in his name, and even more.

That is why women of faith persevere in love and pray without ceasing, "giving thanks in the name of our Lord Jesus Christ to God the Father" (1 Thes 5:17; Eph 5:20). Keeping watch, persevering in supplication, fasting, and praying enable us, with the help of grace, to overcome our struggles with dullness, laziness, presumption, or lack of zeal.

We learn in Scripture, and from our experience of humble, trusting, persevering love, three enlightening and life-giving truths about prayer [2743-2745]:

(1) It is always possible to pray, in whatever state, be it tempest or rest, one finds oneself;

(2) Prayer is not a luxury for an elite few but a vital necessity for everyone;

(3) Prayer and Christian living are inseparable.

In the end, the efficacy of our prayer can be proven only by the charity and compassion that flow from it.

Questions for Reflection
and Faith Sharing

1. What place do you give the name of Jesus in your prayer life [2680]? Are you aware when you pray that the Holy Spirit is "the interior Teacher of Christian prayer" [2681]?

2. What role does Mary play in your womanly life of prayer? How often do you entrust your supplications to her, pray in communion with her, ask her blessing on the Church [2682]?

3. Was it in your Christian family that you first experienced formation in prayer [2694]? What do you remember of your initial upbringing in the faith that affects your way of praying today?

4. What "spiritual battles" affect your prayer life [2752]? Has the Lord shown you how to be victorious? When and how have other Christians modeled for you the way to "persevere in prayer"?

EIGHTEEN

The Heart Praying
As Jesus Taught

This word of thanks to the Lord for his mysterious plan regarding the vocation and mission of women in the world is at the same time a concrete and direct word of thanks to women, to every woman, for all that they represent in the life of humanity.

—Pope John Paul II
Letter to Women, 2

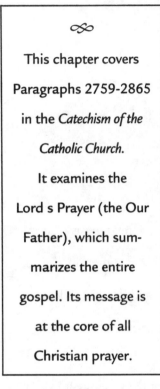

This chapter covers

Paragraphs 2759-2865

in the *Catechism of the*

Catholic Church.

It examines the

Lord s Prayer (the Our

Father), which sum-

marizes the entire

gospel. Its message is

at the core of all

Christian prayer.

"Lord, teach us to pray" (Lk 11:1). This simple request by the disciples gave rise to the prayer that the Church Father Tertullian calls "truly the summary of the whole gospel"[1] [2761]. This is the prayer we learn as children and never forget as adults. These are the sacred words we incorporate into the major events of our life—from the birth of a baby to the death of a family member or friend.

When women pray as Jesus did, with the heartfelt simplicity and familiar intimacy of "Abba! Father" (Gal 4:6), they receive an inkling of the mysterious mission designated for them by the Son in and through the Spirit to the glory of the Father. Sinner or saint, lost or found, we can dare to address God as Father and approach him with the childlike confidence associated with "the certainty of being loved"[2] [2778].

Jesus taught us to pray. He brings us into the Father's presence through the power of the Spirit. There we stand on holy ground, our hearts cleansed of false, worldly images of God. The most heartfelt word we can say is "Father." However, no earthly image of fatherhood can compare to the mystery of "Our Father who art in heaven." Transcending every paternal category imaginable, the Father is beyond our finite comprehension.

As disciples we share in the personal intimacy that flows between Father and Son. This bond of love goes beyond concepts and feelings. To pray to the Father is to ask for what we need, to intercede for the indwelling of the Spirit in our life and world, and to become the true followers Jesus needs and deserves [2782].

Dispositions of a Woman of Prayer

As adopted daughters of God we are called to continual conversion of heart. Two fundamental dispositions enable new life to blossom: the first is the desire to be restored to the divine likeness in which we have been made. This means, in the words of St. Gregory of Nyssa, to "contemplate the beauty of the Father without ceasing and adorn our souls accordingly"[3] [2784].

The second source of new life is to become so grounded in the humility and trust, the reverence and experience of spiritual childhood (see Mt 11:25; 18:3), that we can speak, in the words of St. John Cassian, "familiarly to God as to [our] own Father with special devotion"[4] [2785].

When a woman says "Our Father," she is not simply praying as an individual but as a representative of the whole faith community. She feels united with God and every other man and woman of prayer. The "Our" in this phrase defines for us a new relationship with God. It confirms the eternal covenant of love between us and God. It is proof that his promise to be with us until the end of time will be fulfilled [2786-2788]. This three-letter word signifies a bonding announced by the prophets and beheld to the full in Christ Jesus. We have become his. We are no longer alone, but part of a loving community on whose fidelity God can count.

To address God in this tender way—"Our Father"—shows that in spite of the divisions among Christians, prayer to "our" heavenly Father "remains our common patrimony and an urgent summons for all the baptized" [2791]. Thus women the world over join in the prayer of Jesus for Christian unity.

To call upon "Our Father" is to ask him to set us free from

"narrow individualism." It is to pray, *"Please help me to exclude no one from the circle of love with you at the center. Hear our plea as women for peace. Let our divisions and oppositions be overcome by the power of your grace."*

The God to Whom We Pray

"Who art in heaven" discloses a new facet of the Lord's Prayer. "In heaven" does not mean a place. It suggests a way of being. According to St. Augustine, "'Our Father who art in heaven' is rightly understood to mean that God is in the hearts of the just, as in his holy temple. At the same time, it means that those who pray should desire the one they invoke to dwell in them"[5] [2794].

God is not "elsewhere" or "out there." His holiness transcends anything we can imagine, yet he is close to hearts that are humble and contrite. The symbol of heaven reminds us of the mystery of the covenant and of the Father's house, for heaven is "our" homeland.

Sin exiled humankind from this land of likeness to the Trinity; it alienated women and men from the covenant. Yet while we are here on earth, our groaning for heaven does not cease. We may spend our lives on earth, "but [we] are citizens of heaven"[6] [2796].

What Women Pray For

Having considered to whom we pray, we ask, *for what do we pray?* The "Spirit of adoption stirs up in our hearts seven petitions, seven blessings" [2803]. The first three focus on God and his glory *(thy name, thy kingdom, thy will);* the final four focus on human concerns *(give us, forgive us, lead us not, deliver us).*

Women ask first that his name be hallowed; that his kingdom come; that his will be done. They pray these petitions from the heart because the Father is not yet "all in all" (1 Cor 15:28). Women know that this hope of glory can only happen if they are healed of sin and victorious over evil. That is why all seven petitions are "strengthened in faith, filled with hope, and set aflame by charity" [2806].

Hallowed Be Thy Name

With this petition I express my homage to you, Holy One, Almighty and mysterious Godhead. I sing your praises. I seek to dwell in your presence all the days of my life. I ask that your name be made holy, that you draw me into your plan for salvation through Christ Jesus. I ask to "be holy and blameless before [you] in love" (Eph 1:4).

This petition contains many reminders of the new life that Jesus came to bring, of the new name he wanted each of us to receive in his Father's name. God revealed his great "I am" by accomplishing this saving work—*hallowed be his name.* God committed himself to the Chosen People, to us, despite our sinfulness; he made of us a "holy" or "consecrated" nation (Ex 19:5-6)—*hallowed be his name* [2807-2810]. The Father has given his Son "the name above all other names, for Jesus Christ is Lord, to the glory of God the Father" (Phil 2:9-11).

The hallowing of God's name has a deep effect on women of prayer. "Justified in the name of the Lord Jesus Christ and in the Spirit of our God" (1 Cor 6:11) in Baptism, we are called to holiness. Both God's glory (his divine forming mystery) and our lives are intertwined when we hallow his name. Hence there is an urgency in the first petition we must not overlook, for as St. Peter Chrysologus says, "this name ... gives salvation to a lost world"[7] [2814].

Thy Kingdom Come

With this petition I ask, O Lord, for the grace to pray unceas-ingly, to keep constantly before my mind's eye the kingdom of God—not the kingdoms of this world. I say with my whole, femi-nine heart, "Come, Lord Jesus" [2817]. I want you in my life here and now, even as I contemplate the final coming of the kingdom of God through Christ's return (Ti 2:13).

This petition points at once to the Church's mission in the world (to the work of the Spirit on earth) and to our desire for the fullness of grace and the contemplation of Christ's work until he comes again. God's kingdom and our prayer for its coming refer also to "righteousness and peace and joy in the Holy Spirit" (Rom 14:17). The Spirit sent by Jesus helps us to overcome sin and live in peace. Then we will be able to say to God, in the words of St. Cyril of Jerusalem, "in action, thought, and word ... 'Thy kingdom come!'"[8] [2819].

This petition invites us also to see a distinction—though not a separation—between God's reign in the world and the progress being made in culture and society. It reminds us that our call to holiness and eternal life "does not suppress, but actually reinforces, [our] duty to put into action in this world the energies and means received from [our] Creator to serve justice and peace"[9] [2820].

Thy Will Be Done on Earth As It Is in Heaven

Heavenly Father, you want all people "to be saved and to come to the knowledge of the truth" (1 Tm 2:4). You are patient with us. You want none of us to perish (2 Pt 3:9). Thus you command us to love one another as you have loved us (Jn 13:34; 1 Jn 3–4). Help me to grasp the spirit behind this third petition of the Lord's

Prayer. I feel the urgency in it. May your divine plan be realized as fully on earth as it is already fulfilled in heaven [2823]!

By uniting his human will with the will of the Father, Jesus built the perfect bridge between earth and heaven. By giving himself up for our sins, he has delivered us from the present age (Gal 1:4) and its ends. By virtue of his suffering and death, we have found the way to freedom through obedience. No longer are we aliens on earth; we are adopted children of God, bound for heaven.

In this petition I ask you, Father, to unite my will with Jesus' spirit. I, too, want to be an integral part of his plan for the salvation of the world. On my own I am powerless to do so, but united with the Son through the power of the Holy Spirit, I can choose, as he did, what is pleasing to you, dear Father. Then I shall do your will on earth as it is done in heaven. Then I can spend my life sincerely seeking oneness with you. Then the Eucharist will sustain me as I seek with Mary, my mother, and all the saints to emulate your obedience unto death [2827].

Give Us This Day Our Daily Bread

Imprint these two words, O Lord, with their bold imperative, on my heart. Let their mark signify my trust in you and your unfailing goodness to me. In them I acknowledge that everything is gift. With them I express my covenant relationship with the Triune God. Through them I belong to God as God longs to be with me. He is all for me. He is the Father of everyone, and so I can pray to him in solitude and solidarity [2828-2829].

The bread for which we pray suggests that the Father, who gives us life, cannot refuse to give us the nourishment this life requires—be it material or spiritual. All goods and blessings come to us from the providence of God. That is why we can approach our heavenly Father with childlike trust (see Matthew 6:25-34), free from excessive worry, strain, and anxiety.

Behind this petition is also a profound social concern. It arouses a woman's commitment to care for the world's hungry, to feed those who lack bread and the basic necessities of life. It compels her to examine her personal responsibility for both the physically and spiritually hungry and poor. In and with Christ, she seeks to bring justice to socially unjust neighborhoods, towns, cities, countries, and nations. The Church's concern for economic justice for all reminds women that we cannot hope to transform the world unless we are willing to reform our own selfish hearts [2835].

The sharing of bread called for by this petition has to be done not out of mere philanthropic duty but out of deep love for people (2 Cor 8:1-15). The abundance the few possess has to be shared with the many who have so much less, if social justice, peace, and mercy are to prevail in an increasingly self-centered society and world.

Men, women, and children not only hunger for bread to eat; they also hunger to hear the word of God (Dt 8:3; Mt 4:4). We live on a planet that is starving spiritually. We need to hear the Good News preached to us. This fourth petition also concerns the Bread of Life: "The Word of God accepted in faith, the Body of Christ received in the Eucharist"[10] [2835]. As St. Augustine says:

> *The Eucharist is our daily bread. The power belonging to this divine food makes it a bond of union. Its effect is then understood as unity, so that, gathered into his Body and made members of him, we may become what we receive ... This also is our daily bread: the readings you hear each day in church and the hymns*

you hear and sing. All these are necessities for our pilgrimage[11] *[2837].*

The words "this day" and "daily" add punch to our prayer of trust in the Lord. It is not so that we need God now and again; God should be our all every minute of every day. These expressions bind us not only to mortal time but to the "eternal now" of God. In the temporal sense, "today" connotes trust without reserve, just as "bread" refers to Christ's Body, called by St. Ignatius of Antioch the "medicine of immortality"[12] [2837]. Its heavenly meaning points to the Day of the Lord, to the feast of the kingdom to come, when the saved shall receive the Eucharist without cease.

And Forgive Us Our Trespasses, As We Forgive Those Who Trespass Against Us

Lord, forgive my sins and help me to forgive those who have sinned against me. Teach me that I dare not ask you to forgive me unless I am willing to see myself as part of a community of sinners in need of salvation. You call us all to belong to the communion of saints, but only forgiveness can pave the way.

The Catechism refers to this petition as "astonishing" [2838]. With the bold confidence of the Prodigal Son, with the humility of the tax collector (Lk 15:11-32; 18:13), we recognize that we are sinners in need of redemption. We ask God to forgive our sins every time we receive the sacraments of the Church. The connector "as" cannot be overlooked. Though it is only a tiny, two-letter word, it makes us aware that this part of the Lord's Prayer presents a profound challenge. The "as" suggests that this outpouring of divine mercy can penetrate our hearts only to the extent that we are willing to forgive others as we have been forgiven by God.

In this same way, Scripture says, we cannot love the God we cannot see if we do not love the brother and sister we do see (1 Jn 4:20). Forgiveness opens closed hearts. It softens the harshness that hinders the flow of the Father's love. That is why this fifth petition is so important. Yet, unforgiving as our hearts sometimes are, we know it is impossible to fulfill it without God's help.

The word "as" also gives us a clue to the covenant mystery on which we can rely for help. We do not have to walk this road to forgiveness of self and others alone. Christ is with us from the start. He says, "A new commandment I give to you, that you love one another; even *as* I have loved you, that you also love one another" (Jn 13:34).

In other words, forgiveness cannot happen if we think of the Lord as removed from the struggles of this world. Were that the case, then who of us could do *as* he did? It is necessary instead for us to think of the *as* as a full and vital entrance into Christ's own forgiving heart. Only then does our forgiveness of others become an everyday occurrence, something that happens at least in spirit every time we pray the Our Father.

As women of faith, our hearts resonate with this invitation of grace. The pain of our own sin and of the way others have trespassed against us is not forgotten, but a path opens in the wilderness. Through the power of this prayer, our hearts can take another turn. We can ask the Holy Spirit to change our wounds into a source of compassion, to purify our memories of them, to make them a prayer [2843]. No wonder forgiveness has such a healing effect on ourselves and others.

This petition has a more serious edge to it. Forgiveness has to extend to our enemies, too. It thus represents a high point of Christian prayer because it configures us to our Master, Jesus. Without a forgiving heart it is difficult, if not impossible, to pray as Jesus does.

Forgiveness sends a powerful message into an unforgiving, revengeful world. It bears witness to the truth that love is stronger than sin. It is the condition for the possibility of reconciliation between all people and God, for we are his children. This being the case, Scripture teaches us that there is no limit or measure to divine forgiveness (Mt 18:21-22; Lk 17:3-4). We are always debtors, always sinners in need of divine mercy.

And Lead Us Not into Temptation

Dear Jesus, if sin is a result of my consent to temptation, then I need your grace to say no. Knowing the depth of my weakness, I pray that you will not allow me to enter into temptation, that you will free me from evil and prevent me from taking that first step on the path toward sin. Urgently I ask you to send me the spirit of discernment to help me to unmask the "lie of temptation" [2847]. To even pray like this implies that I have already made a "decision of the heart" [2848]. Thanks to your being by my side, I want to overcome the struggle I feel in this ancient battle "between flesh and spirit" [2846]. Teach me to know which "tests" are necessary to foster my growth in spiritual maturity and which "temptations" lead to sin and death. Help me to discern between "being tempted" (which happens all the time) and "consenting" to temptation (which I pray for the grace to resist). I know I only delude myself if I try at the same time to serve two masters (Mt 6:21, 24). I have to make the choice on which my whole formation depends. I have to decide where my heart really is: with God or against God? Self-giving or self-centered? Self-seeking only or willing to carry the cross?

To consent to the Spirit's leading gives a woman the strength to resist temptation. It is consoling to know from revelation that God will not test her beyond her strength and that he will give her the grace she needs to endure (1 Cor 10:13).

Discernment and decisiveness are the fruits of a life of prayer. At the start of his public life as well as in his ultimate agony, Jesus vanquished the Tempter by his prayer (see Matthew 4:1-11; 26:36-44). When we pray this petition in union with him, we are united not only with Jesus' struggle but also with his victory.

Christ gives us another arm to lean on, for he also begs his Father in heaven to protect us in his name (Jn 17:11). On our part, through the power of the Spirit, we are to keep watch (1 Cor 16:13; Col 4:2; 1 Thess 5:6; 1 Pt 5:8) until the last temptation, praying to the end for the grace of perseverance [2849].

But Deliver Us from Evil

My Lord and my God, I need protection not only from evil in general but from the Evil One [2850]. You yourself prayed for this favor in your farewell discourse (see John 17:15). The deliverance I seek is not only for myself but for the entire family of humanity. In the drama of sin and death, of liberation and restored life, I am both dependent on God and interdependent. I stand in solidarity with Christ's body, "the communion of saints"[13] [2850], but I am at peril, for as this seventh and final petition reminds me, evil is not an abstraction. It refers to an Other, to Satan, the Evil One, the devil. How intentionally and completely opposed this fallen angel is to your plan and to the work of salvation accomplished in Christ [2851]. Indeed, you must deliver me!

The devil is literally *dia-bolos*, the one who "throws himself across" God's design for us and the work of salvation "accomplished in Christ" [2851]. Through him sin and death entered the world. This liar—this "father of lies"—is "the deceiver of the whole world" (Jn 8:44; Rv 12:9).

When she prays this petition, a woman brings the distress and conflicts of all humankind before the Father. She entrusts herself to God, fully convinced that victory over the "ruler of this world" (Jn 14:30) belongs to Christ. Freedom from the corruption of sin and death was won once and for all when Jesus gave himself over to death. In so doing he gave us new life. His coming through the Virgin Mary, the new Eve, a woman so full of grace that God preserved her from sin and the corruption of death, "deliver[s] us from the Evil One" [2853].

Still, knowing how vulnerable we are to missing the mark, we ask to be delivered daily from the deceiver as well as to be freed from the past, present, and future evils that ensnare our hearts. We implore the Father for the precious gift of peace. We ask for the grace to persevere in expectation of Christ's return [2854]. Thus, with the whole community of faith, we pray during Holy Mass, after the recitation of the Lord's Prayer, these unforgettable words:

> *Deliver us, Lord, we beseech you, from every evil and grant us peace in our day, so that aided by your mercy we might be ever free from sin and protected from all anxiety, as we await the blessed hope and the coming of our Savior, Jesus Christ[14] [2854].*

The Final Doxology

The doxology following the Lord's Prayer, "For the kingdom, the power and the glory are yours, now and forever" [2855], renews the first three petitions we make to God the Father: glorifying his name, praying for the coming of his kingdom, and acknowledging the power of his saving will. The doxology removes from the "ruler of this world" any false claim to kingship, power, and glory

[2855]. Christ, the Lord, restores these titles to his Father and our Father, foretelling the day when the mystery of salvation will be brought to its completion and God will be all in all (see Luke 4:5-6; 1 Corinthians 15:24-28).

To this glorious vision, let us say in rousing unison, "So be it." With one voice, many though we may be, we ratify in word and deed the entire content of our Catholic faith. We say "So be it" to what we believe, to what we celebrate, to what we live, and to what we pray, "In the name of the Father and of the Son and of the Holy Spirit, Amen, now and forever, Alleluia, Amen!"

Questions for Reflection and Faith Sharing

1. Does this description ring true to you: "Simple and faithful trust, humble and joyous assurance are the proper dispositions for one who prays the Our Father" [2797]? Why does the Lord's Prayer affect you in this way?

2. Is your sense of "the true homeland toward which [you] are heading" somehow a part of where you already belong? In other words, do you sense an intersecting of time and eternity when you pray the Our Father [2802]?

3. Which of the seven petitions of the Lord's Prayer best describes your greatest need at the moment? Is it to be nourished? To be healed of sin? To be victorious in the struggle of good over evil [2857]?

4. In reading the Catechism, what message in it has touched you the most? How has it challenged you to live a more Christ-centered life?

Closing Prayer

Thrice holy God,
Overshadowing us, your people,
Called to be holy
And to live holistically,
Gifted to form, reform, and
transform
The community of faith,
Sent to serve our sisters and
brothers
In ministry eagerly, tirelessly,
faithfully,
Renew our hearts by the grace of
God.
Grant us hitherto unknown depths
Of prayer and presence,
As we offer the witness
Of love and healing
In and through Christ
To a world wounded
By violence, hatred, and ill will,
Sick in soul and body because of
sin.
God the Father,
God the Son,
God the Holy Spirit,
Gather us together
As husbands and wives,
As fathers and mothers,
As children and elders,

As friends and relatives,
Into the embracing, caring
Arms of Christ crucified.
Through him help us to shoulder
The responsibilities we as laity,
Clergy, and religious
Must carry with and for
The Church
Into the world.
There we can be found
Reading God's Word,
Distributing Holy Communion,
Communicating our catechetical
tradition
To youth and adults,
Holding decision-making
Positions and remembering
Our responsibility to be ministers
Of the Church, responding
Wherever you place us
To souls hungering
For spiritual deepening,
Not wasting our suffering
But offering it daily
For their and our salvation.
Spirit of fire and light,
Help us as we strive
To build a better world
For our children,
A world revitalized
And renewed by a deepening
Of faith, hope, and love,

A Church recreated
In the image and likeness
Of Christ now and for all ages
To come.
Teach us, Holy Spirit,
To speak with a disciple's tongue,
In fidelity to the treasures
Of our faith and formation tradition.
Give us a spirit of deep prayer,
contemplative, mental, and vocal.
Let the cry of our heart
Be a constant reminder to us
Of your resurrected presence,
Giving us the courage
To carry on; the confidence
To minister to others
Even as we allow them to care for us;
And the compassion to be
Messengers
Of hope and healing in a time
Of transition like our own.
Spirit of truth and goodness,
Teach us to see in our Mother,
Mary, the finest witness to what
It means to be whole and holy.
Help us to imitate her spirit
Of courage and consent,
Of loyalty and dedication,
As she strove to bear
In joy and sorrow
The awesome responsibility
The Father gave her to be

The Mother of our Lord.
May the Word she cherished
Become flesh in us,
As we strive to foster
In our ministry
The ongoing spiritual formation
Of all we hold dear.
In Jesus' name, though many,
In one voice we say,
Amen! Alleluia! Amen!

NOTES

∞

ONE
Believing That a Loving God Loves Us

1. *Roman Catechism*, Preface, 10; cf. 1 Cor 13:8.
2. St. Augustine, *Conf.* 1, 1, 1:PL 32, 659-661.
3. GS 18 § 1; cf. 14 § 2.
4. DV 8 § 1.
5. DV 10 § 3.
6. DV 18.
7. St. Thérèse of Lisieux, *ms. autob.* A 83v.
8. *Dei Filius* 3:DS 3008-10; cf. *Mk* 16:20; *Heb* 2:4.
9. John Henry Cardinal Newman, *Apologia pro vita sua* (London: Longman, 1878), 239.
10. Edith Stein, *The Mystery of Christmas*, tr. Josephine Rucker (Darlington, England: Darlington Carmel, 1985), 13-14.
11. St. Irenaeus, *Adv. haeres.* 5, 20, 1:PG 7/2, 1177.
12. St. Augustine, *Conf.* 10, 28, 39: PL 32, 795.
13. *DV* 8§ 1.
14. *DV* 21.

TWO
Seeking Intimacy with the Trinity

1. St. Ambrose, *Expl. symb.* 1:PL 17, 1193.
2. *Roman Catechism*, I,2,2.
3. St. Teresa of Jesus, *Poesías* 30, in *The Collected Works of St. Teresa of Avila*, vol. III, tr. by K. Kavanaugh, OCD, and O. Rodriguez, OCD, (Washington: Institute of Carmelite Studies, 1985), 386 no. 9, tr. by John Wall.
4. Cf. *Ps* 27:10; *Eph* 3:14; *Isa* 49:15.
5. Niceno-Constantinopolitan Creed; cf. DS 150.
6. Council of Florence (1439): DS 1300-1301.
7. *2 Cor* 13:13; cf. *1 Cor* 12:4-6; *Eph* 4:4-6.
8. Paul VI, *CPG* § 2.
9. *Fides Damasi:* DS 71.
10. Council of Florence (1442): DS 1331.
11. Cf. *Jn* 17:21-23.
12. Prayer of Blessed Elizabeth of the Trinity.
13. Cf. Paul VI. *CPG* § 9.

THREE
Belonging to the Trinitarian Family

1. St. Augustine, *Conf.* 3, 6, 11:PL 32, 688.
2. St. Catherine of Siena, *Dialogue* 4, 13 "On Divine Providence":*LH*, Sunday, week 19, OR.
3. Cf. *1 Cor* 6:19-20; 15:44-45.
4. St. Gregory of Nyssa, *Orat. catech.* 15:PG 45, 48B.
5. Cf. *Jn* 14:9-10.
6. Cf. St. Gregory the Great, "*Sicut aqua*" *ad Eulogium, Epist. Lib.* 10, 39:PL 77, 1097 A ff.; DS 475.
7. *LG* 55.
8. *Col* 2:9.
9. St. Irenaeus, *Adv. haeres.* 3, 18, 1:PG 7/1, 932.
10. St. Irenaeus, *Adv. haeres.* 3, 18, 7:PG 7/1, 937; cf. 2, 22, 4.
11. Cf. *Jn* 13:15; *Lk* 11:1; *Mt* 5:11-12.
12. Cf. *Lk* 18:8; *Mt* 24:12.
13. Cf. *Rev* 13:8; 20:7-10; 21:2-4.
14. Cf. *Rev* 20:12; *2 Pet* 3:12-13.
15. St. Gregory of Nyssa, *De Spiritu Sancto,* 16:PG 45, 1321A-B.
16. *GS* 12 § 4.

FOUR
Enjoying Oneness with a Faith Community

1. Byzantine liturgy, Pentecost, Vespers, *Troparion,* repeated after communion.
2. St. Cyril of Alexandria, *In Jo. ev.,* 11, 11:PG 74, 561.
3. St. Hippolytus, *Trad. Ap.* 35:SCh 11, 118.
4. *LG* 6; cf. *Gal* 4:26; *Rev* 12:17; 19:7; 21:2, 9; 22:17; *Eph* 5:25-26, 29.
5. *Pastor Hermae,* Vision 2, 4, 1:PG 2, 899; cf. Aristides, *Apol.* 16, 6; St. Justin, *Apol.* 2, 7:PG 6, 456; Tertullian, *Apol.* 31, 3; 32, 1:PL 1, 508-509.
6. *LG* 3;cf. *Jn* 19:34.
7. Cf. St. Ambrose, *In Luc.* 2, 85-89:PL 15, 1666-1668.
8. Paul VI, June 22, 1973; AG 7 § 2;cf. *LG* 17.
9. St. Leo the Great, *Sermo* 4, 1:PL 54, 149.
10. St. Leo the Great, *Sermo* 4, 1:PL 54, 149.
11. St. Thomas Aquinas, *STh* III, 48, 2.
12. Acts of the Trial of Joan of Arc.
13. St. Irenaeus, *Adv. haeres.* 3, 24, 1:PG 7/1, 966.
14. St. Clement of Alexandria, *Paed.* 1, 6, 42:PG 8, 300.

15. Origen, *Hom. in Ezech.* 9, 1:PG 13, 732.
16. St. Thérèse of Lisieux, *Autobiography of a Saint*, tr. Ronald Knox (London: Harvill, 1958) 235.
17. *UR* 3; *AG* 6; *Eph* 1:22-23.
18. *LG* 23.
19. Paul VI, *EN* 62.
20. *LG* 23.
21. Cf. *RMiss* 55.
22. Cf. *RMiss* 55.

FIVE
Forming Our Lives in Christian Fidelity

1. Pius XII, Discourse, February 20, 1946: AAS 38 (1946) 149; quoted by John Paul II, *CL* 9.
2. St. Thomas Aquinas, *STh.* III, 71, 4 *ad* 3.
3. *LG* 36 § 3.
4. *LG* 36 § 4.
5. Cf. *LG* 42-43; *PC* 1.
6. Cf. CIC, can. 573.
7. *LG* 43.
8. CIC, can. 604 § 1.
9. Cf. CIC, cann. 607; 573; *UR* 15.
10. *LG* 44 § 3.
11. St. Thérèse of Lisieux, *The Final Conversations*, tr. John Clarke (Washington: ICS, 1977), 102.
12. *LG* 53; cf. St. Augustine, *De virg.* 6:PL 40, 399.
13. St. Augustine, *Sermo* 213, 8:PL 38, 1064.
14. *Rom* 8:11.
15. Lateran Council IV (1215): DS 801; *Phil* 3:21; *1 Cor* 15:44.
16. St. Teresa of Avila, *Life*, chap. 1.
17. St. Thérèse of Lisieux, *The Last Conversations*.
18. *The Imitation of Christ*, 1, 23, 1.
19. Cf. *2 Tim* 1:9-10.
20. St. John of the Cross, *Dichos* 64.
21. *Roman Missal*, EP I (Roman Canon) 88.
22. Cf. *Song* 8:6.
23. *GS* 39 § 1.
24. *GS* 39 § 1.
25. *AA* 2 § 2.

26. Paul VI, *CPG* § 30.
27. Paul VI, *CPG* § 15.

SIX
Celebrating the Liturgy

1. John Paul II, *CT* 23.
2. Cf. *Jn* 14:26.
3. *SC* 112.
4. *Eph* 5:19; St. Augustine, *En. in Ps.* 72, 1:PL 36, 914; cf. *Col* 3:16.
5. St. Augustine, *Conf.* 9, 6, 14:PL 32, 769-770.
6. Council of Nicaea II (787): *COD* 111.
7. St. John Damascene, *De imag.* 1, 27:PG 94, 1268A, B.
8. *SC* 102.
9. Cf. *Jn* 21:12; *Lk* 24:30.
10. Byzantine liturgy.
11. *SC* 103.
12. *SC* 90.
13. Cf. Paul VI, *EN* 63-64.
14. John Paul II, *Vicesimus quintus annus*, 16.

SEVEN
Revisiting the Sacraments of Initiation

1. St. Gregory of Nazianzus, *Oratio* 40, 3-4: PG 36, 361C.
2. *AG* 14; cf. RCIA 19; 98.
3. *Roman Missal*, EP I (Roman Canon) 97.
4. OC 25.
5. Paul VI, apostolic constitution, *Divinae consortium naturae*, 663.
6. St. Ignatius of Antioch, *Ad Eph.* 20, 2:SCh 10, 76.
7. *SC* 56.
8. Council of Trent (1551): DS 1642; cf. *Mt* 26:26 ff.; *Mk* 14:22 ff.; *Lk* 22:19 ff.; *1 Cor* 11:24 ff.
9. St. John Chrysostom, *prod. Jud.* 1:6: PG 49, 380.
10. John Paul II, *Dominicae cenae*, 3.
11. EP III 116: prayer for the dead.
12. *LG* 3; St. Ignatius of Antioch, *Ad Eph.* 20, 2:SCh 10, 76.
13. Paul VI, *MF* 66.

EIGHT
Seeking Sacramental Healing

1. *2 Cor* 5:1.
2. *OP* 46: formula of absolution.
3. *Ps* 51:17; cf. *Jn* 6:44; 12:32; *1 Jn* 4:10.
4. Cf. *Lk* 9:23.
5. Council of Trent (1551): DS 1638.
6. Cf. *LG* 11.
7. Council of Trent (1551): DS 1680 (ND 1626); cf. St. Jerome, *In Eccl.* 10, 11: PL 23:1096.
8. Cf. Council of Trent (1551): DS 1712.
9. Cf. *Pss* 32:5; 38:5; 39:9, 12; 107:20; cf. *Mk* 2:5-12.
10. Cf. CIC, can. 847 § 1.
11. Council of Trent (1551): DS 1694.
12. Cf. *Jn* 13:1.

NINE
Celebrating the Sacraments in Service of Communion and Community

1. *LG* 11 § 2.
2. Cf. *LG* 10; 28; *SC* 33; *CD* 11; *PO* 2; 6.
3. Cf. *Mk* 10:43-45; *1 Pet* 5:3.
4. *LG* 20.
5. St. Augustine, *In Jo. ev.* 5, 15: PL 35, 1422.
6. St. John Vianney, quoted in B. Nodet, *Jean-Marie Vianney, Curé d'Ars,* 100.
7. *GS* 48 § 1.
8. *GS* 47 § 1.
9. *GS* 48 § 1; 50.
10. *OCF* 41.
11. St. Simeon of Thessalonica, *De ordine sepulturae.* 336: PG 155, 684.

TEN
Forming Our Character in Imitation of Christ

1. John Paul II, *SRS* 47.
2. St. Leo the Great, *Sermo 21 in nat. Dom.,* 3: PL 54, 192C.

3. St. John Eudes, *Tract. de admirabili corde Jesu*, 1, 5.
4. *Mt* 5:3-12.
5. St. Augustine, *De moribus eccl.* 1, 3, 4: PL 32, 1312.
6. St. Augustine, *Conf.* 10, 20: PL 32, 791.
7. St. Augustine, *De moribus eccl.* 1, 25, 46: PL 32, 1330-1331.
8. St. Teresa of Avila, *Excl.* 15:3.
9. St. Augustine, *In ep. Jo.* 10, 4: PL 35, 2057.

ELEVEN
Sharing in Divine Salvation

1. St. Augustine, *De natura et gratia*, 31: PL 44, 264.
2. Acts of the trial of St. Joan of Arc.
3. Council of Trent (1547): DS 1546.
4. St. Thérèse of Lisieux, "Act of Offering" in *Story of a Soul*, tr. John Clarke (Washington DC: ICS, 1981), 277.
5. St. Gregory of Nyssa, *De vita Mos.:* PG 44, 300D).
6. *1 Tim* 3:15; *LG* 17.
7. Cf. *LG* 25; CDF, declaration, *Mysterium Ecclesiae* 3.
8. Cf. *Jn* 15:12; 13:34.

TWELVE
Transforming Our Lives Through the First Three Commandments

1. *LG* 42 § 2.
2. *DH* 14 § 4.
3. *DH* 2 § 2.
4. *Sermo de die dominica* 2 et 6: PG 86/1, 416C and 421C.
5. St. Augustine, *De civ. Dei* 19, 19: PL 41, 647.
6. CIC, can. 1246 § 1.
7. CIC, can. 1247.

THIRTEEN
Affirming Respect for Life : The Fourth and Fifth Commandments

1. Cf. *CA* 25.
2. *Acts* 5:29.
3. CDF, instruction, *Donum vitae*, intro. 5.
4. St. Thomas Aquinas, *Sth* II-II, 64, 7, *corp. art.*
5. St. Augustine, *De civ. Dei*, 19, 13, 1: PL 41, 640.
6. Cf. *GS* 81 § 4.

FOURTEEN
*Healing Relationships by Observing the
Sixth and Seventh Commandments*

1. *GS* 17.
2. CDF, *Persona humana* 9.
3. CDF, *Persona humana* 8.
4. St. John Chrysostom, *Hom. in Eph.* 20, 8: PG 62, 146-147.
5. *HV* 11.
6. Cf. *SRS* 32; *CA* 51.
7. *SRS* 47 § 6; cf. 42.
8. P. Hansen, *Vita mirabilis* (Louvain, 1668).

FIFTEEN
*Telling the Truth in Obedience to the
Eighth, Ninth, and Tenth Commandments*

1. St. Augustine, *Conf.* 6, 11, 20: PL 32, 729-730.
2. Cf. St. Augustine, *De catechizandis rudibus* 4, 8: PL 40, 315-316.
3. St. John Chrysostom, *Hom. in Rom.* 71, 5: PG 60, 448.
4. St. Augustine, *De serm. Dom. in monte* 1, 1, 3: PL 34, 1232.

SIXTEEN
Entering into the Heart of Prayer

1. St. Thérèse of Lisieux, *Manuscrits autobiographiques,* C 25r.
2. Cf. *Gen* 32:24-30; *Lk* 18:1-8.
3. Cf. *Am* 7:2, 5; *Isa* 6:5, 8, 11; *Jer* 1:6; 15:15-18; 20:7-18.
4. Cf. *Eph* 1:9.

SEVENTEEN
Renewing the Heart of Praying Persons

1. Guigo the Carthusian, *Scala Paradisi:* PL 40, 998.
2. *Roman Missal,* Pentecost, Sequence.
3. St. Gregory of Nazianzus, *Orat. theo.,* 27, 1, 4: PG 36, 16.
4. St. John Chrysostom, *Ecloga de oratione* 2: PG 63, 585.
5. St. Teresa of Jesus, *The Book of Her Life,* 8, 5 in *The Collected Works of St. Teresa of Avila,* tr. K. Kavanaugh, OCD, and O. Rodriguez, OCD (Washington DC: Institute of Carmelite Studies, 1976), I, 67.

EIGHTEEN
The Heart Praying as Jesus Taught

1. Tertullian, *De orat.* 1: PL 1, 1155.
2. Cf. *Eph* 3:12; *Heb* 3:6; 4:16; 10:19; *1 Jn* 2:28; 3:21; 5:14.
3. St. Gregory of Nyssa, *De orat. Dom.* 2: PG 44, 1148B.
4. St. John Cassian, *Coll.* 9, 18: PL 49, 788C.
5. St. Augustine, *De serm. Dom. in monte* 2, 5, 18: PL 34, 1277.
6. *Ad Diognetum* 5: PG 2, 1173.
7. St. Peter Chrysologus, *Sermo* 71, 4: PL 52:402A; cf. *Rom* 2:24; *Ezek* 36:20-22.
8. St. Cyril of Jerusalem, *Catech. myst.* 5, 13: PG 33, 1120A; cf. *Rom* 6:12.
9. Cf. *GS* 22; 32; 39; 45; *EN* 31.
10. Cf. *Jn* 6:26-58.
11. St. Augustine, *Sermo* 57, 7: PL 38, 389.
12. St. Ignatius of Antioch, *Ad Eph.* 20, 2: PG 5, 661; *Jn* 6:53-56.
13. Cf. *RP* 16.
14. *Roman Missal,* Embolism after the Lord's Prayer, 126: *Libera nos, quaesumus, Domine, ab omnibus malis, da propitius pacem in diebus nostris, ut, ope misericordiae tuae adiuti, et a peccato simus semper liberi, et ab omni perturbatione securi: expectantes beatam spem et adventum Salvatoris nostri Iesu Christi.*

SELECTED
BIBLIOGRAPHY

∞

à Kempis, Thomas. *The Imitation of Christ.* Harold C. Gardiner, ed. Ann Arbor, Mich.: Servant, 1992. See also Thomas à Kempis. *The Imitation of Christ.* tr. William C. Creasy. Notre Dame, Ind.; Ave Maria, 1989.

Augustine, St. *The Confessions.* tr. John K. Ryan. New York: Doubleday, 1960.

Catechism of the Catholic Church. English Translation. United States Catholic Conference. Liguori, Mo.: Liguori, 1994.

Catherine of Genoa. *Purgation and Purgatory, The Spiritual Dialogue,* tr. Serge Hughes, in *The Classics of Western Spirituality.* New York: Paulist, 1979.

Catherine of Siena. *The Dialogue,* tr. Suzanne Noffke, in *The Classics of Western Spirituality.* Suzanne Noffke, tr. New York: Paulist, 1980.

Companion to the Catechism of the Catholic Church. San Francisco: Ignatius, 1994.

Elizabeth of the Trinity. *The Complete Works.* Vol. I. tr. Sr. Aletheia Kane. Washington: ICS, 1984.

_____. *A Practical Guide to Spiritual Reading.* Petersham, Mass: St. Bede's, 1994.

Francis of Assisi. *Writings and Early Biographies.* Marion A. Habig, ed. Chicago: Franciscan Herald Press, 1973.

Gregory of Nyssa. *Ascetical Works,* in *The Fathers of the Church,* Vol. 58, tr. Virginia W. Callahan. Washington: Catholic University of America, 1967.

Gregory the Great. *Pastoral Care.* tr. Henry Davis. New York: Newman, 1950.

_____. *The Lord's Prayer. The Beatitudes.* In *Ancient Christian Writers,* No. 18., tr. Hilda C. Graef. Westminster, Md: Christian Classics, 1954.

_____. *The Life of Moses,* tr. Abraham J. Malherbe and Everett Ferguson. In *The Classics of Western Spirituality.* New York: Paulist, 1978.

John Cassian. *Conférences,* tr. Colm Luibheid. In *The Classics of Western Spirituality.* New York: Paulist, 1985.

John of the Cross. *The Collected Works,* tr. Kieran Kavanaugh, OCD, and Otilio Rodriguez, OCD. Washington: ICS, 1991, 1994.

John Paul II. *Year of the Family.* February 2, 1994. Washington: United States Catholic Conference.

_____. *On the Dignity and Vocation of Women (Mulieris Dignitatem).* Apostolic Letter, August 15, 1988. Washington: United States Catholic Conference.

_____. *Letter to Women.* Washington: United States Catholic Conference.

_____. *The Vocation and the Mission of the Lay Faithful in the Church and in the World (Christifideles Laici).* Post-Synodal Apostolic Exhortation, December 30, 1988. Washington: United States Catholic Conference.

Julian of Norwich. *Showings.* In *The Classics of Western Spirituality.* New York: Paulist, 1978.

Muto, Susan. *Caring for the Caregiver.* Pittsburgh: Epiphany, 1996.

_____. *Celebrating the Single Life: A Spirituality for Single Persons in Today's World.* New York: Crossroad, 1982.

_____. *John of the Cross for Today: The Ascent.* Notre Dame: Ave Maria, 1991.

_____. *John of the Cross for Today: The Dark Night.* Notre Dame: Ave Maria, 1994.

_____. *Pathways of Spiritual Living.* New York: Doubleday. Reprinted Petersham, Mass.: St. Bede's, 1988.

_____. *Light Love Life.* Washington: ICS, 1984.

_____. *Womanspirit: Reclaiming the Deep Feminine in Our Human Spirituality.* New York: Crossroad, 1991.

_____ **and Adrian van Kaam.** *Divine Guidance: Seeking to Find and Follow the Will of God.* Ann Arbor, Mich.: Servant, 1994.

Newman, Cardinal John Henry. *Apologia Pro Vita Sua.* New York: Doubleday, 1989.

Ratzinger, Joseph, and Christoph Schönborn. *Introduction to the Catechism of the Catholic Church.* San Francisco: Ignatius, 1994.

Stein, Edith. *On the Problem of Empathy,* 3rd rev. ed. Washington: ICS, 1989.

Teresa of Avila. *The Way of Perfection.* In *The Collected Works,* vol. 1. 2nd rev. ed. tr. Kieran Kavanaugh, OCD, and Otilio Rodriguez, OCD. Washington: ICS, 1987.

_____. *The Collected Works,* vol. 2. tr. Kieran Kavanaugh, OCD, and Otilio Rodrigue, OCD. Washington: ICS, 1980.

_____. *The Interior Castle* in *The Classics of Western Spirituality,* tr. Kieran Kavanaugh, OCD, and Otilio Rodriguez, OCD. New York: Paulist, 1979.

Thérèse of Lisieux. *Story of a Soul.* Tr. John Clarke, Washington: ICS, 1975.

van Kaam, Adrian. *Looking for Jesus.* Denville, N.J.: Dimension, 1978.

_____. *Traditional Formation. Formative Spirituality Series,* vol. 5. New York: Crossroad, 1992.

_____. *Woman at the Well.* Denville, N.J.: Dimension. Reprinted Pittsburgh: Epiphany, 1993.

_____. *The Tender Farewell of Jesus.* Hyde Park, N.Y.: New City, 1996.

Wuerl, Donald W., STD, Ronald Lawler, OFM, and Thomas Comerford Lawler. *The Teaching of Christ.* 4th ed. Huntington, Ind: Sunday Visitor, 1995.